P9-AGE-098

Modern Language Association of America

Approaches to Teaching World Literature

Joseph Gibaldi, Series Editor

1. Joseph Gibaldi, ed. *Approaches to Teaching Chaucer's* Canterbury Tales. 1980.
2. Carole Slade, ed. *Approaches to Teaching Dante's* Divine Comedy. 1982.
3. Richard Bjornson, ed. *Approaches to Teaching Cervantes'* Don Quixote. 1984.
4. Jess B. Bessinger, Jr., and Robert F. Yeager, eds. *Approaches to Teaching* Beowulf. 1984.
5. Richard J. Dunn, ed. *Approaches to Teaching Dickens'* David Copperfield. 1984.
6. Steven G. Kellman, ed. *Approaches to Teaching Camus's* The Plague. 1985.
7. Yvonne Shafer, ed. *Approaches to Teaching Ibsen's* A Doll House. 1985.
8. Martin Bickman, ed. *Approaches to Teaching Melville's* Moby-Dick. 1985.
9. Miriam Youngerman Miller and Jane Chance, eds. *Approaches to Teaching* Sir Gawain and the Green Knight. 1986.
10. Galbraith M. Crump, ed. *Approaches to Teaching Milton's* Paradise Lost. 1986.
11. Spencer Hall, with Jonathan Ramsey, eds. *Approaches to Teaching Wordsworth's Poetry.* 1986.
12. Robert H. Ray, ed. *Approaches to Teaching Shakespeare's* King Lear. 1986.
13. Kostas Myrsiades, ed. *Approaches to Teaching Homer's* Iliad *and* Odyssey. 1987.
14. Douglas J. McMillan, ed. *Approaches to Teaching Goethe's* Faust. 1987.
15. Renée Waldinger, ed. *Approaches to Teaching Voltaire's* Candide. 1987.
16. Bernard Koloski, ed. *Approaches to Teaching Chopin's* The Awakening. 1988.
17. Kenneth M. Roemer, ed. *Approaches to Teaching Momaday's* The Way to Rainy Mountain. 1988.
18. Edward J. Rielly, ed. *Approaches to Teaching Swift's* Gulliver's Travels. 1988.
19. Jewel Spears Brooker, ed. *Approaches to Teaching Eliot's Poetry and Plays.* 1988.

Approaches to Teaching Eliot's Poetry and Plays

Edited by

Jewel Spears Brooker

The Modern Language Association of America
New York   1988

Copyright © 1988 by The Modern Language Association of America

Library of Congress Cataloging-in-Publication Data

Approaches to teaching Eliot's poetry and plays / edited by Jewel
   Spears Brooker.
         p.   cm. — (Approaches to teaching world literature : 19)
      Bibliography: p.
      Includes index.
      ISBN 0-87352-513-2   ISBN 0-87352-514-0 (pbk.)
      1. Eliot, T. S. (Thomas Stearns), 1888–1965—Study and teaching.
   I. Brooker, Jewel Spears, 1940–.   . II. Series.
   PS3509.L43Z594   1988
   821'.912—dc19   88-13158

Cover illustration of the paperback edition: Marcia Loeb, *Art Deco: Designs and
Motifs* (New York: Dover, 1972), 40

Published by The Modern Language Association of America
10 Astor Place, New York, New York 10003-6981

140155

CONTENTS

PREFACE TO THE SERIES

In *The Art of Teaching* Gilbert Highet wrote, "Bad teaching wastes a great deal of effort, and spoils many lives which might have been full of energy and happiness." All too many teachers have failed in their work, Highet argued, simply "because they have not thought about it." We hope that the Approaches to Teaching World Literature series, sponsored by the Modern Language Association's Committee on Teaching and Related Professional Activities, will not only improve the craft—as well as the art—of teaching but also encourage serious and continuing discussion of the aims and methods of teaching literature.

The principal objective of the series is to collect within each volume different points of view on teaching a specific literary work, a literary tradition, or a writer widely taught at the undergraduate level. The preparation of each volume begins with a wide-ranging survey of instructors, thus enabling us to include in the volume the philosophies and approaches, thoughts and methods of scores of experienced teachers. The result is a sourcebook of material, information, and ideas on teaching the subject of the volume to undergraduates.

The series is intended to serve nonspecialists as well as specialists, inexperienced as well as experienced teachers, graduate students who wish to learn effective ways of teaching as well as senior professors who wish to compare their own approaches with the approaches of colleagues in other schools. Of course, no volume in the series can ever substitute for erudition, intelligence, creativity, and sensitivity in teaching. We hope merely that each book will point readers in useful directions; at most each will offer only a first step in the long journey to successful teaching.

Joseph Gibaldi
Series Editor

PREFACE TO THE VOLUME

The poetry and plays of T. S. Eliot are especially appropriate for the MLA series on teaching world literature. They are important in the liberal arts curriculum, and they are pedagogically formidable. This volume should be helpful in a number of ways. First, simply by inviting attention to the challenge of teaching complex poetry, the volume should stimulate a certain amount of critical and pedagogical rethinking. Second, in presenting a cross section of views, it should be of practical assistance to teachers who are inexperienced or who wish to be more effective. Third, as part of a conversation that includes experienced teachers and scholars, this volume should incorporate certain lessons from the past and in dialectical fashion become the beginning point for many future conversations. The potential for at once preserving and stimulating diverse responses is a major value of this book and of the whole Approaches series.

The idea of education as an ongoing conversation was important to Eliot. In "The Aims of Education," a series of lectures given at the University of Chicago in November 1950 (printed in *To Criticize the Critic*), he suggested that teachers should enable their students not only to adapt to society but also to form an idea of a better society, continually measuring the reality against the idea. Eliot further claimed that teachers must somehow protect both their students and themselves from taking any conception of education too seriously. What they should take seriously is the ongoing conversation about the *is* and the *ought*, the actual and the possible in education. This volume is intended to be part of such a conversation about the actual and the possible, a conversation among the great teachers of the past, present readers and their students, and future teachers emerging from today's classrooms.

Like other volumes in this series, this book is divided into two parts, "Materials" and "Approaches." The first consists of a general discussion of Eliot in the college curriculum, a survey of available texts and popular anthologies, a few suggestions about readings for students and teachers, and a review of available teaching aids. The second part consists of essays by twenty-seven teachers from the United States and Europe. We present these essays not as prescriptions but as suggestions. We will be pleased, of course, if other teachers find our hints and guesses useful in their day-to-day work in and out of the classroom.

In "The Function of Criticism" (*Selected Essays*), Eliot defines criticism as the common pursuit of true judgment. His phrase is equally appropriate as a description of educational endeavors, especially of the present project, which from the beginning has been a collaborative effort. Many teachers have generously shared the insights they have gained in the classroom. I have met few of them personally, but from our common pursuit of excellence I have learned that they are a remarkably conscientious and hard-working group of professionals.

Part of the work for this volume was accomplished in the fall of 1986, during which I benefited from a paid hexennial leave from Eckerd College; and the book was completed in 1987, during which I was privileged to hold a National Endowment for the Humanities Fellowship for College Teachers. I am grateful to the Master and Fellows of St. Edmund's College, Cambridge, where I was a visiting scholar during 1987, and to Michael Halls, modern archivist at King's College, whose courtesy and professional advice have been very helpful in this and other projects.

I have a number of personal debts that are a pleasure to acknowledge. I have learned much about teaching by being taught. My first and greatest teachers were my parents, Mae Johnson and William B. Spears. Regarding Eliot, Joseph Bentley has been my most influential teacher. He will always be the model teacher for me, and now he is my collaborator in several scholarly projects as well. I have also learned about teaching by teaching, so I am grateful to my two children, Emily and Mark, and to my students at Eckerd College. In becoming my students, they also became my teachers.

Concerning the present volume, I am most indebted to Joseph Gibaldi, my MLA editor who from the earliest stages of this project has been sympathetic and helpful. I am grateful to Mildred Meyer Boaz, who helped me compile the list of musical compositions, to my daughter, Emily Hope, who prepared the index, and to Carolyn Johnston, Joseph Bentley, Grover Smith, and Donald Gallup, who kindly critiqued parts of the manuscript. For years of conversation about teaching and for practical help with this volume, I am grateful to Ronald Schuchard and Alistair Duckworth. For suggesting this project in the first place, I am indebted to Aldo Scaglione. I thank Shirley Davis, my department secretary, for her unfailing help and my dean, Lloyd Chapin, for his consistent encouragement. Finally, I am grateful to my husband, H. Ralph Brooker, who despite his own professional obligations is in the most practical ways endlessly supportive of my work.

JSB

Part One

MATERIALS

Jewel Spears Brooker

Eliot in the Curriculum

In response to the MLA survey on teaching T. S. Eliot, teachers from Canada, England, Germany, and the United States indicate that Eliot's writings are central to the college curriculum, appearing in a variety of English courses as well as in more general humanities courses. Most students in the United States are introduced to Eliot's poetry during the first two years of college. Eliot is frequently included in freshman English, especially when composition is combined with an introduction to literature, and in world literature or Western civilization courses. Eliot's poetry and plays are particularly appropriate in general humanities courses, because the writers and traditions Eliot alludes to (Homer, Dante, Shakespeare) are often studied early in the term. Students thus can experience the joy of recognizing, say, Dante in a modern work and can feel more confident with Eliot's palimpsest texts.

The lower-division courses in which Eliot is most often and most systematically taught are the surveys of American and British literature. Almost all instructors teach either or both of these surveys, and most teach Eliot in both. The complexity and richness of his poetry invariably make the duplication fruitful, bearing witness to Joseph Frank's well-known principle, outlined in "Spatial Form in Modern Literature," that modern literature cannot be read, it can only be reread. Other lower-division courses in which Eliot appears include American Literature of the 1920s (described in this volume by Nancy D. Hargrove), Literature between the Wars, Literature and Related Arts (Mildred Meyer Boaz), Literature and Mysticism (John Gatta), and Mythology in Literature. Some lower-division courses seem especially challenging for most freshmen and sophomores: T. S. Eliot and the Development of Personal Values, T. S. Eliot: Reading and Judgment, and Dante / Eliot (Robert W. Ayers).

The upper-division courses most frequently including Eliot are those in twentieth-century literature or twentieth-century poetry. Also popular are major-authors courses for seniors, some featuring Eliot alone and others Eliot and one or two of his contemporaries. Combinations include Yeats-Eliot, Pound-Eliot, Eliot-Stevens, Eliot-Joyce, Yeats-Pound-Eliot, and Pound-Eliot-Stevens. Among other upper-division courses teaching Eliot are Literary Criticism (often required of English majors), Modern Drama (Katherine E. Kelly), Symbolist Tradition in Literature, Modern European Literature, and Twentieth-Century Spanish Poetry. The Spanish course uses Eliot in part to introduce English-speaking students to modernist poetry in their own language before introducing them to modernist poetry in Spanish.

Editions and Anthologies

There is no uniform, definitive edition of Eliot's writings. His poetry and plays are published in a number of volumes, none of which contains the complete works. His prose has not been collected; it is scattered in various periodicals and several published volumes.

Eliot's poetry and criticism are published by Faber and Faber in England and by Harcourt Brace Jovanovich in the United States. The important verse collections are the so-called *Complete Poems and Plays 1909–1950*, the *Poems Written in Early Youth*, the *Collected Poems 1909–1962*, and the *Complete Plays* (in England, *Collected Plays*). *Complete Poems and Plays* includes all the important poems and three plays (*Murder in the Cathedral, The Family Reunion*, and *The Cocktail Party*). *Collected Poems* is the most complete edition of his poetry. *Complete Plays* includes *Murder in the Cathedral, The Family Reunion, The Cocktail Party, The Confidential Clerk*, and *The Elder Statesman*. For courses involving only the poetry, *Collected Poems* is the best volume; for courses including the plays, *Complete Poems and Plays* is most practical. Teachers who wish to assign all five plays may prefer to use *Collected Poems* and *Complete Plays*. Some teachers use *Old Possum's Book of Practical Cats* to show a lighter and more accessible Eliot. The cat poems, which provide most of the lyrics of the popular rock opera *Cats*, are included in *Complete Poems*.

The Waste Land: *A Facsimile and Transcript of the Original Drafts*, edited by Valerie Eliot, contains the early drafts of the poem and shows the collaborative roles played by Ezra Pound and by the poet's first wife Vivien (Vivienne) Eliot. The letters included in Valerie Eliot's introduction provide invaluable background for an understanding of Eliot's life and work. This volume, available in both hard and soft cover, is particularly useful in Eliot (or Eliot-Pound) seminars and in creative writing seminars.

Both Faber and Harcourt publish a number of slim and reasonably priced paperback editions of the poetry. The most popular are *Selected Poems*, The Waste Land *and Other Poems*, and *Four Quartets*. Both paperback collections of the earlier poems include "The Love Song of J. Alfred Prufrock," *The Waste Land*, and *Ash-Wednesday*, but only *Selected Poems* includes the four masterpieces of his student years ("The Love Song of J. Alfred Prufrock," "Portrait of a Lady," "Preludes," and "Rhapsody on a Windy Night"), the quatrain satires (e.g., "Sweeney Erect," "The Hippopotamus," "Whispers of Immortality"), and "The Hollow Men." In addition, *Selected Poems* has a straightforward paperback companion guide by B. C. Southam. Combining the paper editions of *Selected Poems* (or The Waste Land *and Other Poems*) and *Four Quartets* is one alternative to using the hardcover *Collected Poems*.

In the United States, Harcourt publishes paperback editions of all the plays except *The Elder Statesman*; and in England, Faber publishes paperback editions of several of the plays with useful introductions by Nevill Coghill.

Of the various volumes of Eliot's prose, the most important are *Selected Essays* (1950) and *On Poetry and Poets* (1957). Unfortunately, however, some of the most interesting essays are either in periodicals or in other volumes. In response to this situation, Frank Kermode edited *Selected Prose of T. S. Eliot* (1975), a single-volume, reasonably comprehensive and representative collection of Eliot's prose. Available in both paper and hard cover, this volume is an excellent choice for classroom use. Kermode's editing is judicious and his introduction helpful.

For most college courses, literature anthologies are more appropriate than single-author volumes. Unfortunately, the Eliot estate permits no more than one thousand lines of Eliot's poetry to appear in any anthology, a restriction which means that no anthology includes what most scholars consider a minimum selection of the poetry. This limitation accounts for the exclusion of "The Hollow Men," *Ash-Wednesday*, and three of the *Four Quartets* from most anthologies and for the wide variation in anthology presentations of Eliot's work. While teachers probably would not choose an anthology based only on the treatment of Eliot, they should be aware of certain differences among the standard texts.

Teachers of American and British literature surveys use a variety of anthologies. The Norton anthologies are the most popular, for both American literature (ed. Nina Baym et al.) and British literature (ed. M. H. Abrams). The Macmillan *Anthology of American Literature* (ed. George McMichael) and the Random House *American Tradition in Literature* (ed. George Perkins et al.) are also widely used. All these texts include Eliot's indispensable essay "Tradition and the Individual Talent," and Norton adds "The Metaphysical Poets." All three contain "The Love Song of J. Alfred Prufrock" from the Harvard period, *The Waste Land* from the post–World War I period, and one of the *Four Quartets* from the thirties–World War II period. Norton and Macmillan include two of the quatrain satires, and Random House and Macmillan include "Gerontion." Only Macmillan includes "Preludes," a poem that is especially helpful in introducing modernism and in approaching the problem of form in *The Waste Land*; and only Random House includes "The Hollow Men," a poem that is not only representative but remarkably teachable (see the essay by Graham Clarke in this volume). Norton and Random House use "Little Gidding" to represent the *Quartets*, and Macmillan uses "Burnt Norton."

The biggest difference in the three anthologies is in the editorial apparatus, with Norton and Random House offering considerably more interpretive guidance than Macmillan. The introductions are adequate in all three, although Norton's is the fullest and perhaps the most helpful and Macmillan's is the briefest. The Norton and Random House texts have special introductions to *The Waste Land*, commenting on basic themes and explaining such matters as the myth of the Fisher King. Macmillan has little interpretive comment in the general introduction and none with individual poems. Similarly, Norton and Random House offer interpretive footnotes, while Macmillan generally sticks to informational notes. Some of the interpretive notes are helpful, but some are reductive, and many mislead by generating spurious confidence in both teachers and students. A number interfere with the collaboration essential between reader and Eliot. For example, in the footnotes to part 1 of *The Waste Land*, the Norton editor describes "Stetson" as "[p]resumably representing the 'average business man.' " And in the notes to "The Love Song of J. Alfred Prufrock," the Random House editor explains the lines "In the room the women come and go / Talking of Michelangelo" by saying "The lines suggest the futility of 'arty' talk by dilettantes."

The policy governing editoral apparatus leads to another difference, one that for many teachers will make all the difference in teaching *The Waste Land*. Eliot's "Notes" to the poem are a stumbling block to many; and for all who wish to ignore them, his later reference to the notes as "bogus scholarship" provides a proof text. But Eliot, master of irony and lover of intellectual jokes, also claimed that the notes are serious. Moreover, because the poet consistently chose (in edition after edition) to print them with the poem, he must have intended for readers to experience them in conjunction with the poetic text. The notes encourage readers to become active collaborators, physically turning pages, mentally trying to understand parodies and make connections, and, sometimes, abandoning the text in an attempt to recover a poem by Baudelaire or a play by Shakespeare. Of the three anthologies, Macmillan prints the poem as Eliot chose to print it, adding their own footnotes for brief explanations and for translations of foreign lines. Both Norton and Random House distribute Eliot's notes as footnotes rather than as endnotes; both edit the notes; and both have interwoven editorial comments into the notes, with a bracketed "Eliot's note" showing which is which. Treating *The Waste Land* "Notes" as if they were notes to a scholarly paper is to mistake art for life, "bogus scholarship" for straightforward scholarship. The motive, of course, is to be helpful to teachers and students, but the effect is to create an alternative poem.

The three anthologies offer start-up bibliographies: Macmillan and Random House place the bibliography at the end of the introduction, and Norton at the back of the book in a special bibliographic section. All three list some very basic books, with Norton offering the best guide. Random House, oddly, includes without comment several quasi-notorious publications, surely a disservice to beginning teachers and students.

In most of the major anthologies, one misses the authority of the single voice, the sensitive and learned reader with individual taste in poetry. One happy exception is *The Harper Anthology of Poetry*, edited by John Frederick Nims. In this medieval-to-modern collection of English-language poetry, the seductive voice of an informed lover of poetry imparts both unity and charm to the text. Distinguished as a poet, translator, teacher, and also as the editor of *Poetry*, Nims provides adequate introductory biographies and clear explanatory footnotes to the poems. For many poems, especially modern ones, Nims walks the reader through with a personal but apolitical interpretation. The commentaries are included in an appendix so that readers who do not need them can ignore them. Nims is particularly good on modern poetry, and both his footnotes to and interpretations of Eliot's work are sound. Perhaps because they are part of a coherent overall response his notes do not seem reductive. He does follow the majority, however, in distributing Eliot's notes as footnotes and identifying them with a "[T. S. E.]." Nims's section on prosody is also helpful.

For courses in modern poetry, many teachers use the *Norton Anthology of Modern Poetry*, edited by Richard Ellmann and Robert O'Clair, but the Macmillan *Chief Modern Poets of Britain and America*, edited by G. D. Sanders et al., is also popular. The Norton offers an excellent selection of the poetry, including part of the usually omitted *Ash-Wednesday*. The Norton introduction to Eliot, both his life and his poetry, is outstanding, rich in factual information and helpful in interpretation. As in the other Norton volumes, *The Waste Land* notes are included as footnotes rather than as endnotes. The editorial footnotes in the Norton *Modern Poetry* are not always helpful. Regarding "I shall wear the bottom of my trousers rolled" ("Prufrock"), the editors suggest, "Prufrock is eager to keep up with the latest fashion." To the line "After such knowledge, what forgiveness" in "Gerontion," the editors append, "The knowledge, however imperfect, of Christ," a reductive and misleading note that obscures the nature of Gerontion's malaise and complicates the reading of the poem.

Recommended Reading for Students

Our survey of instructors revealed several different attitudes regarding recommended readings for students. One widely shared view is that undergraduates should read only Eliot's poetry because, as one instructor puts it, "the poems speak vividly for themselves." "We don't need to kneel and pray first," M. L. Rosenthal says in his contribution to this volume, "or take Greek lessons, or pass examinations on . . . *The Golden Bough* or Helen Gardner's works." A second attitude is that students should read what Eliot read, or, more modestly, at least sample the works that he knew best. As one instructor suggests, "I think it is absurd that a student to whom Baudelaire is no more than a name should be asked to read a book about Eliot." Practically speaking, a teacher in a modern literature course cannot do much about the gap between Eliot's education and that of today's students, but a surprising number do recommend that students sample the classics, the Bible, Augustine's *Confessions*, and the works of Dante and Shakespeare in conjunction with reading Eliot's poetry. (See the essay by Robert W. Ayers in this volume.) A third line of thought would recommend that students read Eliot's criticism and the criticism of his friends and contemporaries. The Eliot essays most frequently assigned to students are "Tradition and the Individual Talent" and "The Metaphysical Poets" (both in *Selected Essays*). Both are widely available, and both are helpful in getting to central concerns in Eliot's art. (For an approach combining Eliot's poetry and criticism, see the essay by James Torrens, SJ, in this volume.) The contemporary of Eliot's whom most teachers recommend to students is, of course, the early Ezra Pound. Pound's brilliant and provocative literary journalism, including the short pieces on imagism and vorticism, can be found in his *Literary Essays* and in the Penguin anthology of his critical writings. Another contemporary often recommended is T. E. Hulme, whose brief essay "Romanticism and Classicism" is both a landmark of modernism and an introduction to a general position endorsed by Eliot.

Many instructors recommend background readings on modernism and on the intellectual and literary context of Eliot's work, especially for students in upper-division courses. The seventh volume of the *Pelican Guide to English Literature*, a paperback anthology of criticism devoted to the modern period and edited by Boris Ford, includes essays on major writers and on social, intellectual, and literary backgrounds. These essays are intended for the nonspecialist and, although dated (1963), are still helpful. Other valuable anthologies include Irving Howe's *Literary Modernism* and Michael Bell's *The Context of English Literature: 1900–1930*. Two studies of modern poetry, Monroe Spears's *Dionysus and the City* and David Perkins's *History of Modern Poetry*, are often recommended to students. The importance and fascination of Spears's topic, the primitive and the metropolitan in modernism, is evident in *The Savage and the City in the Work of T. S. Eliot* by Robert Crawford. Some instructors suggest that students read *The Pound Era* by Hugh Kenner. Kenner's widely influential concept of the modern period as "Renaissance ii" has been expanded and tightened in books by his admirers, most recently in Jeffrey Perl's *Tradition of Return: The Implicit History of Modern Literature*. Some teachers prefer to assign a single essay on modernism. Good single essays on the period include the introduction to the *Norton Anthology of Modern Poetry*; Nathan Scott, "The Broken Center: A Definition of the Crisis of Values in Modern Literature"; Lionel Trilling, "On the Teaching of Modern Literature"; Harry Levin, "What Was Modernism?"; and Irving Howe's introduction to *Literary Modernism*. For advanced students, several instructors recommend Joseph Frank's "Spatial Form in Modern Literature."

Where literary criticism is concerned, only a few teachers advocate giving students long book lists. Many maintain that a brief basic bibliography is more helpful than a long one, and some believe that assigning secondary material constructs a barrier between student and text. Most teachers in upper-division courses, however, do distribute at least a one-page bibliography. The titles most frequently listed are those classic works that, many say, have "never been equaled." They include the brilliant studies on modern literature that began appearing in the 1930s and that contain chapters on Eliot. Chief among these works are Edmund Wilson's *Axel's Castle*, F. R. Leavis's *New Bearings in English Poetry*, R. P. Blackmur's *Double Agent*, and Cleanth Brooks's *Modern Poetry and the Tradition*. A number of excellent books devoted entirely to Eliot appeared in the 1930s and 1940s, such as F. O. Matthiessen's *The Achievement of T. S. Eliot*, Elizabeth Drew's *T. S. Eliot: The Design of His Poetry*, Helen Gardner's *The Art of T. S. Eliot*, and Kristian Smidt's *Poetry and Belief in the Work of T. S. Eliot*. Also published in the 1940s were the first two of many collections of essays on Eliot: Leonard Unger's *T. S. Eliot: A Selected Critique* and B. Rajan's *T. S. Eliot: A Study of His Writings by Several Hands*.

Other older studies that still appear on the bibliographies distributed to students include George Williamson's *Reader's Guide*, Grover Smith's *T. S. Eliot's Poetry and Plays*, Hugh Kenner's *Invisible Poet*, and Leonard Unger's *Moments and Patterns*. Three books recommended for the plays are D. E. Jones's *Plays of T. S. Eliot*, Carol H. Smith's *T. S. Eliot's Dramatic Theory and Practice*, and E. Martin Browne's *Making of T. S. Eliot's Plays*. Also useful for students are several single-volume paperback introductions to the poet, generally summaries or reiterations. Northrop Frye, Philip Headings, and Bernard Bergonzi are among the authors of such introductions. In the last few decades, a number of works have been published especially with students in mind. The *Dictionary of Literary Biography* entries on Eliot (Brooker on the poetry; Hargrove on the plays, Beehler on the criticism), all written in the 1980s, contain primary and secondary bibliographies, as well as critical introductions to the poetry, plays, and criticism. Of special interest to students is B. C. Southam's straightforward guide to the paperback *Selected Poems*.

Students can sample Eliot criticism most conveniently through the various casebooks and anthologies of criticism, many of which are readily available in college bookstores and libraries. Twentieth-Century Views has a collection of essays edited by Kenner; Twentieth-Century Interpretations has a compilation on *The Waste Land* edited by Jay Martin and one on *Murder in the Cathedral* edited by David Clark. Macmillan has a volume on *The Waste Land*, edited by C. B. Cox and A. P. Hinchliffe, and one on *Four Quartets*, edited by Bergonzi. Allen and Unwin has a collection edited by Sheila Sullivan; McGraw-Hill has one edited by Linda Wagner; and St. Martin's Press publishes The Waste Land *in Different Voices* edited by Moody. The collections of essays intended primarily for students continue to appear from year to year.

The Instructor's Library

Since the present volume is intended to facilitate intelligent resourcefulness, the following list, to a great extent the result of the MLA survey of instructors, is suggestive rather than definitive. Any list of recommendations for beginning instructors is bound to overlap with a checklist for students and, of course, to some extent with any adequate checklist for scholars.

Background Reading

Three books on modern poetry from the 1930s are frequently recommended: Wilson's *Axel's Castle*, Leavis's *New Bearings in English Poetry*, and Brooks's *Modern Poetry and the Tradition*. Also recommended are *The Modern Writer and His World* (1953) by G. S. Fraser, *Romantic Image* (1957) by Frank Kermode, *Poets of Reality* (1965) by J. Hillis Miller, *The New Poetic* (1964) by C. K. Stead, and *The Modern Poets* (1975) by M. L. Rosenthal. Many instructors stress the importance of supplementing background reading with direct experience teaching modern writers, particularly those congenial to Eliot, like Conrad, Joyce, and Pound. Such experience provides the teacher with a rich and recurrent review of the period.

Two anthologies of modernism, one of critical essays and one of primary documents, are especially valuable for teachers. The 1976 Pelican anthology, *Modernism: 1890–1930*, edited by Malcolm Bradbury and James McFarlane, pays special attention to European manifestations of modernism. In attempting to define modernism and its cultural and intellectual climate, the editors include essays on the cities of modernism (London, Berlin, Paris, Vienna, Prague, New York, and others), on the movements (symbolism, imagism, vorticism, and others), and on the major genres (poetry, the novel, and drama). The appendix has a detailed international chronology, an extensive bibliography, and brief biographies of major figures. *The Modern Tradition: Backgrounds of Modern Literature* (1965), edited by Richard Ellmann and Charles Feidelson, is an excellent collection of documents related to the modern period. The editors include materials not only from literature and aesthetics but also from philosophy, theology, anthropology, psychology, history, and other disciplines.

Several teachers insist that "being grounded in Eliot's sources" is the best preparation for teaching his verse. Fortunately, Eliot's sources are generally valuable in their own right; most, in fact, are included on standard reading lists for the liberal arts. One teacher lists "Plato, Dante, the Elizabethans, the Jacobeans, Nietzsche, Frazer, Freud, F. H. Bradley, Irving Babbitt, the French Symbolists, and the 19th-century French and Russian novel."

Some teachers use John Ciardi's translation of the *Divine Comedy*, but others, those who want detailed and readable notes, prefer the superb translations of Dorothy Sayers and of Charles Singleton. Eliot himself used the Carlyle, Okey, and Wicksteed translation, and a few teachers follow his lead. Regarding Frazer's *Golden Bough*, teachers may wish to look at the third edition, the one used by Eliot and most of his generation. For Eliot studies, the most important volumes are *The Dying God* (pt. 3, 1911) and *Adonis Attis Osiris* (pt. 4, 1914). Eliot's graduate studies in Indic languages, religion, and philosophy, reviewed by Cleo McNelly Kearns in *T. S. Eliot and Indic Traditions* (1987), contributed much to the shaping of his mind and art. The poet's unpublished philosophical notebooks are introduced in Jeffrey Perl's fine essay in the *Southern Review* anniversary volume; Eliot's early London years, including his extension lecturing and his relation to T. E. Hulme, are discussed in Ronald's Schuchard's essays; and the formative intellectual experiences are reviewed in detail in Piers Gray's valuable *T. S. Eliot's Intellectual and Poetic Development: 1909–1922* (1982). Eliot's interests during the years of the *Criterion* editorship (1922–39) are chronicled in John Margolis's *T. S. Eliot's Intellectual Development: 1922–1939* (1972).

The Eliot instructor's library should include classical, modern, and contemporary texts of literary criticism, from Aristotle's *Poetics* to Jacques Derrida's *Of Grammatology* and *Writing and Difference*. Since Eliot was himself a major critic and a major influence on subsequent critics, his critical writings should also be represented. Austin Warren's two essays provide an excellent overview of Eliot's criticism and its relation to the poetry. Most contemporary theorists are grounded in Eliot's criticism, and inevitably many work out their theories in dialogue with his early essays. The issues of tradition, influence, literary ancestors, authority, reader response, and many others important in contemporary theory are basic to Eliot's criticism as well.

Bibliographies

A review of critical and scholarly resources related to Eliot is included in *Sixteen Modern American Authors: A Survey of Research and Criticism*, edited by Jackson R. Bryer. The section on Eliot, written by Richard M. Ludwig, is dated (1973) but still valuable.

The standard bibliography for Eliot's own writings is Donald Gallup's splendid *T. S. Eliot: A Bibliography* (1969), a new edition of which is planned to follow the publication of the poet's letters. The major bibliography for secondary materials is Mildred Martin's briefly annotated *A Half-Century of Eliot Criticism, 1916–1965*. Some 1,300 items not included in the Martin bibliography are listed in *T. S. Eliot Criticism in English, 1916–1965: A Supplementary Bibliography*, compiled by Mechthild Frank, Armin Paul

Frank, and K. P. S. Jochum. Another helpful compilation of secondary references is Beatrice Ricks's *T. S. Eliot: A Bibliography of Secondary Works* (1980).

The *MLA Bibliography* is, of course, the single most valuable annual bibliographic resource for teachers of language and literature. The *Annual Bibliography of English Language and Literature* (ABELL), the British approximation of the MLA work, is also extremely useful. The *Journal of Modern Literature* includes an annual bibliography of Eliot criticism. More current listings can be found in the *Humanities Index*, a quarterly, or the *Literary Criticism Register: A Monthly Listing of Studies in English and American Literature*. For teachers who would like a brief summary of articles, the best index is the quarterly *Abstracts of English Studies*. The *T. S. Eliot Newsletter* (1974), which was succeeded first by the *T. S. Eliot Review* (1975–77) and then by the *Yeats Eliot Review* (1978–82), which was revived in 1987 under a new editor, contains some items of interest. The first number of the *T. S. Eliot Annual*, edited by Shyamal Bagchee, was published by Macmillan in 1988.

Biographies

Eliot's letters have not been published, and other materials important for his biography are unavailable to scholars. The letters are being prepared for publication by Valerie Eliot, who has indicated that there will be four volumes and that the first will appear in 1988. In her introduction to the facsimile edition of *The Waste Land*, she included a sample of the letters in her possession. From this sample, it is clear that the Eliot letters are of the first importance for both biographers and critics. The forthcoming volumes will not, unfortunately, include the many Eliot letters sealed at Princeton University until the year 2020. No Eliot biographer has had access to the letters in Valerie Eliot's possession, and, of course, none has seen the collection sealed at Princeton. All Eliot biographies, then, regardless of the competence and the humility of the biographer, are incomplete and speculative. Perhaps the most reliable are the simple chronologies. The fullest chronology is *T. S. Eliot: A Chronology of His Life and Works* (1983) by Caroline Behr.

The most detailed biography is Peter Ackroyd's 1984 *T. S. Eliot: A Life*. Ackroyd did not have access to the poet's private papers, but he researched his topic diligently and assembled much data. Over the years, a number of memoirs have appeared that, despite their subjectivity, do reveal glimpses of the poet in various contexts (e.g., Robert Sencourt's *T. S. Eliot: A Memoir*). Perhaps the most interesting of the memoirs are the brief ones collected in birthday symposia or memorial volumes. For the poet's sixtieth birthday

(1948), Richard March and Tambimuttu assembled tributes from over twenty of his friends, including Conrad Aiken, Clive Bell, Wyndham Lewis, and Frank Morley. For Eliot's seventieth birthday, Neville Braybrooke put together an interesting and entertaining collection of tributes, including material from schoolchildren and literary critics. In 1966, the year after the poet's death, Eliot's friend Allen Tate assembled a collection of brief and poignant remembrances by many friends and co-workers, including Conrad Aiken, Ezra Pound, Frank Morley, Cleanth Brooks, I. A. Richards, and E. Martin Browne. Herbert Howarth's *Notes on Some Figures behind T. S. Eliot* is still valuable, for Howarth's "notes and sketches" include substantial chapters on St. Louis and Eliot's family background, Boston and his college years, his studies in France, the early London years, and his work as editor and dramatist. A. D. Moody's 1979 *Thomas Stearns Eliot: Poet*, which combines biography and criticism, contains basic chronologies for each period of the poet's life. Many instructors indicate that they find Moody's work particularly useful in lecture preparations.

Literary Criticism

Two special resources will help the teacher sort out the most useful publications on Eliot before the 1980s. The first is Richard M. Ludwig's survey of research and criticism, mentioned above. The second is Robert H. Canary's *T. S. Eliot: The Poet and His Critics* (1982). Part of the American Library Association series The Poet and His Critics, which explores and evaluates literary criticism on major American and British poets, Canary's guide summarizes the most important English-language scholarship on Eliot and assesses "the current state of Eliot criticism in addressing the central issues raised by his work." Chapters are devoted to the personal poet (psycho-biographical-critical studies), the impersonal poet (theory of poetry, use of personae), the social critic, the religious poet, the traditional poet (Eliot's use of, and place in, Western literary tradition), and the modern poet (studies of modernism and of Eliot and his contemporaries). The topics overlap, but with the help of an unusually full index (writers, titles, topics), the scheme works. Canary reviews and evaluates Eliot studies and generalizes about overall strengths and weaknesses. His bibliography includes not only the articles and books under review but many others, topically organized in "Selected Additional Readings."

Michael Grant's *T. S. Eliot: The Critical Heritage* (1982) is also a basic resource. The Critical Heritage series, designed to show the reception given a writer by his contemporaries and near contemporaries, preserves early reviews, letters to editors, and other brief notices. Grant has collected two volumes of documents on Eliot and added an introductory essay on Eliot's reputation from 1916 until his death in 1965. Limiting his attention to the poetry and plays, Grant includes much interesting material (e.g., Arthur Waugh's 1916 remarks on "Prufrock" and Edmund Wilson's 1922 review of *The Waste Land*).

Much Eliot criticism (and criticism generally) from the 1950s to the 1980s can be associated with reinterpretations of literary history, with the relation of biography to art, and with theories of philosophy and language in poetry. Whereas most early critics of Eliot and of modernism argued that literary history is discontinuous (i.e., that the twentieth century is separated from earlier centuries by a revolution in intellectual history), recent critics have argued that literary history is continuous (i.e., that the nineteenth and twentieth centuries are both romantic periods). Early critics also maintained that continuity is the basic principle of form in nineteenth-century art but that discontinuity is the dominant twentieth-century principle. In this view, the modern arts are radically new, different in kind from those of preceding centuries. This position, which finds support in the history of science, politics, and philosophy and also in Eliot's stated opposition to Romanticism, was clearly articulated by T. E. Hulme before World War I and was taken up in the thirties by influential critics such as Leavis and Brooks. The idea that modernism is fundamentally different from Romanticism continues to be supported in Miller's *Poets of Reality*, which maintains that not only Eliot but also Yeats, Stevens, and Williams all wrote a new kind of poetry, and in Spears's *Dionysus and the City* (1970), which (following Hulme) describes modern poetry as an elaboration of several types of discontinuity.

In the past few decades, critics have disputed this version of literary history, emphasizing modernism's continuity with Romantic and Victorian literature. (See the essay by David Spurr in this volume.) In *The Poetry of Experience* (1957), a study of the dramatic monologue, Robert Langbaum maintains that the poetry of the twentieth century, like that of the greater Romantics and Victorians, is rooted in the primacy of immediate experience. Langbaum devotes considerable attention to Eliot as an exemplar of the poetry of experience. In *Romantic Image*, Kermode emphasizes the continuities running from the Romantics through the symbolists to the modernists. He argues that Eliot's notions of the image and of the poet are fundamentally romantic. Helen Gardner, in *T. S. Eliot and the English Poetic Tradition* (1966), also stresses continuity between the poetry of Milton, Pope, and the Romantics and that of Eliot. The insistence on Eliot's kinship with the Victorians and Romantics continues in George Bornstein's *Transformations of Romanticism in Yeats, Eliot, and Stevens* (1976). Bornstein separates Eliot's poetry from his prose as wheat from chaff, the poetry preserved as part of the harvest of Romanticism and the chaff cast into the fire. Bornstein begins and ends his book with Stevens (not Yeats), filtering both Yeats and

Eliot through Stevens's poetics. Edward Lobb in *T. S. Eliot and the Romantic Critical Tradition* (1981) and Gregory Jay in *T. S. Eliot and the Poetics of Literary History* (1983) reclaim Eliot's prose as an essential link between Romanticism and modernism. Arguing that Eliot is the literary father of Harold Bloom, Jay calls the second section of his book "Eliot in Bloom." Bloom is at the center of the movement to rehabilitate Romanticism, to supplant Eliot as critic, and to integrate him as poet into the Romantic tradition. As Eliot once referred to himself as "Anglo-Catholic, Royalist, and Classical," Bloom in the introduction to his 1985 collection of essays on Eliot refers to himself as "Jewish, Liberal, and Romantic." And he announces that Eliot has been absorbed back into the Romantic tradition that he struggled to disown. That the prodigal son has been taken in, Bloom reassures us, "is hardly a defeat; absorption is not rejection, and Eliot's poetry is securely in the canon" (6).

A second and related trend revolves around the issue of "impersonality," associated by Eliot and some of the older critics with a new twentieth-century classicism. Following the publication of the drafts of *The Waste Land* and *Four Quartets* and concurrent with a rehabilitation of Romanticism, more and more critics have focused on the personal origins of Eliot's poetry. Several pyscho-critical-biographical studies have appeared, the best of which is Lyndall Gordon's *Eliot's Early Years* (1977). Gordon's Eliot is from the beginning a mystic seeker after salvation, and her reading of the poetry parallels it with his spiritual quest. John Soldo's *Tempering of T. S. Eliot* (1983) is also a psycho-biographical reading of the poet's early years. Ronald Bush's *T. S. Eliot: A Study in Character and Style* (1984), a book with affinities to Bornstein's *Transformations of Romanticism*, reads Eliot's character (a misnomer) as torn between romantic yearning for freedom and classical longing for order and argues that the poet's style reflects this polarity. Armin Paul Frank's "The 'Personal Waste Land' Revisited" reviews studies emphasizing the confessional element in Eliot's poetry.

A third and overlapping tendency in Eliot studies is concerned with idealist philosophy, with the nature and limitations of language, and with contemporary literary theory. Following the publication of Eliot's doctoral dissertation (on F. H. Bradley) and concurrent with an interest in the importance of language in twentieth-century philosophy, a number of critics have turned to Eliot's studies in philosophy and to his concept of language. The focus on Eliot's philosophical studies and the interest in placing him in a modern tradition of subjectivity intersect in Miller's *Poets of Reality*. In *What the Thunder Really Said* (1973), Anne C. Bolgan, who edited Eliot's dissertation, claims that an understanding of modern idealism is necessary for interpreting Eliot's poems. In *T. S. Eliot: The Critic as Philosopher* (1979), Lewis Freed relates Eliot's literary criticism to his studies of Bradley, arguing that Eliot's critical language is to a large extent derived from Bradley. (See the essay by Glenn P. Wright in this volume.) Many recent critics have abandoned the search for "meaning" and focused on the logocentricism of texts and on the nature of language. Michael Edwards's little-noticed but brilliant *Eliot / Language* (1975) is informed by close readings not only of Eliot but of the French symbolists and contemporary French philosophy. William Spanos in 1978 contributed "Hermeneutics and Memory: Destroying T. S. Eliot's *Four Quartets*," followed in 1979 by "Repetition in *The Waste Land*: A Phenomenological De-struction." In 1985, Ruth Nevo published a much briefer and more down-to-earth article, "*The Waste Land*: Ur-Text of De-construction," useful for easing uninitiated students into discussions of contemporary theory. Harriet Davidson's *T. S. Eliot and Hermeneutics: Absence and Interpretation in* The Waste Land (1985) and Michael Beehler's *T. S. Eliot, Wallace Stevens, and the Discourses of Difference* use Derrida and other contemporary theorists as backdrop for their readings of Eliot. Sanford Schwartz's *Matrix of Modernism* (1985), a rich account of modernist poetics and developments in philosophy and science, is also informed by an awareness of postmodern literary theories. Schwartz's long chapter on the philosophical assumptions underlying Eliot's poetry is excellent.

Two of Eliot's earliest and most helpful critics, Grover Smith and Helen Gardner, have continued to publish books that should be on the instructor's shelf. In 1983, Smith published a study of *The Waste Land* that bulges with information about the poem and its origins. In 1978, Gardner published *The Composition of* Four Quartets, the one indispensable book on that poem. Gardner's study of the growth and development of the poetic sequence makes available and elucidates much of the material that lies behind the published version of the poem. The instructor should also have on hand two collections of essays. In 1973, A. Walton Litz edited *Eliot in His Time*, a group of essays commemorating the fiftieth anniversary of the publication of *The Waste Land*. In 1985, James Olney, whose *Metaphors of Self* contains an excellent chapter on *Four Quartets*, edited a handsome collection of essays on Eliot. Illustrated with previously unpublished photographs, it is one of the fiftieth-anniversary issues of the *Southern Review*, a journal with historical connections to Eliot and classic modernism.

Several commemorative volumes have been announced for 1988 as part of the celebration of the centenary of Eliot's birth. Further, the *Dictionary of Literary Biography*'s 1988 yearbook includes a collection of centennial essays. The *DLB* tribute includes essays by older figures such as Muriel Bradbrook, Katharine Worth, and Grover Smith, and by younger critics such as Cleo McNelly Kearns and Robert Crawford, whose books on Eliot appeared in 1987. Bradbrook's contribution, "Growing Up with T. S. Eliot," is a tribute not only to Eliot, but to an era in literary history.

Aids to Teaching

About half of the teachers responding to the MLA survey on Eliot use no teaching aids; some, in fact, maintain that to use anything other than the printed word is to compromise with a postliterate generation. Other teachers report that they have experimented with recordings, films, and other aids and that their experiments have been enjoyable and productive for both themselves and their students.

Recordings: Poetry

Many teachers are dubious, quite rightly, of the typical procedure of asking students (each at his or her own desk) to read a poem (in silence, to avoid disturbing roommates or being thrown out of the library) as preparation for talking about the poem at the next class. The relation of hearing a poem (if only in the mind's ear) to knowing it will be missed by most students unless the teacher organizes the first hearing. One instructor recommends that students pair off and read poems to each other. Some teachers call on students to read in class (see Rosenthal's essay in this volume). One teacher has students tape readings of the poems: "My students present 25-minute discussions on tape, with the stipulation that at least two voices be used, one for the poetry quoted and another for the critical discussion." Several teachers arrange reader's theater productions of either *Murder in the Cathedral* or *The Cocktail Party*.

Many teachers use recordings of Eliot reading his poetry. Several maintain that the poet, regardless of his or her ability as performer, is the best reader (see Clarke's essay); others hold that a professional reader is most effective with students. Whatever the choice, it is important that the listening experience be planned and perhaps related to a special problem in the poetry. Prolonged playing of recordings in class, of course, can do more harm than good.

Teachers of Eliot's poetry can choose from a wide variety of tapes and records. Caedmon has three recordings, available on LP or tape, of Eliot reading his poetry. *Poems and Choruses* includes "The Love Song of J. Alfred Prufrock," "Portrait of a Lady," "Preludes," "Mr. Eliot's Sunday Morning Service," *Ash-Wednesday*, "A Song for Simeon," "Marina," and selections from *Coriolan, The Rock, Murder in the Cathedral*, and *The Family Reunion*. The second recording, The Waste Land *and Other Poems*, includes *The Waste Land* in its entirety, "The Hollow Men," "Journey of the Magi," "La Figlia che Piange," "Landscapes," "Morning at the Window," "Sweeney among the Nightingales," "Whispers of Immortality," "Macavity:

The Mystery Cat," and selections from *Coriolan*. The third recording is a studio reading of *Four Quartets*. Eliot's voice is also preserved on a tape from Harvard University Press. In 1978, Harvard came out with tapes of readings given at the university between 1933 and 1970 by thirteen major poets. The Eliot tape includes "Gerontion," "The Hollow Men," "A Song for Simeon," "Fragment of an Agon," "The Love Song of J. Alfred Prufrock," "Journey of the Magi," "Preludes," and "Sweeney among the Nightingales." Eliot's reading of the Sweeney dramatic fragment, with its jazzy rhythms and modernist themes, its juicy little missionary stew and its cream of a nightmare dream, is sheer fun. Students may get the "hoo-ha's" from this reading, but they should also understand more vividly the difference between naturalistic and stylized form in art.

For teachers who prefer a professional reader, Decca Record Company has records of Alec Guinness reading *The Waste Land, Four Quartets*, and several shorter poems, and Caedmon has a record of John Gielgud and Irene Worth reading *Old Possum's Book of Practical Cats*. Guinness, a personal friend of the poet's, has appeared in numerous performances of Eliot's plays, including the original production in 1950 of *The Cocktail Party*. Two of Eliot's plays, *Murder in the Cathedral* and *The Family Reunion*, both featuring Paul Scofield, are available on LP and tape from Caedmon.

Recordings: Music

Some of Eliot's poems have been used in musical compositions. The most famous is *Old Possum's Book of Practical Cats*, which provided most of the lyrics for Andrew Lloyd Webber's 1981 rock opera *Cats*. This musical played on London's West End and New York's Broadway, winning the Tony award for best musical in New York. Eliot himself loved the music hall (see, e.g., his essay on Marie Lloyd in *Selected Essays*) and probably would have taken special pleasure in *Cats*. Be that as it may, the musical can be used to counter the stereotype of the poet as overserious, pessimistic, and humorless.

In a brief essay in Braybrooke's symposium for Eliot's seventieth birthday, the composer Denis ApIvor expresses the view that "no poet writing in English this century can offer the equal of [Eliot's] musicality, his sonorous lyricism, and his dramatic impact" (91). ApIvor, who has based compositions for voices and instruments on both "The Hollow Men" and "Landscapes," maintains that such verses are already "halfway to music." Several other major composers have used Eliot's verse. Vincent Persichetti's composition *The Hollow Men*, for trumpet and string orchestra, available on record, is a haunting work. *The Dove Descending*, Igor Stravinsky's anthem based on

Four Quartets, is particularly interesting in view of the Eliot-Stravinsky friendship and of the modernist breakthrough in form achieved by both. Benjamin Britten also used Eliot's verse in several compositions. Teachers of Eliot's verse and of the humanities who wish a fuller list of music using or inspired by Eliot's poetry should consult "Recordings" and "Selected Musical Compositions" following "Works Cited" in this volume.

Some teachers use music to illustrate certain principles of form used in Eliot's poetry (see the essay by Mildred Meyer Boaz). Preludes by Chopin, rhapsodies by Brahms or Liszt, and quartets by Beethoven or Bartók are just a few of the possibilities. Many literature teachers would not feel comfortable using this particular teaching aid, but most would be able to use, say, a nineteenth-century love song to help students understand the irony in "The Love Song of J. Alfred Prufrock," or a ragtime composition to help students with *The Waste Land*'s 1912 hit, the "Shakespeherian Rag." In an appendix to her book on *The Waste Land*, Helen Williams has a helpful list of rag titles probably known by Eliot. Three of our respondents use Stravinsky's *Rite of Spring* as part of their introduction to modernism and to *The Waste Land*, and two use melodies from Wagner (see the essay by Armin Paul Frank in this volume).

For students brought up on the Beatles and other rock groups, it is instructive to point out the influence Eliot has had on modern popular music, especially on lyricists such as John Lennon (e.g., "A Day in the Life") and Paul Simon (e.g., "The Sounds of Silence"), both well aware of modern literature. A striking instance of Eliot's presence in contemporary rock can be seen in an album by Genesis called *Selling England by the Pound*. "The Cinema Show," one of the songs in this album, has lyrics intelligently adapted from the typist-and-clerk scene from part 3 of *The Waste Land*. *The Waste Land*'s great themes of automatism, sterility, and lovelessness are captured in the lyrics; more interestingly, the "spatial form" that Joseph Frank attributed to the poem is illustrated in the song.

Films

Four of Eliot's plays have been televised by the British Broadcasting Company: *Murder in the Cathedral*, *The Family Reunion*, *The Cocktail Party*, and *The Confidential Clerk*. In 1951, in close collaboration with the poet, *Murder in the Cathedral* was adapted for film by George Hoellering (see Hoellering, "Filming *Murder in the Cathedral*"). At its world premiere in Venice, *Murder in the Cathedral* won prizes for "Best Film in Costume" and "Best Art Direction." Hoellering wanted Eliot himself to play the role of Becket. Eliot declined, but did agree to allow his voice to be used as that of the invisible Fourth Tempter. Some teachers assign the play and show the film. The difference in the play and the film can be instructive and lends itself to interesting assignments.

A film portrait of the poet, *The Mysterious Mr. Eliot*, is available from McGraw-Hill. Co-produced by the BBC and WNET, this 62-minute combination of documentary footage, interviews, and dramatic episodes explores the connection between the poet's life and his work. The film includes remembrances by Robert Lowell, Stephen Spender, I. A. Richards, Valerie Eliot, and others. A one-hour documentary on Eliot, included in the 1988 *Voices and Visions* television course, is available for classroom use. This film is valuable for its generous inclusion of Eliot reading his work and giving public speeches and for its presentation of the places associated with his life and art. This film is limited in that it was produced before the publication of his letters and without the collaboration of his estate and also in that it neglects the American Eliot, leaving the impression that he is primarily a British poet.

Miscellaneous

Two of Eliot's best poems ("Preludes" and "Rhapsody on a Windy Night") were first published sandwiched between a review of contemporary art by Wyndham Lewis and a painting by Etchells in the vorticist journal *Blast*. *Blast* was short-lived, but its two issues (1914, 1915), published in facsimile in 1981 by Black Sparrow Press, vividly show the close connection between modern poetry and painting. The shocking-pink cover of *Blast* 1 and the strikingly modern cover (painting by Lewis) of *Blast* 2 convey something of the excitement and even outrage produced by modernist art. Students instantly see the difference between a painting by Ingres and one by Picasso or Lewis and can be led to see analogous differences in Tennyson and Eliot. In a brief 1960 article and in this volume, Jacob Korg describes some of the possibilities that an intelligent awareness of movements like vorticism and cubism can open up for literature teachers.

Part Two

APPROACHES

INTRODUCTION

The following essays represent the views and practices of twenty-seven teachers of Eliot's poetry and plays. The contributors, topics, and approaches illustrate the great diversity and richness that exists in the teaching profession. Our contributors, from North America and Europe, represent several types of institution, ranging from secondary school to university. The editor of this volume and nine of the contributors are women, and one of the essays discusses the women in Eliot's poetry. Some of Eliot's first critics as well as distinguished critics from the past few decades are joined by several more recent voices in scholarship and pedagogy.

Most of the essays focus on specific poems or plays. We offer two contrasting readings of "Prufrock," Eliot's most frequently taught poem, by scholars who have been teaching the poet for many decades, Cleanth Brooks and Grover Smith. Graham Clarke and A. D. Moody write on two works, "The Hollow Men" and *Ash-Wednesday*, that are particularly helpful in introducing students to modern themes and techniques. Seven subsequent essays place *The Waste Land* in numerous contexts: the Western epic (Bernard F. Dick), Indic mythology (William Harmon), secular culture (Douglas Fowler), and the breakdown of community (Jewel Spears Brooker); Jacob Korg and Armin Paul Frank emphasize the contemporaneity of the poem's form, while Nancy D. Hargrove puts the poem in the context of the Jazz Age in America. Three essays broach *Four Quartets*, an especially difficult poem to teach. M. L. Rosenthal shows that the techniques used in reading simple poems are very useful in reading difficult ones like the *Quartets*; John Gatta puts the sequence in the tradition of mysticism; and Marilyn R. Chandler indicates the thematic and structural correspondence between the poem and both ancient Eastern thought and modern physics.

And what of the plays? Should they be dismissed, as they sometimes are, as a "historical curiosity"? Carol H. Smith addresses that question and demonstrates the distortion that comes from excluding the plays from the teaching canon. Katherine E. Kelly shows how the plays work effectively in courses on modern drama. Linda Wyman emphasizes poetic language in her essay on *Murder in the Cathedral*, and Ann P. Brady underscores humor in her approach to *The Cocktail Party*.

These specific approaches are placed within appropriate contexts by a number of essayists, especially in the first section. J. P. Riquelme addresses the constructive role that must be played by the reader of Eliot's poetry. Mildred Meyer Boaz discusses the music of the poetry; Joseph Bentley, the mythic dimensions of gender in Eliot's poems. Among background essays are David Spurr on the continuity of Eliot's work with the Romantics and Victorians, Robert W. Ayers on a course in Dante and Eliot, and Glenn P. Wright on Eliot and the British idealist Francis Herbert Bradley. James Torrens explains how he uses Eliot's essays as a bridge to the poetry.

Many of the approaches to specific works involve general issues as well. The problem of form in *The Waste Land* and in the modern arts generally is central in Korg's essay on the visual arts and Frank's on the cinema. (The question of form is also basic in Riquelme, Bentley, Brooker, Harmon, and Dick.) A number of essays are concerned with religion: Carol H. Smith and Ann P. Brady on the Christian center of Eliot's plays; Gatta on the tradition of mysticism that culminates in the *Quartets*; Moody on *Ash-Wednesday* and the idea of Christian community; and Fowler on religious poetry in a secular age. Hovering behind the essays by Moody and Brooker is the issue of a Christian poetic. Eliot's critical ideas, the topic of the Torrens essay, are also central for Grover Smith, who is concerned with both unified sensibility and tradition.

The nature and shape of these pedagogical essays reflect the pragmatic as well as the scholarly. See, for example, Rosenthal's explanation of the game of "Idiot's Delight" in teaching the *Quartets*, Brooks's step-by-step reading of "Prufrock," and Brooker's outline of assignments and class discussion for *The Waste Land*. Finally, essays dealing with specific pedagogical contexts include Jeanne Gunner on Eliot in literature-based composition courses and Rex McGuinn on introducing the poet in secondary school.

We dedicate the essays that follow to improved teaching and scholarship and to a greater understanding of Eliot's work.

GENERAL APPROACHES

Poetic Creation and the Double in Eliot's Poetry

J. P. Riquelme

Students encountering Eliot's poetry, whether the text be an early one, such as "Prufrock," or a late one, such as *Four Quartets*, are invariably puzzled by the pervasive discontinuities. It is possible to channel their puzzlement into a coherent response to the textual difficulties by placing the poems within the tradition of the dramatic monologue. This can be done by having students read an example, such as Browning's "My Last Duchess," or by reminding them of the form's characteristics, which Eliot would have come to know well as he became acquainted with the poetry written by his Victorian predecessors. The description of the dramatic monologue provided by M. H. Abrams in *A Glossary of Literary Terms* is a good place to begin.

If asked to compare "Prufrock" to the dramatic monologue as Abrams describes it, students will often see that Eliot was relying on his readers' familiarity with a poetic tradition that he was in the process of transforming. They may note that "you and I" and "us" in the first verse paragraph of "Prufrock" and elsewhere in the poem can be interpreted in various ways: as suggesting, in the tradition of the dramatic monologue, a speaker and a silent listener in an external scene; as presenting the speaker taking on the role of listener as well in silent, interior dialogue with himself; and as encouraging the reader to fill the role of listener, since "you" can be read as an instance of direct address. In this last possibility, the reader could be the listener either in a dramatized scene or within the speaker's mind.

Such a discussion can lead in many directions, depending on the group's background and interests. The class might focus attention on details of style, especially on ways that the poem's language differs from our expectations of a dramatic monologue. Or the discussion might concern itself with the responses evoked in readers by those stylistic details. Or it might explore the possible reasons Eliot decided to renovate this particular traditional form rather than another.

This last topic can be developed to encompass the other two. Eliot is trying both to create a new style, one distinctly different from the conventional styles he encountered in his reading of nineteenth- and early twentieth-century poetry, and to encourage a particular kind and degree of engagement in the reader. By approaching this dual attempt in terms of literary history, a teacher can make students aware of Eliot's relation to the English Romantic poets as well as to the Victorians. Without going into much detail concerning texts that are unknown to the class, a teacher can pass on the fact that the dramatic monologue arose as a response to the conventions of Romantic poetry, that it is one way to create distance between the writer and the fictitious speaker in the poem. (Robert Langbaum's discussion of the dramatic monologue in the second chapter of *The Poetry of Experience* provides useful information on this topic. Alan Sinfield's response to Langbaum in his *Dramatic Monologue*, especially chapter 6, "The Victorians," is also helpful.) This fact can help sensitize relatively inexperienced students to a poet's choice of personae. Once students understand that Romantic poets wrote lyrics whose "I" was generally not distinguished from the "I" of the writer, they can begin to see that many of Eliot's poems involve a more complicated swerve from Romantic conventions than do the Victorian dramatic monologues. His poems are often interiorized dialogues in which one half of the speaker's mind is quiet, but, as in the dramatic monologue, the speaker seems at times to be addressing a real person, whose role the reader assumes. Since Eliot does not situate the speaker as a historical personage in the way Browning does, the reader's assumption of the listener's role takes a new form. The reader is being addressed in a familiar, even an intimate way by the speaker, who says things that he might not say to a stranger. Because of the interiorized aspect of the poems, this intimacy can encourage us to feel that we are not only the listener in a dramatized scene but also the interior listener. We oscillate between roles in our response.

As in Romantic poetry, we are encouraged by some details of style to identify with the speaker, but in a different way, since we do not take on the role of the poet's "I." The difference involves the doubling of the poet, the fictitious speaker, and the reader. As in the dramatic monologue, the poet presents himself in two roles as both the writer of the poem and the "I" who speaks but is not identical with the writer. (A comparison with the way actors take on roles in dramatic performances will often make the doubling clearer to readers who do not normally think of poetic speaking as this sort of active performance and role-playing.) In addition, the use of "you and I" suggests the interior doubling of the poem's speaker into a speaking and a listening self. Through partial identification with the speaker encouraged by the use of "I," the reader also experiences doubling in two ways. First, we are identifying with a speaker who is double, who is both listener and speaker. And, like poet and actor, we are performing a role, assuming a part that we know differs from our normal sense of "I." These various doublings are overlapping and mutually defining. That is, the speakers and listeners suggested by "you and I" tend to align both poet and reader with the doubled speaker and therefore with each other. Through the acts of writing and reading, both poet and reader perform the text through doubling. That doubling so forcefully and persistently evoked by Eliot's poems gives us a sense of how consciousness operates that is distinctly different from the one produced by the Romantic and Victorian traditions his poems modify. The mental processes suggested by the poems' discontinuities and ellipses are differential. They do not depend on, and in fact undermine, the notion that the self or ego is unified and consistent. Instead, we observe and experience the mind in flux, moving in surprising and contrary directions, jumping without logic or association from image to image, oscillating between positions, and always engaging in dialogue.

Through our shared performance of the poem with the writer, we can come to understand that we are the co-makers of the poetry. Students who recognize in these texts the suggestion of collaboration between writer and reader are often encouraged to rethink the process by which writing—not only a poet's but theirs—can take place. For Eliot, as for all of us, writing involves a process of revision that depends on the help of readers. Eliot's readers were sometimes other poets. The dedication of *The Waste Land* to Ezra Pound, who gave Eliot detailed advice for revisions, suggests the importance of collaboration. The documentary evidence of Pound's advice in the widely available facsimile edition of *The Waste Land* usually captures students' attention. But writers are always their own readers and rereaders in the process of revision, and that interior doubling of roles in the dialogue of revision meshes well with the interplay of roles between and within reader and writer evoked in Eliot's poetry. The evocation can emerge in discussion if Eliot's poetry is compared to Romantic poetry concerned with the process of aesthetic creation. "Prufrock," of course, does not deal directly with the problem of writing poetry, but it is concerned with the more general difficulty of speaking at all. The "I," for instance, worries throughout that he may not be able to speak at the crucial moment. Even the speaking that we take the poem itself to be may be only interior and not actual speech. The poem may be the preamble for the "I"'s *not* actually speaking. The difficulty of writing poetry is more explicitly presented in the later poetry, especially in *Ash-Wednesday* and *Four Quartets.*

As early as *The Waste Land* the nature of poetic creation is vividly suggested, for example, in the powerful lines of part 2 presenting the myth of Philomel depicted on the wall:

> Above the antique mantel was displayed
> As though a window gave upon the sylvan scene
> The change of Philomel, by the barbarous king
> So rudely forced; yet there the nightingale
> Filled all the desert with inviolable voice
> And still she cried, and still the world pursues,
> "Jug Jug" to dirty ears.
> And other withered stumps of time
> Were told upon the walls.

The connection to Romantic evocations of poetic creation can be made by citing such poems as Keats's "Ode to a Nightingale." As in the contrast between "Prufrock" and the dramatic monologue, the differences from Romantic representations are instructive here. Among the more important differences is Eliot's suggestion of intense pain and suffering as the source of the nightingale's voice. Instead of proceeding from a visionary gleam, the bird's singing (and, by extension, the poet's) arises from pain of the sort Philomel suffered when she was raped by her brother-in-law, who then cut out her tongue. And even though singing does still occur, Eliot stresses the problem of an audience lacking understanding, to whose "dirty ears" the song sounds like "Jug Jug." Those last words—if that is what they are—can be used effectively to suggest the reader's performative role, for they can be read aloud as garbled, strangled phrases, almost vomited out as JOURG, JOURG. So performed, they are the attempt of Philomel to speak without her tongue, the stump of which is glanced at in the phrase "withered stumps of time." The grotesque quality of the passage provides an absolute antithesis to Romantic presentations of inspiration. But the passage requires the reader's active, performative participation for its full effect.

The "stumps of time" suggest the source of poetic speaking in another, different way, if we understand them as referring to literature of the past. *The Waste Land* encourages us to interpret them this way through its abundant allusions, those fragmentary references to other texts that contribute substantially to our difficulty in reading the poem. Many discontinuities and doublings similar to those of "Prufrock" reappear in this longer work and can be similarly interpreted. But the allusions add something arrestingly new. They suggest the doubling of reader and writer, but not in exactly the same way as in "Prufrock." Now by means of the multiple allusions, the poetic speaker is cast in the role of the reader of the literary tradition. It is a tradition that has withered and nearly died because of the problem of audience implied in the passage about Philomel. Like Ezra Pound and the reader, who as readers help bring the poet's work to life, the poetic speaker gives new life to the texts he has read by inscribing them in his own for new purposes. He creates a voice for himself by taking fragments—explicitly mentioned in the final stanza—and making them provisionally his own. The issue involves silence, especially how to break the silence of the dead poets and at the same time earn a voice for oneself. The placing of Tiresias in the poem's center helps focus our attention on this issue, particularly if we remember Tiresias's role in *The Odyssey* as one of the dead whom Odysseus enables temporarily to speak.

The clearest and most accessible presentations of poetic creativity as the dead's coming back to life and speaking occur in *Four Quartets*, especially in the first two sections of "Little Gidding." "Midwinter spring" in part 1 can be read as the frozen land coming briefly back to life; this might refer specifically to creativity in old age, or it could mean more generally the return of creativity in the midst of a long, winterlike absence. In *Four Quartets* the allusions are not so intrusive and persistent as in *The Waste Land*, particularly since there are no notes, but they are still abundant. Readers who know the earlier poem may well see the allusions as again resurrecting the moribund literary tradition. In this passage, Eliot is resurrecting his own work as well by reconsidering and rewriting the beginning of *The Waste Land*, with its focus on spring disturbing the winter. And he is sending us back to such Romantic poems as Wordsworth's "Tintern Abbey," which also concerns a visit to a ruined religious shrine. The reference to "the hedgerow" in the first stanza of "Little Gidding" recalls the mention of hedgerows at the beginning of Wordsworth's poem. The differences between Eliot and the Romantics persist, however, especially in Eliot's skepticism. At the end of "Ode to the West Wind," for example, Shelley declares optimistically, "O, Wind, / If Winter comes, can Spring be far behind?" Not only does Eliot's speaker say there is "no wind," he goes on to ask, "Where is the summer, the unimaginable / Zero summer?" Like the blossoms of snow decorating the hedgerow, the returning ability to create may not be real; this brief spring may be a delusion that will be followed by no productive summer.

The long passage concerning "a familiar compound ghost" in the second part of "Little Gidding" also sends us back to its sources in the literary tradition. Most frequently Yeats is identified as one of the primary elements in the compound. Dante is an important precursor, too, as is Shelley, who

uses terza rima in "The Triumph of Life" to present a dead master. But
Eliot is also reconsidering his own earlier work again, for the passage recalls
the one at the end of the first part of *The Waste Land* in which the speaker
encounters his dead friend Stetson. That passage ends with an allusion to
Baudelaire in a line "You! hypocrite lecteur!—mon semblable,—mon frère!"
that clearly invites the reader as a double to be part of the poem's performance. In "Little Gidding," Eliot shifts the emphasis from the reader as his
double to his relationship with writers he has read as one of doubling. The
entire passage of over seventy lines is worth close discussion in this regard,
but the following segment presents the doubling most obviously:

> I caught the sudden look of some dead master
> Whom I had known, forgotten, half recalled
>   Both one and many; in the brown baked features
>   The eyes of a familiar compound ghost
> Both intimate and unidentifiable.
> So I assumed a double part, and cried
> And heard another's voice cry: "What! are *you* here?"
> Although we were not. I was still the same,
>   Knowing myself yet being someone other—

Parts of this passage could be used to describe "Prufrock" in the way I
suggested earlier. We encounter a speaker in that poem who is "[b]oth
intimate and unidentifiable," and in response we assume "a double part" in
various senses. But the passage refers more immediately to the role of the
poetic speakers in *The Waste Land* and *Four Quartets*, in which evocations
of the literary tradition are so pervasive. As the poet writes, he encounters
the ghosts of dead writers whom he has read and only partially remembers.
That is, the literary language in his memory becomes revivified and transformed by his process of poetic speaking. This process includes assuming "a
double part," taking on the role of another writer by crying out in that other's
voice. This differential process of "[k]nowing myself yet being someone
other" is the process of writing that Eliot encourages his readers to share
with him through the discontinuities and ellipses of form evident even in
such an early poem as "Prufrock." In reading Eliot we can engage actively
in a process of doubling and discover that reading is the double of writing.

Eliot, Modern Poetry, and the Romantic Tradition

David Spurr

In his introduction to *The Use of Poetry and the Use of Criticism,* Eliot recalls the "new world of feeling" that opened to him when, at about the age of fourteen, he read FitzGerald's *Rubáiyát of Omar Khayyám:* "It was like a sudden conversion; the world appeared anew, painted with bright, delicious, and painful colours. Thereupon I took the usual adolescent course with Byron, Shelley, Keats, Rossetti, Swinburne" (33). This confession reminds us of Eliot's debt to the Romantic tradition—his well-known anti-Romanticism notwithstanding—and suggests that his poetic career evolves in relation to a deep and original identification with his Romantic forebears. The inevitable complexity and ambivalence of this relation have become a central topic of inquiry for a course I teach on modern poetry and the Romantic tradition.

My approach to this subject begins with the assumption that students need a historical sense of the sources of modern poetry. They must learn to see the modernist aesthetic, Eliot's in particular, not as isolated from historical context but as a natural descendant of the Romantic revolution in literary form and sensibility. This assumption also implies that students themselves must learn to recognize Romantic influence in modern poetry and to apply that recognition toward their own acts of interpretation and analysis. In practical terms, a course in reading poetry ought to provide students with a critical vocabulary that allows them to think imaginatively and coherently about what they read. This essay suggests one way to create that vocabulary.

I begin the class with a two-week crash course in Romantic poetry, in which we read a few selected poems from Wordsworth, Coleridge, Shelley, and Keats. Once the conventions of the Romantic mode have been established, we spend roughly three weeks each on Yeats, Eliot, and Stevens, emphasizing the particular ways in which each poet carries forth or responds to Romantic tradition. Eliot's anti-Romanticism—a position he reaches partly in reaction to his adolescent passion—can thus be seen in contrast to Yeats's late Romanticism and Stevens's "new romanticism." In this light, modernism itself is understood as a natural outgrowth of the poetic tradition.

This evolutionary notion provides a thematic thread running through the course—that modern poetry not only reflects the historical background of Romanticism but also extends and transforms the basic principles of Romanticism: sensation as primary experience, transcendence of time and space, organic form, the sympathetic and visionary imagination. Apart from these fundamental values, modern poetry also carries forward certain Romantic conventions of poetic practice: the enlivening attention to concrete particulars, the uses of suggestion and ambiguity, the spontaneity and naturalness of diction and syntax, the merging of tenor and vehicle, the fusion of literal and figurative language, and the correspondences, in the sense implied by Baudelaire's poem of that title, among different objects in the natural landscape.

To the extent that a modern poet such as Eliot espouses these principles and relies on these conventions, his work can be seen as a late movement in the development of Romanticism. But at the same time, Eliot's poetry defines itself as specifically modernist precisely in those places where it distorts, inverts, or otherwise transforms Romantic conventions for his anti-Romantic purposes.

The initial crash course in Romanticism introduces a common set of referents both for students who have studied Romanticism and for those who are encountering it for the first time. During these two weeks we read some of the familiar poems of the period: "Tintern Abbey," "Frost at Midnight," "Kubla Khan," "Mont Blanc," "Ode to a Nightingale," "Ode on a Grecian Urn." These poems are chosen for their brevity, for their representative quality in incorporating standard Romantic conventions, and for their formal similarity: each can be read as an example of the genre defined by M. H. Abrams in "Structure and Style in the Greater Romantic Lyric."

According to Abrams, the greater Romantic lyric begins with a description of a landscape; some aspect of the landscape then leads to an inward turning of the speaker's mind, toward memory, thought, feeling, or visionary anticipation—a meditative process that nonetheless remains connected to the outer scene. Often the poem ends with a return to this outer scene, but with a renewed understanding of it as a result of the intervening meditation. In addition to this outline of a basic formal procedure in Romantic poetry, I also rely on such works as William K. Wimsatt's "Structure of Romantic Nature Imagery." The idea is to provide my students with a series of structural criteria—Romantic building blocks—that are combined in various ways by the inversions and innovations of modernism.

In Yeats, Eliot, and Stevens I focus on what are regarded as the major poems, with a view to showing both the internal development of each poet's career and its place in the evolution of Romanticism. Many of the great modernist poems follow the form of the greater Romantic lyric, and virtually all of them can be read as commentaries on or transformations of Romantic convention.

"The Love Song of J. Alfred Prufrock," for example, relies heavily on such conventions. Like most of the Romantic poems cited above, "Prufrock" can be read as a loosely discursive, first-person narrative concerning the quest for the identity of the self. The poem appears to begin at a given moment and place, moving forward from there through the particular form of meditation that George Bornstein in *Transformations of Romanticism* has called, following Stevens, "the poem of the act of the mind" (2). Throughout the poem the outward aspect of the scene unfolds in close association with the process of thought, memory, and emotion taking place in the speaker's mind, creating a metaphoric as well as metonymic relation between inward mental action and the outward movement through time and space. In the poem's opening lines, the "muttering retreats" and the "Streets that follow like a tedious argument" make this relation between mental and spatial movement quite explicit. Eliot even uses the device in Romantic nature imagery that Wimsatt calls the fusion of tenor and vehicle: the catlike fog of the third stanza merges subtly into a foglike cat, so that the hierarchy of metaphorical relation is dissolved into a more fluid system of natural referents where the boundaries between objects, as well as their ontological status in the world described by the poem, become vague and indistinct.

In all these respects "Prufrock" resembles a poem like "Tintern Abbey" or "Mont Blanc." But whereas in Romanticism these poetic structures come together in establishing the unity of the self through the poet's vision of harmony in nature, in Eliot's modernism they become instruments of alienation. The grounding in a particular time and place, a device that in Romantic poetry brings about a sympathetic relation between the subject and the subject's natural surroundings, now has quite the opposite effect in "Prufrock," where a hostile environment—now urban rather than natural—only increases the speaker's paranoia and sense of isolation. The narrative movement of the poem leads not toward self-realization but toward anticlimax, with the speaker unable to "force the moment to its crisis." Likewise, the meditative process behind the narrative ultimately leads to no conclusion, but instead merely calls into question its own value as meditation: "And would it have been worth it, after all. . . ." The Romantic assertion of self-identity takes place here only in the negative sense, with the speaker testifying, however ironically, to his own marginality: "I am not Prince Hamlet, nor was meant to be." The fusion of subject and object, or of tenor and vehicle, that one associates with Romantic imagery is used by Eliot for purposes of disaffection rather than organic unity. The principal exception to this rule comes with the final six lines of the poem, where the speaker finds refuge in a dreamlike vision controlled by traditional principles of Romantic order.

Once students begin to understand "Prufrock" as the inversion of specific rhetorical structures in Romanticism, they are prepared to read *The Waste Land* as a radical extension of this anti-Romanticism—as a complete disruption rather than a simple distortion of Romantic principles. Though full of local scenes, the poem lacks orientation in a particular time and place. Though rich in historical allusion, it represents no historical moment. *The Waste Land* presents its landscape as a natural projection of an inner life, but it does so to express alienation from the corrupted processes of nature: "Lilacs out of the dead land." Where Romantic nature imagery takes the form of fullness and continuity, Eliot's images are those of absence and discontinuity: "the dead tree gives no shelter, the cricket no relief."

The mental action of *The Waste Land* makes yet another departure from Romantic tradition. Jessie Weston and the Grail legend notwithstanding, the poem escapes any controlling narrative development of the kind one recognizes in Wordsworth or Shelley. At least, the development is circular and cumulative rather than linear, so that it may be followed as a series of increasingly complex variations on a theme. The analogy with musical form works better here—especially for students brought up on music—than the one with quest romance. The absence of a conventional narrative development in the poem can be attributed to a meditative process characterized in part by fragmentation and reversal but also by the absence of an identifiable speaking subject. In contrast to the faithful if evolving continuity of the subject in Romantic poetry, the speaking subject of *The Waste Land* metamorphizes itself variously as Dante in the *Inferno*, as a middle-class English husband, as Tiresias, as Augustine, and so on. The poem plays itself off against the Romantic theme of self-identity through a profusion of different voices that relegates the speaking subject to relative anonymity.

Against this background of inverting or disrupting Romantic principles, the final stage of Eliot's poetic evolution may be seen as a partial reconciliation with Romanticism. The first section of each of the *Four Quartets* conforms to the structure and to the general thematic concerns of the greater Romantic lyric, where the poet works through the natural surroundings to a transcendent vision. The opening section of "Burnt Norton," for example, begins by identifying a coherent speaking subject—"My words echo / Thus, in your mind"—and by establishing a particular time and place, the moment in the rose garden, as a setting charged with emotional value. The outer movement toward the center of the garden corresponds to an inner movement through memory, "Into our first world," and toward the spiritual vision of the "heart of light" apprehended in the drained pool. Still following the general scheme of the greater Romantic lyric, the speaker is recalled from this vision in order to contemplate its meaning for a limited and finite world that "cannot bear very much reality."

In addition to this overall structure, other Romantic devices fill the first section of "Burnt Norton"; the return to a childhood world, the communication from and among elements of the landscape, the unheard music and unseen guests—all have their counterparts in the poems by Wordsworth, Coleridge, Shelley, and Keats that I have already cited. The remaining sections of "Burnt Norton" may be read as a series of attempts to interpret the essentially Romantic experience of section 1 for Eliot's own post-

Romantic sensibility. Eliot's career as a whole, in fact, can be seen both as a struggle with the emotional and spiritual influences that connect him to Romanticism and as an extensive reworking of the concrete formal methods he inherited from the Romantic poets.

The written assignments for this course treat the question of Romantic influence as a matter of technique and as a thematic concern in modernism. In one paper, students are asked to analyze a single modernist poem (e.g., Yeats's "The Wild Swans at Coole") as a greater Romantic lyric; in a second, longer paper, they are asked to compare the treatments of a single Romantic principle in two of the modernist poets, for example, organic form in Eliot and Yeats or androgyny in Stevens and Eliot.

In making transitions between major parts of the course, I rely to some extent on the prose writings of each of the three modern poets. In passing from the Romantics to the early Yeats, I discuss Yeats's essays on Shelley and Blake and his treatment of Romantic themes in *A Vision*. In the same way I use Eliot's prose commentaries in *The Use of Poetry and the Use of Criticism* dealing with Yeats and with Eliot's youthful experience with Romanticism. Eliot's impersonal theory of poetry ("Tradition and the Individual Talent"), moreover, can be read as a restatement of Romantic values in its identification of deep feeling and the unconscious life of the poet as primary sources of inspiration. When Eliot speaks of the poet as not a personality but rather a "medium . . . in which impressions and experiences combine in particular and unexpected ways" (*Selected Essays* 9), he comes close to Coleridge's idea of the eolian harp that "trembles into thought" when touched by influences from beneath and beyond the realm of conscious experience. As I attempt to show in *Conflicts in Consciousness*, however, Eliot's critical appraisals of the Romantics betray a profound ambivalence toward the poetic unconscious.

Although the course does not arrive at Eliot until its sixth week, it prepares for him in Yeats's mysticism and in Yeats's later poems, which introduce the ironic voice of the "embittered heart," announce an end to the Romantic era ("Cool Park and Ballylee, 1931"), and repudiate the poet's earlier "allegorical dreams" (*Collected Poems* 336). Yeats's idea of the mask anticipates Eliot's theory of impersonality, a debt that Eliot implicitly acknowledges in his 1940 essay "The Poetry of W. B. Yeats." Here Yeats is praised for having the impersonality of "the poet, who, out of intense and personal experience, is able to express a general truth; retaining all the particularity of his experience, to make of it a general symbol" (*On Poetry* 299).

In reading Stevens at the end of my course, we refer back to Eliot mainly to show the radical difference in his conception of a poetic universe. This difference can be seen by comparing any of Stevens's major poems with any of the *Four Quartets*. Stevens creates a decentered poetic universe, with order imposed on the world through the creative act itself. In "Sailing after Lunch," tired of the old Romanticism that has become a pejorative word, he envisions a new romanticism based in the imagination of the artist who continually renews the world, giving "that slight transcendence to the dirty sail" (Stevens 112). Eliot's own vision may be understood in contradistinction to this aesthetically grounded ideal. For all his anti-Romantic claims, Eliot comes close to the traditional Romantic ideals of the imagination as the vehicle for apprehending the sublime and of a supreme metaphysical order. This is in any case the dream, even if "never here to be realised" (*Collected Poems* 199).

Some Notes on Eliot's Gallery of Women

Joseph Bentley

The question comes up each time I teach the poetry of T. S. Eliot: "Why does he dislike women?" Until recently my answers were defensive and vague, usually ending with a warning to take poems as works of art and not as clues to biography. Such questions, invariably from women, left me with an accumulating sense of regret and clearly deserved to be taken seriously.

I asked myself a fundamental question: What does Eliot's use of female figures imply? Since virtually none of them seems to be happy or fulfilled, at least from male points of view, there must be something wrong with them. But Eliot's women are not his only unhappy personae; his male figures are also unhappy and unfulfilled. I decided that Eliot must be concerned with a situation comprehending both sexes and that his theme must be the perennial idea that life cannot be happy without a harmonious relation between the sexes. This answer, though embarrassingly simple, appeared promising because it precisely parallels the abstract philosophical question that constantly preoccupied Eliot: the issue of relation itself. In his poetry, criticism, and philosophical writings, he repeatedly examines the question of how individuals relate to one another and to the community, how the artist relates to tradition, how subject relates to object, modernity to myth, reason to emotion, human to divine, poetry to religion, falling in love to reading Spinoza. His treatment of these problematic relations is awesomely complex, but his quest is as readily stated as the old notion about the sexes: Without self-transcendence, without at least a sense of movement toward unity, life is impoverished and dismal.

The issue of relation, then, is at the heart of Eliot's poetry. On one level, his poems are accounts of failed relations, particularly of the ways men and women fail each other. The quickest way to make a case for this assertion would be to examine the figures in *The Waste Land*, along with the implications of the writings about philosophy and myth ancillary to the poem. In the classroom, the case could be introduced with a brief preliminary sketch of some of the feminine presences in Eliot's earlier and later work, such as the following: Prufrock fears cultured women who seem cool and unapproachable; the young man in "Portrait of a Lady" cannot clarify his feelings about a woman whose friendship he allowed to slip away; Gerontion laments his loss of a woman once close to him; and Sweeney deals with women by ignoring their hysteria—"he knows the female temperament"—and by fantasizing about murder and dissection followed by residence on a tropical isle where the facts of living are reduced to birth, copulation, and death. From his earliest poems to his late comedies, Eliot seems unusually aware of female victims. In "The Death of Saint Narcissus," a martyr ruminates on his past incarnation as a girl who was raped and killed by a drunken old man in the forest. In the unpublished "Love Song of Saint Sebastian," a saint fantasizes about sexual murder in a mood reminiscent of Swinburne's "Anactoria" and Robert Browning's "Porphyria's Lover." Much later, in *The Cocktail Party*, Celia, a sympathetic character, becomes a missionary in prelude to a dreadful martyrdom: she is eaten alive by ants.

Some have taken examples of this kind, along with the snobs, neurotics, and pathetic figures who abound among Eliot's women, to mean that the poet was a connoisseur of female misery. Such a conclusion ignores the way his figures are placed into carefully designed relations with men and the way most of them suffer because of masculine ineptitude or exploitation. Consider two poems from Eliot's earliest period, "Portrait of a Lady" and "La Figlia Che Piange." Both are detailed pictures of women in the process of being abandoned by men. The "lady" is a formal opposite of Prufrock. She speaks of her loneliness, of her need for friends, of her fears and regrets. In doing so, she prompts the man to retreat from her intimacies. He acts the way Prufrock fears women will act if he speaks directly and sincerely to them. The language of growing close fails in both poems.

In "La Figlia Che Piange," a manipulative male examines a dissolving love affair. As he meticulously "places" both himself and his beloved in this scene, he seems to savor the picture he has created:

> So he would have left
> As the soul leaves the body torn and bruised,
> As the mind deserts the body it has used.

Nothing could be more direct: Man is to woman as soul is to body, and the abstract deals with the physical only to exploit it until it is used up. In the years immediately following the composition of this poem, Eliot learned an immense amount about life, love, ideas, and art, but he did not substantially alter the equations rendered in these lines. They become emblematic of the perplexity and pain of failing relationships. Just as the Harvard philosopher knew how much genius had been expended on the hopeless but perennial questions of souls, minds, and bodies and on how the questions interpenetrate, so the husband, poet, and young man came to know in ever more problematic ways the most complex of human relations, that of marriage.

The equations suggested in "Portrait of a Lady" and "La Figlia Che Piange" can be developed by considering the mythic backgrounds Eliot used in *The Waste Land*. (The most useful works in understanding these mythic backgrounds are, of course, Frazer's *Golden Bough* and Weston's *From Ritual to Romance*.) The tradition of interpreting myths as traces of early fertility magic focuses directly on those aspects of myth that concern the contrary fertility functions of men and women. In the waste-land myths, the well-being and health of a king and those of his land are mysteriously related, with the impotence or guilt of the king resulting in the barrenness of the land. In mythic terms, the king is the guilty male, and the land is the woman whose health is impaired, whose fruitfulness is lost. The male carries the responsibility both for the plague and for its removal. He suffers both physical pain and the anguish of separation from his land. The woman also suffers, but she is neither responsible for her suffering nor capable of relieving it. This pattern assigns all blame to the male figure, divides suffering between male and female, and makes the healing of the female contingent on the suffering and death of the male. In philosophical terms, the male is a subject, the female an object. Unity of subject and object, either before or after an analytical process, is a condition of simplicity designating well-being—both health and love. The irresolvable dualism in the analytical center is the triumph of relational knowledge that locks both into closed systems and prevents communion.

Consider, further, that the main epistemological analogues of mythic male and female are, respectively, reason and direct perception. Reason (under some conditions, faith) is the means of knowing what cannot be directly perceived. These analogues are corroborated in myth by the remoteness of mythic fathers and the immediacy of mythic mothers. Mythic fathers live in the sky and bring their seed and messages from a distance. When they visit the earth to engender heroes and kings in the wombs of mortal women, they come in disguise. Their presence is usually unknown until it is announced by an oracle after their departure. The existence of sky fathers is an inference based on reason or faith. Mothers, by contrast, whether earth mothers or mortal mothers of half gods, are present in the flesh to be directly experienced. These distinctions in myth are equivalent to the distinctions drawn from common experience. We know our mothers empirically, in the womb and at the breast, but we must know our fathers, if at all, by believing what we are told.

In epistemological terms, then, myths on the failure of men and women to merge satisfactorily are symbolic renderings of the logical concept that the two kinds of knowledge, rational and empirical, cannot be validated when they are isolated from each other. The fundamental assumption in most epistemological thought is that reliable knowledge can be achieved only when rational conclusions can be verified by observations or when observations fit into a rationally coherent pattern. Though both modes are mental, reason is experienced as a subjective process and observation as an objective one. The interdependence of reason and observation is another variation on the need for a harmonious and complementary coexistence of the polarities of self and other, male and female. This cursory review of sexual, mythic, and philosophical analogues should reveal to students that the well-educated Eliot, at once strikingly intelligent and profoundly human, does not write thoughtlessly of females or of sexual relations.

Before returning to Eliot's poetry, however, we should consider one more item in our review of gender in myth, an item that is fundamental in understanding *The Waste Land*. In myth, there is an interdependence between linear time, leading inevitably to death, and circular time, leading to new life. Individual existence for men is achieved by emerging from the cycles of nature and stepping into a sequence of irreversible moments ending in death. Heroes and kings must move on a rectilinear time line, for their deaths are essential for the fruitfulness of the land. "By this, and this only, we have existed," Eliot says in the last section of *The Waste Land*, by the "awful daring of a moment's surrender / Which an age of prudence can never retract." These lines are usually interpreted as a statement of modern existentialism, but their first significance is mythic. Selfhood is attained only by the awful daring of existence in rectilinear time, existence characterized by irreversible moments. The price of this selfhood is mortality, a final fact that closes the frame around the life and individualizes it with a last irreversible event. The paradox of this mythic biography, however, is that it both represents and makes possible the curvilinear immortality of the earth. Without individuality, there are no heroes or kings, and without them, there is no one whose death and burial can rejuvenate the barren land; without individuality, there is no one to unify and fructify the land through a symbolic merger between male and female.

When mythic women become individuals, they do so, like Jocasta and Queen Gertrude, by the same process of transcending nature and paying the price of mortality. They too become human by becoming mortal, but although their humanity is placed at the center of focus, their suffering is not a redemptive event that unifies and fructifies the land. They merely suffer and merely die. Their catastrophes are not last events that move the gods to take away famine, plague, and political disorder. Their condition is for this reason more painful than that of the heroes. The women too give up immortality, but even though they are isolated from the primal female condition of being the oscillating earth itself, they cannot become significant sufferers. The way is now prepared for an understanding of Eliot's gallery of unhappy women in *The Waste Land*. After reviewing his descriptions of women in part 2, "A Game of Chess," we will return to these mythic analogues as stimuli to discovery in approaching the problems of harmony between the sexes.

"A Game of Chess" can be divided into two approximately equal panels, each one a portrait of a woman. In presenting these two women, Eliot alludes to several famous females from myth and literature: Cleopatra, Dido, Eve, Philomel, and Ophelia, figures whose biographies corroborate observations made in our discussion of gender roles in myth. The most remarkable aspect of Eliot's first portrait is that his long description never refers to the woman herself. We know the glow and glitter of her ornate surroundings, the smoke rising from her candles, the mingled odors of her perfumes, minute details about her art works, but nothing whatsoever about her as a person or even as a physical presence. She is a blank area at the center of a vivid field of sensations. We know nothing of her age, her appearance, her place in history, or even whether she is the same person who speaks at line 111. We seem to hear her speak desperate words to her visitor, but beyond her affluent status and her dependence on a male for some structure to impose on her life, we know nothing of her. Except for her hair, she remains invisible.

The second portrait of a "lady" in "A Game of Chess" is a studied contrast to the first. Lil belongs to a lower social class, anticipates major changes in her life "if Albert makes off," recalls past events that can have profound consequences, and seems to exist in a public rather than a private place. Further, while light dominates the first scene, rapid speech is the entire medium of the second, with the narrator competing with the bartender for attention. The woman in the boudoir panel is present but invisible, while Lil, the focal figure of the pub scene, is not present but vividly and empathetically evoked. We know no details about the first woman, but of Lil we know that she has bad teeth, has borne five children (one of them named George), has ruined her health with an abortion induced by drugs, is thirty-one years of age, looks much older, is married to a man who was recently in the army, and has misspent her allowance. We even know what she once served for Sunday dinner. We are as overwhelmed with personal data here as we were with information about decor in the earlier scene. What, we must ask, do these contrasting methods imply?

Some answers emerge when we superimpose the two female figures. The first is a voice speaking from a blank area in a picture. The second is a clear picture with a past, a probable future of abandonment, and no voice at all. The first, to put it another way, has no body. She exists beneath the seeable qualities of light and shadow. The second has a body that is a severe burden to her and a husband who exists only to exploit it on the rare occasions when he is present. The first feels the stress of having no structure to give meaning to her repetitious days and nights; the second feels the stress of being structure-bound, of being trapped in an ongoing nightmare that makes her both a victim of biology and a victim of mistaken attempts to alter bodily processes. Lil is being destroyed by both fertility and an effort to avoid it and as a consequence is likely to lose her only source of security, Albert, who is also the main source of her suffering. Too little sense of structure in the first woman is matched with too much in the second. The result of the superimposition of the two is a complete portrait of a woman, the victim of both male incapacity and her own inability to see a way out through personal initiative. Eliot's technique here is cubistic, presenting us not with one figure but with an overlapping, faceted, layered structure. When we superimpose Marie, the hyacinth girl, the typist, and other females in the poem, we glimpse Eliot's cubist portrait of a woman, his complete female structure, the suffering presence not only at the center of his great poem but also at the center of the ruined land itself.

Returning to the traditional associations of gender in myth, we discover the perspective from which this portrait can be seen as a coherent whole. The barrenness caused by the male, the dependence on the male for rejuvenation, and the denial of significance to female suffering are all much more easily grasped by students if placed in the context of the waste-land myth. As the land in the myth is unhealthy and barren, so the women in the poem are barren and bereft. The first woman is mentally distressed and virtually paralyzed. "Stay with me. / Speak to me. Why do you never speak. Speak," she pleads. Desperately dependent on the male, she cries, "What shall I do now? What shall I do? . . . What shall we do to-morrow? / What shall we ever do?" But the man in her life has too many problems of his own—he thinks, "we are in rats' alley / Where the dead men lost their bones." His inaction dooms her, for she cannot imagine taking action on her own. Lil, to say the least, is also unhealthy and now perhaps barren, directly from the effects of the abortifacient but indirectly from the effects of being used by a male. As in myth, the lives of these women represent the circularity of the seasons. Their endlessly repetitive lives are structured by and contingent on male potency. The "stay with me" of the first figure is the counterpart of Lil's fear that Albert will leave her. The feeling established by the allusions makes it certain that neither male will stay, that both the bored man in the boudoir and Albert will vanish. Both women will suffer, but neither will be permitted the significant redemptive suffering of males. Like Prufrock, who thought of himself as a secondary character, only an "attendant lord" in the story of his own life, these women are supporting players in their own narratives of personal existence.

The value of seeing Eliot's poem in the context of myth can be underscored by reference to the analogy with epistemology. Myth associates females with direct experience and males with reason, revelation, or faith. Female closeness and male remoteness form the complementary conditions on which the sense of knowledge and well-being are based. Regarding the other associations I have discussed—health, circularity, dependency, and quality of suffering—Eliot's women are similar to the women in myth. But regarding modes of knowing, Eliot's women are sharply contrasted with those of myth. The first woman sees what is not there, and she misinterprets what she hears, "the wind under the door." She smells only her "strange synthetic perfumes." Further, she herself cannot be seen by the reader, just as the absent Lil cannot be seen by the characters in the tavern. In a variety of ways, the empirical is defeated or distorted both by the senses of the women and by the method of presenting them in verbal colors and sounds. The intangibility of the first woman and the inaudibility of the second are further ways in which the perceptual is transformed into an unclassifiable array of unstable relations or "broken images."

The failure of men to cohere with these women is, from the perspective of myth, the failure of rational processes to cohere with observations. The objects of reason and faith are abstract, like Eliot's first woman, and the objects of perception are empathetic, like his second woman, Lil. But in "A Game of Chess," we can know the first lady only through an act of faith and the second only through an act of empathy. In neither case is there the complement of opposites that is basic to both health and knowledge. One implication is that androgyny is a mythic analogue of knowledge. Tiresias, thus, sees all because he is a complete, self-contained structure of male and female. In the absence of androgyny, collaboration between the sexes is a necessary condition of health and knowledge. One of Eliot's major points, certainly, is that the categories we normally separate into isolated mental compartments are complementary. The categories are, first, erotic life and, second, intellectual life. In "The Metaphysical Poets" (*Selected Essays*), Eliot located their dissociation in the English poetic tradition, but he was clearly aware that the divorce of eros from intellect, pleasure from knowledge, was a recurring catastrophe in history and before it. The separation was, if myth meant anything, the basis of both religion and art. The challenge is to remarry the two modes. *The Waste Land* presents the unlikelihood of that reconciliation but does so in a way that at least provides us with a dubious hope.

We can see now that to be evasive when our women students inquire about the wretchedness of Eliot's women is to perpetuate, to reenact, the disaster the poet presents in his writings. It is not women he deplores but what history has done to them. Both men and women are victims of the heresy of self-sufficiency. They are also victims of the notion—Gnostic, idealistic, or scientific—that mind is somehow superior to matter, that the abstract can exist apart from the concrete. Eliot's most famous concept is the "objective correlative," which proclaims that ideas, emotions, and objects must be united in poetry. Seeing how the idea extends to the much larger issues of love, logic, and religion releases us from the conventional perception that Eliot's women and men are negativistic images. They are illustrations of the need for harmony and the necessity of finding it—at least within isolated moments.

Eliot's Essays:
A Bridge to the Poems

James Torrens, SJ

In his fifty years of reflecting in prose upon the poetry of others, T. S. Eliot intimated, or even directly said, most of what matters about his own. His essays continually probe the quality of an author's presence in poetic writings by means of a term favored in the Romantic tradition, *sensibility*; his own sensibility at any given time, formed in the process of his writing as much as by his reflection on the writing of others, was the norm. While writing about others, he was "dealing with his facts," like the great poet-critics whom he admired. Walton Litz, in maintaining that Eliot "would not want us to read his poetry through his criticism," also admits that we cannot but do so, for the criticism lies along the "route to the work's structure and meaning"; but we need "good sense and judgment" (12–13).

Eliot's convictions about poetry, that ideal way of experiencing the real (to express the matter in Bradleyan terms), show remarkable consistency. And his favorite themes, pervading both poetry and prose, are already in evidence at the start of "The Function of Criticism" (1923): the artist's struggle against the ego, the path of heroism leading to "surrender or sacrifice," the superior value of offering oneself "to a common action." Austin Warren, in his essay "Continuity and Coherence in the Criticism of T. S. Eliot," extensively traces the constants in Eliot's criticism, the threads of his extended argument.

The notion of continuity in Eliot, nevertheless, needs severe qualifying. The world certainly did not stand still around him during his productive years, nor was his inner life placid. With the seriousness of Matthew Arnold, whom he both lampooned and admired, he labored as book reviewer, editor, lecturer, and writer of prefaces, sifting through "the best that is known and thought in the world," forever clarifying his convictions, revising estimates, correcting focus. To see the distance he came, consider the two essays dated 1917 in *To Criticize the Critic* (1965). They appear as foreign objects in that collection.

The poetry of Eliot too is a continuum with many phases. In a pattern like Yeats's gyre, he keeps circling back on early themes to take them up in a new way. We can chart in Eliot's poetic life a cycle of brief, intense activity and long rests. He would get something out of his system—exorcize it, as he said—according to his resources of rhythm and language and his insights at a given time. Then, reluctant to repeat himself, he awaited what would be a new explosion of inventiveness.

Giant steps take us from "Prufrock" to "Gerontion" to *The Waste Land* to *Sweeney Agonistes* to *Ash-Wednesday* to *Coriolan* to *Murder in the Cathedral* to *Four Quartets* to *The Cocktail Party*. The critical essays prepare for such leaps, and mirror them, and above all help us understand them. It remains here to suggest which essays go hand in hand with which poems and to show how. *The Selected Prose of T. S. Eliot* (ed. Frank Kermode) gives a judicious and fairly wide choice of his best essays and passages. (In this article sources are cited in parentheses for those essays that are not in Kermode's volume.)

The early versification of Eliot, his stepping out of the exquisite symmetry and smooth rhythms that came to him from the Victorians into the loose-line, underrhymed style of "Rhapsody on a Windy Night," is the background to "Reflections on Vers Libre" (1917). From that essay we can learn much about the training of his ear and about the deliberateness of his flexibility. He calls for "the ghost of some simple metre" and teaches a respect for rhyme even while showing how it can be hidden.

The few paragraphs excerpted by Kermode from "Henry James" (1918) help us approach "Portrait of a Lady," for the Jamesian title tells us that Eliot wants to do something like the master. Eliot too has a version of the "social entity" and aims to reproduce James's "mastery over, his baffling escape from, ideas." Eliot always relished the stolen title, the reference, intact or barely retouched; it let him express his esteem for a model even while making his ironic comment or modifying its argument. "Tradition and the Individual Talent" (1919) sums up, in the waspish way appropriate to the *Egoist* (1917–19), this engagement with the work of other writers, his adjustment both to it and of it. His poetic confession of debt will come a quarter of a century later, in the invocation and imitation of Dante in "Little Gidding."

The most challenging match one can make in the Eliot canon is between the essay "Hamlet" (1919) and "The Love Song of J. Alfred Prufrock." In "Hamlet," Eliot points out the importance of focusing upon the play as a whole rather than on the tragic hero and his personality, for it is only in the larger construction that one finds "in the form of art" Shakespeare's pained feeling about the self and the world. Eliot claims that a solid interpretation of *Hamlet* involves learning what material in it emerges as hauntingly distinct from the revenge motif that it inherits from earlier dramatic versions. The world-weariness, disgust with sexuality, anger at sham and duplicity, and self-doubt, Eliot argues, are in excess of any revulsion to be evoked by the "negative and insignificant" Gertrude (*Selected Prose* 48). Where does this excess come from? According to Eliot, something in the author's inner, resonating life seeks out an "objective correlative" to itself—a symbolic equivalent ("as if a magic lantern threw the nerves in patterns on a screen") rather than a logical explanation—yet, for whatever reason, cannot find or create an adequate context for itself.

Eliot's essay "Hamlet" is suggestive regarding "Prufrock." The poem is, in certain ways, a satire, but one in which the reader is forced to identify with the persona and is not allowed to laugh at him. The poem is also a confession. Prufrock, the hyper–self-conscious modern, would love to be heroic—to be both the romantic hero and the philosophical hero raising the great questions about human aloneness before the Absolute. But, post-Romantic creature that he is, he cannot emerge from the pain of mere velleity. Hamlet eventually (and somewhat ironically) resolves himself. Prufrock, prematurely cautious and nostalgic, lacerates himself in a rhetorical pattern that is reminiscent of Hamlet's. Hamlet also presents himself as "old," overmature in thoughts, the opposite of his immature elder, Polonius, who would need to back up toward him, crablike. Prufrock imagines himself "scuttling" in avoidance of reality, futile like Polonius yet in solitary pain like Hamlet. By analogy with the link Eliot sees between Shakespeare and *Hamlet*, one may be led to assume some linkage between "Prufrock" and Eliot himself. Perhaps "Prufrock," like *Hamlet*, can be interpreted as a "form of emotional relief" for the author.

Eliot's Harvard experiments in poetry and self-scrutiny led, on contact with Jules Laforgue and the French symbolists, into the first outcropping of finished works. Then he went dormant; little would come until Ezra Pound proposed that they both try imitating the French Parnassian Théophile Gautier. Eliot produced a series of clipped, obscure, cheeky quatrain poems. To appreciate these poems, we can turn to "The Metaphysical Poets" (1921), an essay also relevant to "Gerontion" and *The Waste Land*. In this review essay, he discusses "rapid association of thought," the yoking by violence of the "most heterogeneous ideas," a "telescoping of images and multiplied associations" (*Selected Prose* 60), all of which are characteristic of Elizabethan and Jacobean dramatists. Delineating with mock elegance his primitives (Burbank, Sweeney, Grishkin), Eliot is illustrating, as theme, and trying to reverse, in style, the "dissociation of sensibility."

"Gerontion," however, is closer to Eliot's true vein than are the quatrain poems. In this meditation on the breakdown of his own postwar age, he drew on the gloomy assessments of Julien Benda, Henri Massis, and Paul Valéry; he also drew on the work of the Jacobean playwrights who spun their horror stories at the downturn of the Renaissance. "Philip Massinger" (1920), "Ben Jonson" (1919), "Seneca in Elizabethan Translation" (1927), and the conclusion to "Thomas Middleton" (1927) (all in *Selected Essays*) are especially useful in understanding "Gerontion."

A passage from *The Use of Poetry and the Use of Criticism*, chapter 5, provides a key to the dense final section of "Gerontion," besides helping with the *Tempest* allusions in *The Waste Land*. Eliot, speaking of Coleridge's "Kubla Khan," discusses the "saturation" of certain imagery "with feelings too obscure for the authors even to know quite what they are" (*Selected*

Prose 90–91). The compression and polyvalence that he prized in poetry have entranced readers of *The Waste Land*. We might, noting the irony, call the poem a virtuoso performance of "Tradition and the Individual Talent." Much more to the point would be Eliot's brief appreciative notice of James Joyce, "*Ulysses*, Order, and Myth" (1923). Eliot had watched from the sidelines while Ezra Pound and the lawyer John Quinn fought to get *Ulysses* through censorship into print. In a few acute paragraphs about the text, Eliot not only sums up Joyce's method—"manipulating a continuous parallel between contemporaneity and antiquity"—but also intimates his debt to it: "Mr. Joyce is pursuing a method which others must pursue after him" (*Selected Prose* 177).

"The Hollow Men," a spin-off from *The Waste Land* and also, in its way, a generalization of "Prufrock" ("Between the emotion / And the response / falls the Shadow"), speaks in a newly abstract and reverberant manner predictive of *Ash-Wednesday*. The wordplay of "The Hollow Men" leaves us at a metaphysical impasse; in *Ash-Wednesday*, taking his cue from the religious wit of Lancelot Andrewes, Eliot resorts to religious paradox as an opening within what hitherto was hopelessly closed. His 1926 essay on Andrewes draws us right into lines 1 to 10, section 5, of *Ash-Wednesday*: "If the lost word is lost. . . ."

The 1929 essay "Dante," the most ambitious of Eliot's critical pieces, may be considered a prose companion to *Ash-Wednesday*. The shift in Eliot's poetry out of the narrative and dramatic mode, that is, away from the invention of traceable situations and personae, into a symbolistic pattern where the voice, the "I," is more generalized, will not surprise the reader familiar with this essay. Twenty years of reading Dante had convinced Eliot that "the allegorical method makes for simplicity and intelligibility" and affords "a peculiar lucidity" unattainable in confessional writings. *Ash-Wednesday*, like *The Divine Comedy* in its ascent to God, but even more like the *Vita nuova*, that pure-love allegory, deals in visions, the "high dream," which is a more "disciplined kind of dreaming" than the erotic fantasy, or "low dream," given such status by the psychoanalysts (*Selected Prose* 209, 207, 209). In "Dante" what Eliot says about the *Vita nuova* tells the most about the sensibility and mode of *Ash-Wednesday*.

Ash-Wednesday, as I argued in my 1974 *PMLA* essay on Eliot and Dante, is about Eliot's own "New Life," the purging of distortions of love in view of beatitude. We find in the poem a figure of woman as tutor-intercessor, which corrects the biting portraits of women in the early poetry. "The silent sister" of this poem is a composite of Matilda, Lucy, Beatrice, and the Virgin Mary, drawing subtly on passages in Dante where they appear.

In 1922 Eliot memorialized the music hall performer Marie Lloyd, that "expressive figure of the lower classes" (*Selected Prose* 173). He praised the "selection and concentration" in her comic sketches, a quality for which he was striving in *Sweeney Agonistes* at the same period. To call the *Sweeney* "unfinished" does not do it justice, any more than does the same adjective applied to *Coriolan*. *Coriolan* chronicles the paganizing of all classes, who have shifted their response of awe from the divine to that haunting presence of the 1930s, the dictator. Eliot conveys in this diptych the crying need for interiority in the era of the loudspeaker. And what he says in *The Idea of a Christian Society*, at the decade's end, helps explain *Coriolan*.

Murder in the Cathedral (1935) grew out of Eliot's partiality for poetic drama and his interest in the links of drama to ritual, voiced in 1928 in "A Dialogue on Dramatic Poetry" (*Selected Essays*). He gave his mature views on this subject, with autobiographical comment, in "Poetry and Drama" (1951; *On Poetry*). Of especial value is a passage about poetic drama in "John Marston" (1934; *Elizabethan Essays*), which refers us to "a kind of doubleness in the action, as if it took place on two planes at once." This doubleness, which is at the very core of *The Cocktail Party*, is also observable in *Murder*.

Murder in the Cathedral is contemporaneous with "Religion and Literature," written in the vein and after the model of John Henry Newman's lectures on the sensitive Christian reader. Eliot draws the line between devotional poetry, "the product of a special religious awareness," which is generally a "limited awareness," and "a literature which should be unconsciously, rather than deliberately and defiantly Christian." *Murder in the Cathedral* is devotional in the best sense; Eliot gives us a glimpse of its mainspring in a sentence of the essay: "What I believe to be incumbent upon all Christians is the duty of maintaining consciously certain standards and criteria of criticism over and above those applied by the rest of the world" (*Selected Prose* 99, 100, 105). Such criteria are open in *Murder*, mostly latent and veiled in *The Cocktail Party*.

In "Burnt Norton," the first of the *Quartets*, Eliot opened up a broad field of religious awareness. He begins in an impersonal, philosophic voice, one heavy with paradox but shifting often to the communal "we." His subject is the yearning for Eden and lost innocence. Section 2 starts as a tightly metrical, mythical version of the cosmic cycle; it then relaxes into long-line probing for those privileged moments when we can be free of "the enchainment of past and future." In section 3, treating of the false and the true way, he images, in a London underground, first the way of superficiality and distraction and then the mystical way of negation. (He treats the way of affirmation at the end of section 5.) Section 4, in subtly rhymed free verse and traditional images, suggests the natural cycle—love against death, movement slowing to stillness. Section 5 reproduces the ceaseless artistic struggle—words straining for a brief hold on contemplative stillness.

In the above outline one can detect the structure of favorite topics and meanings that Eliot pursued in the other three *Quartets*. Musical structure was a governing analogy for this poem; he gives us the working principles of it in "The Music of Poetry" (1942). This essay calls for "transitions between passages of greater and less intensity" in a long poem, "to give a rhythm of fluctuating emotion"; it points out that words, however rich in association, are beautiful only when attuned to context; it describes a poem's music as constituted of its rhythms plus "the secondary meanings of words" (*Selected Prose* 112, 133). Eliot loved to draw these double senses from Latinate words.

One concept dominates "The Music of Poetry" and its companion pieces in *On Poetry and Poets*—the "common style." In the days of the London blitz Eliot exercised a kind of piety toward the formative power of language over a people. Poetry's role was to refine feeling and thought, foster maturity, spiritually communicate. This is the theme of "The Social Function of Poetry" (1945; *On Poetry*) and the keynote of all Eliot's later work: Find the music latent in the common speech.

The "Dantescan Voice":
A Course in Dante and Eliot

Robert W. Ayers

His was the true Dantescan voice.

Ezra Pound in memory of T. S. Eliot

Early in my teaching of Eliot's poetry, I realized that I could not communicate to students a sense of the coherence of an Eliot poem so long as its heart seemed to lie outside its body in footnoted allusions to other works always unfamiliar, and often even unknown, to them. Moreover, the footnotes seldom disclosed the functions of the allusions to which they pointed: in quoting and alluding, Eliot characteristically used the tonality and thematic emphases of a whole work, not just the immediate context. For these reasons, some genuine prior familiarity with the whole of his more important sources and influences is essential for the reader who would grasp Eliot's meanings more than sporadically. The compound analogues and allusions fundamental to Eliot's poetry are multiplying mirrors intended to direct the reader to their ideal center and to incorporate both those contexts and that center in his own poem. Eliot's aesthetic of allusion, then, led me to broaden my course to include direct prior study of that writer whose poetry Eliot in 1950 described as "the most persistent and deepest influence" on his own verse (*To Criticize the Critic* 125).

But Dante, like Eliot, was a traditional poet, aware of the timeless qualities of great works of the creative mind, and he too re-creatively incorporated the contexts of earlier poets' works in his own. Thus the Dantean contexts in their turn demanded augmentation in a number of pre-Dante readings. The consequence was the evolution of a one-semester course that in its present form moves from biblical, classical, patristic, and modern background texts in the Christian tradition (2 weeks), to Dante (5 weeks), to Eliot (6 weeks), with ever-increasing complexity and comprehensiveness. A final week is devoted to rereading one biblical text, one classical or patristic background text, and one part of the *Divine Comedy*, in an effort to understand Eliot's statement in "Tradition and the Individual Talent" that "Whoever has approved this idea of order [that the existing monuments of art form an ideal order among themselves, which is modified by the introduction of the new work of art among them] . . . will not find it preposterous that the past should be altered by the present as much as the present is directed by the past" (*Selected Essays* 5).

The Bible was of course of special importance to both writers; both had it not only in their heads but in their hearts. In a sharply focused selection, we read Genesis 1–22, 37, 39–41, 50; Exodus 1–17, 19–20, 32–33; Ezekiel 2, 6, 10, 17.1–10, 22.23–27, 31.1–14, 47.12; The Song of Solomon; Matthew 1–3, 12–14, 16–17, 20–28; Luke 24.13–35; John 1.1–28; Acts 2.1–13; 2 Corinthians 12.2–5; and the Apocalypse. The usefulness of these readings for storing the mind with traditional ideas and images for later application to Dante's and Eliot's poetry can be illustrated by the Book of Genesis. Within the first minutes of the first day we find ourselves perforce discussing the garden "which was the beginning" ("Little Gidding"), as well as other biblical gardens (and woods); the cursing of the ground with its consequent transformation into a waste land; and the expulsion from the garden. From the story of Adam we move to that of Cain and Abel, in which Cain (humanity) is cursed from the earth, and, as in his exile he begins "our life's journey," he becomes "a fugitive and a vagabond . . . in the earth" (Gen. 4.12). The story of the flood introduces the theme of death by water, both destroying and salvific. That of Nimrod and the building of the Tower of Babel leads us to discuss the symbols of the city and the falling tower; the failure of human communication represented by the various Babelic languages; and isolation, destruction of community, as the first consequence of sin.

The importance of Exodus for the *Divine Comedy* is evident especially in the initial canto of each of the *cantiche*; and in the letter to Can Grande della Scala, Dante himself interpreted the *Paradiso* in terms of the Exodus story (Ps. 114). Aspects of the biblical story also appear in the desert imagery of *The Waste Land* and *Ash-Wednesday*. The Song of Solomon, introducing another garden, is the clearest poetic expression in the Bible and Christian tradition of the love theme and the marriage metaphor that underlay Dante's introduction of Beatrice in the latter cantos of the *Purgatorio* and Eliot's allusion to Spenser's *Prothalamion* in *The Waste Land*. As the most adequate allegory of the soul's communion with its Maker, the Song of Solomon became the epithalamium of the soul married to Christ.

Ezekiel, 2 Corinthians 12.2–5, the Apocalypse, and the Gospel of Nicodemus should be grouped with book 6 of the *Aeneid* in an apocalyptic tradition of formative power in the poetry of both Dante and Eliot. Ezekiel, explicitly alluded to by both, is notable not only for the splendor of its visions but for its call to the prophet (the poet?) to prophesy against a backsliding people "a whoring after their idols" (6.9) and for the unforgettable image of the valley of dry bones as a metaphor for the spiritual death and dissolution of the community. The few verses from 2 Corinthians record Paul's vision of being caught up into the third heaven. The Pageant of the Church, beginning in canto 29 of the *Purgatorio*, drew to some extent from Ezekiel, but much more from the Apocalypse. Those cantos, acknowledged by Eliot to have been of special importance for him, are intelligible only in terms of these biblical texts. The Gospels are concerned primarily with the life and death of Christ, to which there are many allusions in both the *Divine Comedy* and Eliot's poems and plays (especially *Murder in the Cathedral*).

Three classical readings are all by Vergil. Book 3. 239–452 of the *Aeneid* relates how the wind scatters the palm leaves on which the Sybil's prophecies were inscribed and renders her auguries indecipherable; the passage was certainly used by Dante, and probably by Eliot in *The Waste Land*. Book 6 of the *Aeneid* was constantly before Dante's eyes during the composition of the *Divine Comedy*; it is reflected in the physical plan of Dante's Hell in countless details, and it became fundamental not only for the *Divine Comedy* but for all later poetry of the hereafter. Although in eclogue 4 Vergil was actually celebrating the birth of a son to the well-placed Asinius Pollio, Dante's traditional interpretation of lines 5–7 as a prophecy of the birth of Christ is responsible for Vergil's presence as Dante's guide through Hell and Purgatory.

One apocryphal text included in the background readings, the Gospel of Nicodemus, relates Christ's descent into Hell during the three days' interment. As another apocalyptic text, it is analogous to Aeneas's descent into Hades in book 6 of the *Aeneid*. Like that text, it had as prototypes a series of old Greek descents into Hell—of Orpheus, Heracles, and Pythagoras, for example; both had Dante's descent in the *Inferno* and Eliot's in "Burnt Norton," pt. 3, as literary successors. Augustine's *On Christian Doctrine*, books 1–3, is an introduction to interpretation of the Bible basically as Dante read it, and it established for all time a grandly reasoned love of God as the bound and scope of Christian righteousness. Moreover, in simple and lucid language it constitutes a collection of Christian topoi and metaphors useful in reading Christian literature such as Dante's or Eliot's. Augustine's *Confessions* generally presents a paradigm of the faltering and inconstant progress of the Christian penitent, helpful in understanding the content and the movement of *Ash-Wednesday*. In book 11, which is specifically assigned and emphasized, past and future are conceived as apprehensions of a continuing present through modes of memory and anticipation, in a fashion that enables understanding of the concatenation of temporally discrete events in the *Divine Comedy* and understanding of the concept of memory as means to redemption of time in *Ash-Wednesday* and *Four Quartets*. Boethius's *Consolation of Philosophy* explores the metaphysical labyrinth of chance and destiny, of prescience and free will, of time and eternity. "A golden volume not unworthy of the leisure of Plato or Tully," as Gibbon said (*Decline and Fall* 125), it is not unworthy of the attention of college students, who generally much admire it. Boethius adapts the Augustinian argument on time to reason that God sees immediately what seems to us a succession of choices and actions, that there is thus neither divine foreknowledge nor foreordination, and that there is consequently freedom of the human will. But the

Consolation is useful in other ways as well. From the time of the *Psychomachia* of Prudentius to the *Romance of the Rose* of Guillaume de Lorris and Jean de Meun, desirable human qualities were personified, usually in the figure of a gracious or seductive woman. The intervention of Beatrice (as Theology) with Vergil on behalf of Dante in *Inferno* 2 closely resembles *Consolation* 1, prose 3, where Lady Philosophy appears to aid Boethius. Both are traditional predecessors of the Beatrice-Mary figure in Eliot's poems, wherever she enters.

Two modern texts—*The Bible and the Liturgy* by Jean Danielou and *The Sacred and the Profane* by Mircea Eliade—complete the list of background readings. The first studies the sacraments as efficacious signs, helping to prepare students for understanding the ritualistic final cantos of the *Purgatorio* or *Murder in the Cathedral*, and it articulates a Christological and sacramental typology within which a purified Dante or Becket can be understood and accepted as a type of Christ. The second considers the mythic experience of space and time in a world charged, like both Dante's and Eliot's, with religious values. While this pre-Dante portion of the course is perhaps strenuous, because of the need for the readings to be done and discussed in at least summary form within the first two weeks or so, it is not intrinsically difficult for good freshmen. The readings are intellectually congruent and often in useful ways even duplicative.

But Western cultural and literary tradition came to Eliot in its most urgent and animating complex of forms through Dante, and there can be no doubt that for Eliot the *Divine Comedy* was the greatest poem of the Christian tradition. He alludes to it or quotes from it almost countless times and repeatedly expresses his admiration particularly for its structure, which he describes as "an ordered scale of human emotions" (*Sacred Wood* 168). As we move through the Dante and Eliot segments of the course, my procedure in class, as in my comments here following, is to emphasize both those traditional elements essential to an independent comprehension of the *Divine Comedy* and those to which Eliot points, either implicitly in his poetry or explicitly in one or another of his essays. Since Eliot was both a devoted and a perspicacious reader of Dante, these interests are usually served by the same emphases. And from this time forward in the course, I attempt to sustain in the students a sense of continuity and tradition by constantly asking questions such as: Have you encountered these ideas before? Have you read of these (or similar) events, individuals, or objects before? Where? What images were associated with them in the earlier contexts? What were their symbolic values? What images are associated with them here? What are their symbolic values?

Cantos 16–18 of the *Purgatorio* constitute both the numerological and the thematic center of the *Purgatorio* and the *Divine Comedy*. In these cantos

Dante is instructed by Marco Lombardo and Vergil in the Augustinian idea that all actions of both Creator and creatures necessarily spring from love, and in the Boethian concept that the Creator endows human beings with reason to enable them to distinguish that which should be loved from that which should not and with freedom of the will to choose between the two. Thus in the Dantean moral order love and will are one, and, notwithstanding the uncontrollable operations of heredity and environment, every person is responsible for his or her own salvation.

The implications of this identity of love and will ray out through and structure the Dantean universe. Since love emanating from God impels the motion and the action of the whole living universe, those who do not love turn willfully away from God, exclude themselves from active participation in his universe, and destroy the bond of charity. Thus Hell is populated by self-centered souls to whom community or common endeavor of any kind is impossible. In the *Inferno*, they continually quarrel and attack one another; the damned move away from the shores of Acheron "one by one" (3) and are always ferried across the infernal rivers alone. As Satan's situation shows, their isolation is the very essence of damnation.

But as in a thousand ways Dante emphasizes the alienation and isolation of the damned in Hell, writhing in the torment of their own willfully and perpetually perverted natures, so he stresses the penitents' free exercise of the will to choose God, their participation in his universe, and their acceptance of Purgatory's flames, because there suffering "makes them clean." As a consequence, in Purgatory there is great stress on harmony, community of goods, and prayer for one another. In addition to cantos 16–18, the final six cantos of the *Purgatorio*, dedicated to the Earthly Paradise and acknowledged by Eliot to have been of particular interest and importance to him, call for special attention. These cantos dramatize the Apocalypse, atonement, redemption, and penance, all of which are fused in the meeting of Dante and Beatrice, and in them Dante has focused the whole human endeavor on the dream of return to original innocence.

In the *Paradiso*, community becomes communion, and beginning with Piccarda's speech "His will is our peace" (3.85, qtd. by Eliot in the 1929 essay on Dante [*Selected Essays* 226] and in *Ash-Wednesday* [sec. 6]), there is constantly reiterated emphasis on the perfection of the will in love. And these major themes are augmented by the emergence of others, especially the Incarnation (how, Dante wonders, can the timeless be incorporated in time?) and predestination (how can a human being exercise freedom of choice in a universe in which God's will must be done?).

Much of the most recurrent imagery from the first line of the *Inferno* to the last of the *Paradiso* is that of the garden (wood, waste land); to this dominant imagery the *Paradiso* adds imagery of light, music, and dance of such magnificence that Eliot expressed his "awe at the power of the master who could thus at every moment realize the inapprehensible in visual images" (*Selected Essays* 228).

In the *Paradiso*, as throughout the two preceding *cantiche*, there are insistent allusions to the harrowing of Hell, the exodus, the Babylonian exile, and the fall of the Tower of Babel. Springing directly from the last of these is the topos of the inexpressibility of the beatific vision by one who remains in the land of the living; and paradoxically related to it is Dante's grand conception of the universe as a book bound together by love in which the Creating Word has incarnated himself.

With such background, then, the students in this course come to direct study of some of the prose, poetry, and drama of Eliot. Here, reading of "Tradition and the Individual Talent" (1920) and "Dante" (1929) (both in *Selected Essays*) is followed in chronological order by "The Love Song of J. Alfred Prufrock" (1917), *The Waste Land* (1922), "The Hollow Men" (1925), "Animula" (1929), *Ash-Wednesday* (1930), *Murder in the Cathedral* (1935), and *Four Quartets* (1936–42; 1943). The first essay declares that the historical sense "involves a perception, not only of the pastness of the past, but of its presence" (4), a consciousness "not of what is dead, but what is already living" (11), and that therefore "the existing monuments [of art] form an ideal order among themselves, which is modified by the introduction of the new . . . work of art among them" (5). For students who are already familiar with the Augustinian argument on the simultaneity of past and future in the continuing present and who come to Eliot's essay with a background of constant emphasis on elements that persist through the various background readings and the *Divine Comedy*, these are not difficult concepts. In the "Dante" essay, most attention is directed to what Eliot says is to be learned from the *Divine Comedy*: from the *Inferno*, "that the greatest poetry can be written with the greatest economy of words, and with the greatest austerity in the use of metaphor, simile, verbal beauty and elegance," and that "the language of Dante is the perfection of a common language"; from the *Purgatorio*, "that a straightforward philosophical statement can be great poetry"; from the *Paradiso*, "that more and more rarified and remote *states of beatitude* can be the material for great poetry" (213, 214). These will be touchstones in the analysis of Eliot's own accomplishment.

The central Dantean theme of the identity of love and will, which Dante himself found in Augustine and Boethius and elsewhere, is also the central theme of Eliot's poetry and plays. The successes or failures of all his central characters are perceived and presented within the terms of this identity, although it is perhaps most fully expressed in "Prufrock," "Animula," and *Ash-Wednesday*. The theme of isolation, a major theme in the Bible (particularly in Genesis) and in the *Divine Comedy* (especially in the *Inferno*), is a dominating concern in all Eliot's work. *Ash-Wednesday* and *Murder in the Cathedral*, for example, are embodiments of these biblical and Dantean themes; in addition, they exemplify Eliot's use of the Mass as a structural paradigm and control, a strategy he almost certainly learned from Dante's practice in the later cantos of the *Purgatorio*. But together the major themes, images, types, and topoi that the course has traced from the beginning and for which we above found a focus in the *Divine Comedy* constitute a context incorporated most completely into the splendor of *Four Quartets*.

To consider how Eliot's texts can be enriched by prior purchase on our background contexts as mediated through the *Divine Comedy*, let us look at the first movement of "Burnt Norton" and the concluding five lines of "Little Gidding." Lines 1–10 of "Burnt Norton" are a straightforward Augustinian meditation on the possibility that if past and future are both present, a different choice (the door we never opened) must lead only to the same consequence (end). Mention of the rose garden immediately recalls the ideas and the complex imagery associated with the celestial rose of the *Paradiso*, which in turn summons echoes of the Earthly Paradise of the *Purgatorio*, the Garden of Gethsemane (sacrificial love), the garden of the beloved in the Song of Solomon (erotic love spiritualized), and finally the "garden planted eastward in Eden" (Gen. 2.8). Under the prompting of the Spirit (the voice of the bird; see Matt. 3.16–17) the speaker in memory goes back "through the first gate, / Into our first world"—Eden. What would have been the pattern of our history, and what the character of our end, had Adam chosen differently there? The "unheard music hidden in the shrubbery" suggests "the presence of the Lord God amongst the trees of the garden" (Gen. 3.8), recalls the music imagery of the *Paradiso*, and hints at paradisal potential. The speaker's vision of movement "in a formal pattern . . . into the box circle" in the rose garden figuratively recalls the thoughts of Dante as he experiences the beatific vision (*Par.* 33): within an abyss of light, he beholds three circles (the Trinity), the second of which (the Son) is a reflection of the first but is colored with a human image. Yearning to know the principle indicated, the principle of the Incarnation, that is, and how the timeless can intersect with time, Dante gazes in rapturous contemplation, "Like a geometer wholly dedicated to squaring the circle."

The consummate concluding lines of "Little Gidding" move into an elevated, enveloping, and altogether serene expression of faith that "All manner of thing shall be well / When the tongues of flame are in-folded / Into the crowned knot of fire / And the fire and the rose are one." Here Eliot certainly recalls lines Dante had set down relating to the same beatific vision to which Eliot alluded in "Burnt Norton," part 1: "Within [the Eternal Light's] depths I saw ingathered, bound by love in one mass, the scattered leaves of the universe: substance and accidents and their relations, as though together fused, so that what I speak of is one simple flame" (*Par.* 33; Eliot's trans., *Selected Essays* 228).

That Eliot did not merely take his resolution from Dante is evident at the end of "Little Gidding," for Dante does not directly fuse the purgatorial flame with the celestial rose. All the same, if we would know Eliot we must know Dante, for as Eliot himself said in "Tradition and the Individual Talent," "we shall often find that not only the best, but the most individual parts of [a poet's] work may be those in which the dead poets, his ancestors, assert their immortality most vigorously" (*Selected Essays* 4).

"You Are the Music": Tuning in to Eliot

Mildred Meyer Boaz

To teach poetry through music produces a range of questions, some problems, and many joys. In any interdisciplinary approach, one needs to consider what is most appropriate for the work itself and for the class, as well as one's own background. With Eliot's poetry and some of his plays, using music can help students to grasp the rhythmical, subjective meanings in ways that traditional methods might not achieve. I usually begin by illustrating musical references in the titles of the poems and allusions within the works, then move to discuss broader issues, such as modernism, by citing examples in music that parallel textural elements in the verse.

The basis for this approach comes from a range of critics, from Aristotle to Eliot. In "The Music of Poetry," Eliot asserts "that a 'musical poem' is a poem which has a musical pattern of sound and a musical pattern of the secondary meaning of the words which compose it" and that "these two patterns are indissoluble and one . . ." (*On Poetry* 26). Eliot also addresses the musicality issue in essays on Johnson, Milton, and Shakespeare (in *On Poetry*) and on Tennyson (in *Selected Essays*).

While not the usual starting point for literature teachers, this interdisciplinary approach appeals to many students. First, they generally enjoy music and with some coaxing can discuss musical elements, such as melody, rhythm, tone colors, and formal structures. On a surface level, teacher and students alike can hear varied melody lines, syncopated rhythms, the differences in sound between violins and trumpets, repeated phrases or sections of a work. Such awareness of musical elements can help students distinguish corresponding elements in poetry: its rhythms, voices, patterns. In doing so, they can become active learners in analyzing the musicality of verse.

In addition, students begin to understand how the sound and the sense of a work are interdependent and operate on abstract levels. Often we concentrate on teaching the sense of a poem to the exclusion of its sound. My interdisciplinary approach sensitizes students to those sounds. Finally, students can move from discussing concrete musical elements to considering abstract concerns, how poetry and music may go beyond language and notes. From such a perspective, they may better grasp Eliot's own interest in going "*beyond poetry*, as Beethoven, in his later works, strove to get *beyond music*" (qtd. in Matthiessen 90).

Eliot's poems contain actual references to music and musical forms. One might search out particular compositions for the sake of understanding the allusions, but a class might also investigate the particular forms and their relations with the poetry. For example, "Preludes," "The Love Song of J. Alfred Prufrock," and "Rhapsody on a Windy Night" all contain references to musical form in their titles, and the first part of "Portrait of a Lady" to "the latest Pole" who can "[t]ransmit the Preludes, through his hair and fingertips." To explore these musical references is to give students insights into both form and meaning.

"Preludes" provides a fairly easy approach for both teacher and students. While many composers have written preludes, those by Frédéric Chopin (the earlier Pole) are particularly accessible. His Twenty-four Preludes, op. 28, are available in a variety of recordings. Many students have heard or played them—in particular, no. 7 in A major, no. 15 in D flat (the "Raindrop" Prelude), or no. 4 in E minor (played by Jack Nicholson in *Five Easy Pieces*). Preludes are usually thought of as pieces that introduce longer works, but each of Chopin's compositions is free-standing and built on motifs or fragments worked out within the particular prelude. Thus one can choose a single prelude to make connections with Eliot's poetry.

In using music to teach poetry, most teachers like to begin with the entire work. Usually they have students listen to recordings; in braver moments, some of us have tried performing. One time I taught a class in a room with both a phonograph and a grand piano so that I could play melody lines on the piano after the class had listened to a professional performer on a recording. Some of my amateur performances helped clarify certain concepts. For example, in Chopin's Fourth Prelude the left hand sustains a regular rhythmic pattern while the melodic line in the right hand hovers around the one note of B. According to some critics, Chopin himself kept very strict rhythm in the left hand and allowed certain freedoms with the melodic line in the right. For students to hear those two lines is informative; for them to hear and see a performer's two hands at work is still more illuminating. Then perhaps they can understand how a poem may be constructed of iambic feet yet have a movement of line and stanza that works in counterpoint to the basic rhythm.

In Eliot's "Preludes," there is the contrast between the rhythmic pattern of the line and other verse patterns. The rhythmic pattern is predominantly iambic. The setting, however, varies, changing from passageways and vacant lots to coffee stands and the interiors of a "thousand furnished rooms" back out to the "city block" and the final "vacant lots." The time of the poem also moves—from six o'clock in the evening, to morning, to evening, to night. Listening to the music of Chopin may help students to develop their response to literature and to the shifting imagery, absorb the larger rhythmic time shifts, and hear (perhaps with their inner ears) the iambic beat of the line.

In addition, the moods of Chopin's preludes vary somewhat as do the moods in the sections of Eliot's poem. Chopin's Prelude no. 4 is often described by critics in poetic terms. While it is fairly quiet, lacking some of the tumult of other preludes, it has moments of tension, of pathos. Likewise, in Eliot's "Preludes" the tone is subdued with a kind of brooding quality, evoked by the images of "burnt-out ends of smoky days," of "the hands / That are raising dingy shades / In a thousand furnished rooms." That mood is also present in "Portrait of a Lady" where the man and woman have a nonconversation about the performance of the "latest Pole," their comments revealing their self-containment, their inability to communicate. In the man's mind, "a dull tom-tom begins / Absurdly hammering a prelude of its own." The "capricious monotone" he hears is reminiscent of the melody line in the Fourth Prelude that hovers around the one note.

In the Fourth Prelude the second part basically repeats the first but with a difference. Exact repetition is impossible. One cannot cross the same river twice. So too in "Preludes," each section both differs from and resembles the other sections. To examine these concepts, I have used a modern work, Erik Satie's *Gymnopédies*, a collection of three essentially similar pieces that differ in melody, rhythm, and mood. After the class listens to the three works, I use some transparencies of the score to illustrate particular features: the melodic line with some of its variations, especially the inversions, from one gymnopedia; the opening and closing bars from each piece, showing shifts in the resolutions of each. When possible, I have also played the works on the piano so students can watch as the left hand maintains a steady rhythm and the right presents a melodic line that seems to move detached and independent from that rhythm.

That both Eliot and Satie refashion earlier materials into a modern context also makes their works suitable for comparison. In addition, both Eliot and Satie work with arts that exist in time, yet readers and listeners experience a sense of simultaneity that superimposes one section or gymnopedia on the other sections and gymnopedias. The music and poetry exist on an immediate, concrete level as well as on an abstract, philosophical level.

Other early Eliot poems can be taught effectively through music. "The Love Song of J. Alfred Prufrock" can be contrasted in tone and style with love songs ranging from those of Eliot's day, such as "Ah! Sweet Mystery of Life" and "Let Me Call You Sweetheart," to songs of our time, sung by Frank Sinatra, Barry Manilow, or another current vocalist. Clearly none of these crooners likens evenings to "a patient etherised upon a table." By hearing recordings of these love songs, students may gain an awareness of traditional love songs and then hear how *table* in the third line of the poem is a jarring deviation from the opening rhymes of *I* and *sky*. In "Prufrock" the only song is that of the mythic mermaids, who are hardly fit recipients for a love song—an irony not to be lost.

Moving to Eliot's middle period and, in particular, *The Waste Land*, a teacher can point to musical allusions from opera, jazz, and pop songs, discussing the significance of those allusions within the poem and their discordant, juxtaposed effects. Two allusions to Wagner occur in the poem: *Tristan and Isolde* in "The Burial of the Dead" and the *Ring* in "The Fire Sermon." Isolde's "Liebestod" from *Tristan* is moving for most operagoers, especially after they have waited nearly four hours for it, but undergraduates generally listen to it only with much cajoling. Perhaps music of the Rhine Maidens from *Götterdämmerung* is more suitable. According to critics, there are anywhere from seventy to two hundred leitmotifs in the *Ring*. Each is associated with a particular dramatic idea, such as fate, death, redemption, Siegfried, and Valhalla. These motifs are varied as changes occur in the drama of the opera. In a comparable fashion, motifs in *The Waste Land* are interwoven into the drama of the poem. Memory, desire, the drowned sailor, the unreal city, water, bones, the fisherman—all these images recur within the poem but in different contexts. The themes of death, sex, power, greed, and destruction are present in both Eliot's poetry and these Wagner operas.

To convey the discordant effect of the Wagnerian allusions in *The Waste Land*, the teacher may consider juxtaposing Wagner's music with jazz. For examples of jazz, students may suggest their own favorites: perhaps Scott Joplin, Louis Armstrong, Jelly Roll Morton, Benny Goodman, or Keith Jarret. The musical spread from Wagner to Jelly Roll is shocking to most ears. Experiencing these musical extremes may help students experience the discordance in the poem's imagery and structure.

To move beyond musical references and allusions to musicality, I relate *The Waste Land* to Stravinsky's *Sacre du Printemps*, a major work of modern music. The Eliot-Stravinsky alliance is supported in their lives and their works. Both worked with mythic materials, placing them in a modern context. The fertility themes and the primitive quality of the forms convey deeper psychological and philosophical truths. In his 1921 "London Letter" column Eliot expressed his interest in Stravinsky's music, suggesting that Stravinsky was translating the "despairing noises [of modern life] into music" (453). Eliot tried to do the same in *The Waste Land*. He had written *The Waste Land* several years before hearing *Le Sacre*, but the fragmentary motifs, the rhythmic structure both in the lines and within and between sections provoke comparisons (Boaz, "Musical and Poetic Analogues"). Modern life is just such a collection of displaced voices and experiences.

Because of the scope of *The Waste Land* and *Le Sacre*, I use a two-fold approach: (1) analysis in class of the opening eighteen lines of "The Burial of the Dead" and selected portions of *Le Sacre* and (2) required listening out of class to a recording or taping of *Le Sacre* on reserve in the library or listening lab. I also place on reserve a recording of Eliot's reading of the poem, so the student can experience the total work. I ask students to listen to as much of the music as possible to get the effect and then to listen selectively, focusing on the basic musical elements. Is there an apparent melody? What rhythms are striking? Are the tone colors or sounds of the instruments distinctive? Are harmonies apparent? Most students react to the rhythms and varied tone colors in Stravinsky's *Sacre*. Such identification of the musical elements leads well into a discussion of Eliot's use of rhythms and of poetic voices.

In class, using the first eighteen lines of the poem, I discuss the units within the first paragraph: the clusters of lines—the first four, the next three, the following four, the interpolated line of German, the next four lines, and the closing two. I examine sound patterns closely, following specific approaches discussed by Kenneth Burke in "On Musicality in Verse." Burke discusses cognate phonetic sounds, acrostic structure, chiasmus, augmentation, and diminutions. Such analysis concentrates on the sound patterns, almost to the exclusion of the sense of the verse, and so some modifications are desirable.

Working through the large structure of "A Game of Chess" can yield comparable insights. Students may be asked to examine the imagery and diction of the first section and to observe the abrupt effect of "Jug Jug," comparable to the effect of the German in the first eighteen lines. The truncated dialogue in the middle, the diminution of "Speak," "What?" "Think" clearly exemplify Burke's point. Tracing the use of "I said," "she said," "the chemist said" illustrates a kind of syncopation, and the positioning of the line "HURRY UP PLEASE ITS TIME" illustrates a rhythmic displacement, very much like the displacement of musical motifs and rhythms in Stravinsky's *Sacre*.

The alliance between poetry and music is strongest in *Four Quartets*. The title alone evokes the works of numerous composers. Many critics have focused on the Eliot-Beethoven connections, but others (Howarth, Boaz) have cited the quartets of Béla Bartók. Of the late Beethoven quartets, no. 15 in A minor, op. 132, is particularly appropriate for study with Eliot's *Quartets*. Structurally, they are similar in that both have five movements, but they differ in other respects. In Beethoven's work, the third movement, entitled "A Sacred Song of Thanks," is the structural and the philosophical, nearly religious center. In Eliot's *Quartets*, the third sections of the four poems are structurally important, but the lyrical and philosophical centers are asymmetrically placed generally in the lyrics of the fourth sections, sometimes in the resolutions of the fifth sections. To use Beethoven with Eliot is to compare the music of a Romantic composer with the poetry of a modern writer. To illustrate the modernity of Eliot's work, especially the tensions between the symmetry of structure and the asymmetry of theme placement, I prefer to use the string quartets of Béla Bartók.

These quartets, which reveal Bartók's interest in folk music and early musical forms yet are modern in effect, convey both the intimacy of the quartet form in general and the structure and texture of modern music and Eliot's poetry in particular. I like to use nos. 4 and 5. No. 4 has five movements with a slow third movement at its center. One Bartók scholar, Erno Lendvai, analyzes the structure of Bartók's music by using the golden section and the Fibonacci number series (17–18). The study becomes fairly technical, but his discussions of the music's arch forms are especially relevant to Eliot's poetry (see Boaz, "Aesthetic Alliances"). By following the tone colors of the instruments and listening to the work several times, one can follow the progression and inversion of sounds. The circular structure of the sound echoes Eliot's own efforts: "In my beginning is my end," "In my end is my beginning." Like the music, Eliot's *Quartets* contains symmetries (four elements, four settings, four seasons) and asymmetries (five movements, golden sections). While an analysis of all the particulars requires more time than is available in any one course, introducing the musical quartet as a form provides students with a sense of its delicacy and strength, properties also present in the poetry.

Eliot's *Quartets* is a vehicle for discussing most of the issues present in an interdisciplinary approach to poetry and music. His title suggests his interest in the musical form as well as in the abstract dimension of musicality apparent in his early work. The four voices of the four poems move independently yet together, much as voices do in a string quartet. In the poetry, however, the four parts cannot be read simultaneously. The reader must reread and retain all four parts in mind. In this task, the recurrent imagery, the rhythms, and the telling phrases are particularly helpful. Most of these factors are also present in music, where one hears repeated phrases, sounds of different instruments, and varying rhythmic patterns working together to produce unity. The interdisciplinary approach advocated in this essay reveals much about both literature and music, and although it may ultimately reveal more differences than similarities, it is especially rewarding in exploring the musicality of Eliot's poetry.

Bradleyan Idealism
and Eliot's Cast of Mind

Glenn P. Wright

Unlike some verse for which students may need only a good dictionary and a handbook of literary terms, Eliot's poetry cannot be fully understood without access to special information, some of it rather arcane, outside the text. His allusive method obligates the attentive reader to study Frazer as well as Shakespeare, Dante as well as Wagner, Ezekiel as well as Hindu scriptures. Few modern writers make such demands on their readers. Nowhere is this point more evident than in the debt that Eliot owes to the British idealist Francis Herbert Bradley, whose epistemology was the subject of Eliot's Harvard dissertation (1914–16). Eliot's debt to Bradley need not be taken up in survey courses, but in more advanced undergraduate courses, the doctrines of Bradleyan idealism can be presented without distortion and used to elucidate Eliot's poetry, even for students who come to it with little preparation in the history of ideas.

Surely the initial step must be to clarify the major terms of Bradley's philosophy and distinguish them from their look-alikes in colloquial usage. Because of his study of Bradley, certain terms become charged with specialized meanings for Eliot: the Absolute, immediate experience, relations, finite centers, and transcendence. Advanced students, those with a solid background in philosophy, might on their own read selections from Bradley's *Appearance and Reality* (1893) or his *Essays on Truth and Reality* (1914), and perhaps then tackle Eliot's dissertation, published in 1964 under the title *Knowledge and Experience in the Philosophy of F. H. Bradley*. But these works lie outside the ken of most undergraduates and indeed are absent from the libraries of some colleges. Accordingly, some exposition of Bradley's concepts can help to clarify themes in Eliot's poetry and criticism and to indicate something of the poet's general cast of mind.

Idealism and the Absolute

Bradley devoted his career to developing a systematic philosophy that would avoid the inconsistencies and contradictions he found in arguments for utilitarianism and pluralism. He believed, above all, that the universe was one, a unity in which all disparate elements were subsumed and reconciled. A world divided into selves and objects, Bradley reasoned, relied on the principle of relations; and since each term in a relation depended for its meaning on another term, no one term could lay claim to being ultimate. Reality must be nonrelational; it had to be a unified whole. Although it could "contain" a multiplicity of terms and relations, nothing could stand in relation to the Absolute, since that would require yet a more comprehensive whole to contain them both. Adding up all the "parts" of a world, one must eventually arrive at an ideal construction, a whole that is somehow larger than the mere sum of its parts. In Richard Wollheim's terms (and Bradley's), the universe is a "system" rather than a mere "collection" of its parts (38). An alteration in any one part is therefore an alteration in the whole.

Immediate Experience

The doctrine of immediate experience is the foundation of Bradley's metaphysics, his epistemology, and his psychology (*Essays* 189). To talk about it at all is to use the language of metaphor, because immediate experience cannot be discursively analyzed. It is not, properly speaking, an object of knowledge, although we can—indeed we must—infer that it exists; and we can "know" it as an idea or "ideal construction" (*Essays* 412). Some students will want to argue that experience posits the existence of a self, an individual for whom the terms *my* and *mine* can be attached to the experience. Nothing could be further from Bradleyan doctrine, as Eliot explains in the first chapter of his dissertation: "Immediate experience . . . is a timeless unity which is not as such present either any*where* or to any*one*. It is only in the world of objects that we have time and space and selves" (*Knowledge* 31).

Students need to understand that the key word in Eliot's definition is *unity*, by which he and Bradley mean a condition without distinction between subject and object. Bradley often uses the phrases "felt unity" and "felt background" to emphasize that immediate experience resides in "feeling" (*Essays* 176, 177). Here is yet another term to try the unwary reader, for by "feeling" Bradley and Eliot do not mean the psychologist's feeling (pain, pleasure, ennui) or mere sensation or sense-data (Eliot, *Knowledge* 22–24). Rather, from the viewpoint of metaphysics, feeling is the condition in which subject and object are fused; it is neither subjective nor objective. Immediate experience, moreover, is not to be equated with the unconscious or identified with a self aware of its thoughts and emotions. An analogy, if not pressed too literally, can help. Students may respond to the image of a molecule of oxygen in which the shared electron has no sense of belonging to either oxygen atom and no concept of "self" or separateness from the other parts of this unity. If the molecule becomes part of a cloud or combines with another element, the new state can be discursively analyzed, but the experience of felt unity cannot be analyzed or known in any empirical sense.

Bradley's own definition of immediate experience is clear enough for students to grasp and useful for class discussion:

> We in short have experience in which there is no distinction between
> my awareness and that of which it is aware. There is an immediate
> feeling, a knowing and being in one, with which knowledge begins;

and, though this in a manner is transcended, it nevertheless remains throughout as the present foundation of my known world. And if you remove this direct sense of my momentary contents and being, you bring down the whole of consciousness in one common wreck. For it is in the end ruin to divide experience into something on one side experienced as an object and on the other side something not experienced at all. (*Essays* 159–60)

Immediate experience, in other words, is not a "stage" that is left behind or that ceases to exist; on the contrary, it is always present since it exists outside of time (*Essays* 178).

The world Bradley describes, therefore, is all of a piece. Alter any part, and the whole is altered; add an element—a new work of literature, a new perspective on a moment in a rose garden—and the whole needs to be reinterpreted, relearned. A word like *experience*, then, Eliot understood in a more technical sense than does the average reader who is unaware of its philosophical import. For Eliot and Bradley it means much more than a mere event; in the sense of immediate experience, it is the foundation of epistemology, for out of it arises the perceiving self as opposed to the objects of perception. This transcendence of immediate experience gives rise to the relational world of objects and selves, the world of partial realities or "appearances," as Bradley calls them.

The Doctrine of Relations

In discussing immediate experience in chapter one of his dissertation, Eliot uses the example of viewing a painting in which, if one is "sufficiently carried away," the experience unites the perceiver and the object in a wholeness of feeling (*Knowledge* 20). As soon as the perceiver objectifies the painting and begins to be conscious of its blend of forms and colors, the immediate experience is broken up into subject and object; it is not "lost," but it is in a sense transcended. This is a necessary activity, part of the human condition, because mere feeling itself is not and cannot become knowledge. As Jewel Spears Brooker points out in her essay "F. H. Bradley's Doctrine of Experience," analytical and discursive thinking creates a dualistic world "of the self and the not-self, the knower and the known" (152). If this apparent reality is granted an undeserved ultimacy, if the self becomes preoccupied with analysis and continues to fragment the world of experience, then the result is the paralyzing condition of Prufrock, trapped by paranoia and isolation. The same situation can be seen in the cry of the Thames daughter in the third part of *The Waste Land*: "I can connect / Nothing with nothing."

Eliot's position on the fragmentation of modern culture is well known, and on this issue we can conclude that he found in Bradley a kindred spirit. As a philosophical poet, Eliot sought for and achieved a unity of thought and feeling that he said in "The Metaphysical Poets" distinguished the poet from the ordinary person whose "experience is chaotic, irregular, fragmentary. The latter falls in love, or reads Spinoza, and these two experiences have nothing to do with each other, or with the noise of the typewriter or the smell of cooking; in the mind of the poet these experiences are always forming new wholes" (*Selected Essays* 247). This now famous description of the "dissociation of sensibility" provides an important means of understanding Eliot's cast of mind, his assumptions about the nature of reality and experience that determined the course taken by both his poetry and his criticism.

Finite Centers and Transcendence

Before empirically minded students lose all patience with these distinctions, they might be directed to Bradley's discussion of the "finite center" as it appears in his essay "What Is the Real Julius Caesar?" At the heart of this important essay lies a question often explored in Eliot's poetry: Can we know another person? If so, how? Arguing against Bertrand Russell's extreme empirical view that Caesar, because he no longer exists, cannot be a constituent of any judgment we can make, Bradley goes to great lengths to show that the view that one is bounded by birth and death accords an undue ultimacy to the physical body, which, like the soul, is an "appearance" (*Essays* 414–21; *Appearance* 262). Again, students need to understand that Bradley and Eliot use the term *appearance* not to mean illusion but to mean a partial or incomplete manifestation of reality. Failure to perceive the relational nature of these "appearances" fragments experience and pushes one toward despair and solipsism that both Bradley and Eliot explicitly reject.

One antidote, paradoxically, is the work of the intellect, which, although responsible for the construction of these appearances in the first place, can in a sense move beyond them. This kind of transcendence comes from the most arduous and disciplined activity of the mind. Brooker calls the state beyond relational experience "transcendent experience," a condition in which "*thinking* and feeling" are unified ("F. H. Bradley's Doctrine" 152). According to Anne Bolgan, this corresponds to the development of the "significant self," that which transcends the merely "empirical and phenomenal self" (137–40).

The importance of the move toward transcendence cannot be emphasized too much. It is the activity not only of the Fisher King at the end of *The Waste Land* but also of every reader who seeks to unify all the fragments of experience, including those of characters from other literary works alluded to throughout the poem. In fact, it is epitomized by Tiresias, who, as spectator rather than character, "sees" the substance of the poem and unites all. Less successful attempts to unify fragmentary experience and to transcend the phenomenal self can be seen in many of the first-person speakers (Prufrock, Gerontion) of Eliot's poems. Transcendent experience, students must recognize, is not mere euphoria; it is difficult, painful, and demanding because it is the realization of the pattern that is new at every moment.

At this point, an example from the poetry may be illuminating and may itself be illuminated. Accepting Bradley's definition of the finite center as a sphere of influence not bounded by one's birth and death, Eliot shows in "East Coker" how the mere private experience of the first-person speaker ("In my beginning is my end") is transcended as several points of view are synthesized:

> In that open field
> If you do not come too close, if you do not come too close,
> On a Summer midnight, you can hear the music
> Of the weak pipe and the little drum
> And see them dancing around the bonfire
> The association of man and woman. . . .

Class discussion of this passage should lead students to see that the point of view (finite center) is extended through the quotation from Thomas Elyot's treatise *The Boke Named the Governour*, as the speaker's voice merges with that of his ancestor, so that by the end of the first section, the "I" transcends the merely private experience of the man (Eliot) who visited the village in 1937. Thus the section concludes with the lines "I am here / Or there, or elsewhere. In my beginning." Students once exasperated with Eliot's assumed "imprecision" may, after the philosophical background is filled in, come to see that these lines are not imprecise at all. The personal pronoun is significant because it has ceased to designate an individual self and cannot be associated with a particular place or time. For all we know, the words *here* and *there* can refer to the village of East Coker, to the sea where "the dawn wind / Wrinkles and slides," or to the place of burial for those "long since under earth / Nourishing the corn." By the same token, the word *beginning* can refer to 1937, the year Eliot visited the village, or to 1531 when Elyot wrote *The Governour*, or to the present moment when we are reading the poem. The point is that the reference is to all of them, with the result that the pronoun loses its sense of the merely personal. The speaker in "East Coker," like Julius Caesar in Bradley's essay, transcends the boundaries of his birth and death and is present "wherever his knowledge extends, even if that knowledge is of the unseen present or of the past or future" (*Essays* 424).

Other applications of Bradleyan philosophy to Eliot's poetry will help elucidate some of these concepts. Brooker, for example, uses Bradley to explain the structure of "Gerontion," one of Eliot's most difficult poems. Specifically, Brooker shows how an understanding of Bradley's notion of transcendence clarifies Eliot's structural image of "houses within houses" ("Structure" 321). Gerontion's literal house, one of many houses in the poem, is situated in a number of increasingly comprehensive houses, including the nation of Israel, the Christian Church, modern Europe, history, and hell; and it is the relation among all these houses that controls the meaning of the poem.

Whatever the nature of Bradley's and Eliot's beliefs, it is clear that they do not equate the Absolute with God. According to Bradley:

> God for me has no meaning outside of the religious consciousness, and that essentially is practical. The Absolute for me cannot be God, because in the end the Absolute is related to nothing, and there cannot be a practical relation between it and the finite will. When you begin to worship the Absolute or the Universe, and make it the object of religion, you in that moment have transformed it. (*Essays* 428)

The religious quality of Eliot's later poetry is, of course, one of the most important aspects of his cast of mind. Advanced students may wish to try to understand where Eliot's philosophical approach intersects with that of Christianity, or whether they intersect at all. No issue is more central to understanding Eliot, especially the Eliot of *Four Quartets* and of the plays with their combination of philosophy and religion. Bradley recognizes that philosophy in the end demands "what may fairly be termed faith" (*Essays* 15), and Eliot echoes this idea when he argues that no object can be "known" directly, that knowledge "involves an *interpretation*, a transmigration from one world to another, and such a pilgrimage involves an act of faith" (*Knowledge* 163). As another term for *transcendence*, this transmigration is the basis of Eliot's epistemology and the key to some of the most challenging concepts in his poems and plays.

A teacher should exercise restraint in introducing undergraduate students to Bradleyan metaphysics, lest the philosophy become yet another obstacle to the poetry. The task, of course, is not to make the literature accessible by simplifying it; rather, it is to put students in command of materials that can help them to become better readers. As Eliot remarks in his 1929 essay on Dante, it is "better to be spurred to acquire scholarship because you enjoy the poetry, than to suppose that you enjoy the poetry because you have acquired the scholarship" (*Selected Essays* 199).

Poetic Voice(s):
Eliot in Literature-Based Composition Courses

Jeanne Gunner

At first reading, inexperienced students typically find the poetic structure of *The Waste Land* inaccessible, its content disjointed, its voice(s) mystifying. As they read, they become confused, for the poem sounds almost conversational to them, calling up expectations of prose communication that, with continued reading, are soon frustrated. One way around the frustration that students are certain to encounter when they attempt to read the poem as prose is to follow Eliot's own path, as we see it in The Waste Land: *A Facsimile,* and to attempt to "do the [poem] in different voices." By having students focus on the poem's voices, instructors can teach what is both a critical reading skill for the student of literature and a writing skill for the student in a literature-based composition course. The instructor can use the poem to help the student recognize different discourses, learn how they operate, and adapt them to his or her own writing style. The student learns how a writer creates a voice, in poetry or prose.

The Waste Land presents students first with a fundamental reading challenge. They expect a traditional poetic voice (if they make such an assumption at all; many read the poem, and probably all poems, as prose narratives). What happens in such an approach? All goes well for several lines; the reader can concentrate on the statement "April is the cruellest month" without having to identify the speaker. The first uncertainty is likely to arise with the line "Winter kept us warm"; suddenly, a speaker and some other person(s) intrude, in the form of a first-person-plural pronoun. From this point the reading problems increase with each new sentence, causing many students to suspend their prose reading skills (which are not working effectively in this case) without being able to engage a more appropriate approach. Thus, with the poem's opening lines and the students' concomitant confusion, an opportunity arises to teach a different kind of reading skill: that of recognizing poetic language and identifying poetic voices.

Addressing the reading difficulty can take two forms, one a prose-based approach, the other poetry-based. An instructor can begin with the concept of authorial voice in prose compositions and then move on to the poetic counterpart; if a student can compose in a clear authorial voice as well as recognize voice(s) in the prose work of others, he or she should readily grasp poetic voice as a parallel technique. Or the instructor can work with poetic voice first, as described below. In either approach, however, the lesson begins with reading.

The poetry-first approach works best as an in-class exercise. To begin the exercise, one student is selected to read the first line of *The Waste Land* aloud and then to continue reading all lines spoken by the same poetic voice.

The other students interrupt if they think the reader has moved into a new voice. Then another student reads until the next poetic voice begins, and so on. The method has several benefits:

1. The careful reading we do as a class models the critical reading process students should be—but often are not—performing on their own.
2. As we identify different voices, students gain a sense of why the poem seems disjointed and how the poet has achieved that effect, and they begin to read the poem as poetry, not narrative; they also see that their initial sense of confusion, alienation, and so on is related to the poet's design and that poetic structure and content interact.
3. By reading the poem aloud, students explore tone through expression in their own voices, adopting a persona, in effect, and further developing their sense of poetic-authorial voice.

Once students can identify the different voices of *The Waste Land*, they can move on to describing the nature of each voice: What characterizes the individual speakers? What is the tone of each? The pronouns change; what stylistic differences accompany the shift? Does the diction reveal the persona in any way? Does thematic repetition in the section help identify the voice? Does one voice tell a story, another reminisce, another converse? Who, finally, *is* the voice, and how do the various voices relate to one another?

Analyzing the poem's voices can lead into a complex analysis of the poem as a whole. The very complexity of *The Waste Land* makes it valuable material for teaching students how to read for poetic voice; in its division by voices, the poem's structure makes the voices almost visible on the page, in turn making it easier for students to grasp the concept. In contrast, students can read single-voice poems without having to analyze the speaker in any systematic way. When *The Waste Land* is followed by readings such as "Prufrock," "Gerontion," or "Journey of the Magi"—or any other poem with a single identifiable voice—students can then read with an improved sense of the speaker as an entity they can recognize, describe, examine for point of view, relate to thematic content; in short, they can begin to read the poem as poetry. The skill developed in the above exercise is a transferable skill, one students can apply in their next reading assignment.

In a literature-based composition course, I teach the poem early in the semester to illustrate two basic ideas: that through careful reading students can learn to recognize different kinds of discourse and that they can adapt poetic techniques to their own prose compositions (voice being the specific focus of the lesson). Since literary style is in essence a form of linguistic distortion (that is, a purposeful, self-conscious, nonconversational use of language), it provides us with exaggerated models of how authors manipulate language to produce an effect related to their theme or purpose in writing. Using different literary pieces in a composition course allows us to heighten the contrast between different kinds of language, making it easier for students first to grasp the concept of style in itself and then to see how the use of voice(s) within a given style further enriches stylistic possibilities.

To enhance the students' comprehension and to help them develop a voice in their own writing (and further to show how that voice can be something other than their speaking selves or other than an approximation of the disembodied academic voice), I have them take one section of *The Waste Land* and translate it into a prose narrative, written from the point of view of the particular voice in an isolated passage. I suggest that they use a section that has one clear, prevailing voice, such as the Madame Sosostris sequence; the voice of Tiresias as he details the clerk-typist encounter is a more ambitious possibility. The assignment organizes itself: students must first read critically; they must identify the voice in terms of its characteristic diction, tone, attitude, syntactic patterns; they must then experiment with imitating the voice, expanding the themes of the poem at the same time as they fill out the narrative equivalent, moving from imitation to invention in their own writing. The task exercises their skill in several levels of stylistically sophisticated writing and, again, feeds back into their skill in handling the next reading assignment.

Recognizing the authorial control that goes into what is, to the student eye, an apparently anarchic writing style is a valuable experience for students of literature and of writing in general. By teaching a poem such as *The Waste Land*, we can help our students to attain that control in their own writing and to appreciate it in "difficult" poetry.

Teaching Eliot in High School

Rex McGuinn

Because many of our best writers intimidate the beginning reader, high school teachers often hesitate to teach them, choosing Sinclair Lewis over William Faulkner, Kate Chopin over Virginia Woolf, or Carl Sandburg over T. S. Eliot. But not infrequently we are sending our students on to colleges or vocational schools where they will read little or no writing by major authors. Some of our nation's most prestigious schools require no English courses for degrees, and many others have only minimal requirements. It is our duty, a joyous one, to give the students we teach for three or four years the opportunity and ability to read outstanding modern writers. If we recognize the student's legitimate fear of failure on first confronting these writers, then we can succeed in teaching their prose and poetry. By anticipating students' narrative expectations and their desire for linear development in literature, we can teach them a new way of reading that will enable them to appreciate and comprehend modernist methods such as allusiveness and juxtaposition.

The education of our students into a new way of reading cannot be done in a day and will make it necessary for us to give up notions of covering the canon. But in giving up comprehensive coverage of all the major and minor writers, we free ourselves from superficial, relatively unsuccessful survey courses. By encouraging our students to study a handful of major writers in depth, we can strengthen existing reading and writing skills and develop new skills. A course that includes several poems by T. S. Eliot further requires both teacher and students alike to examine the process of reading itself.

In my own Eliot classes I have found that once students discover that they must participate in Eliot's poems and once they feel confident that they have the ability to help Eliot complete the poem in the process of their own reading, most of them get excited about the texts. Using teaching techniques that confront passivity, I begin by working with the assumptions students bring to poetry: that literature ought to tell a story, that poetry has nothing to do with prose, that verse is an arcane and eternally mysterious mode of communication. When I teach *The Waste Land,* for example, I first encourage my students to discover narratives within the poem. I have each student study a different stanza of the poem in class for ten to twenty minutes, and then I ask who has found a story and who hasn't. As we discuss passages like the meeting between the typist and the clerk, students grow more comfortable with the poem and gain a little confidence in their ability to read Eliot. But they also come to recognize that many passages such as the poem's last stanza cannot be understood in terms of action linked by cause and effect. We must go beyond plot.

After reading the typist and clerk passage (if not before), students realize that there are many characters in the poem that resemble those they have encountered in novels. It is useful to have them identify as many characters as they can: Marie, Madame Sosostris, the woman sitting in a chair "like a burnished throne," Lil and her friend, Mr. Eugenides, and so forth. I encourage the class to develop character sketches of each person, either through paragraphs written in class or through discussion, and we note characters' similarities and differences. We discuss what each one has in common with the Sibyl of the epigraph and how the line "April is the cruellest month" might apply to each. A more comprehensive picture of the poem begins to take shape as our discussions of narrative and character lead inevitably to speculation about themes. Lil's five children, her exhaustion and abortion, for example, concretely illustrate why for some April is the cruellest month. We are still in the comfortable world of the novel, however, the world of narrative, character and theme, and much of the poem remains beyond our reach. Although students have learned that questions they ask about novels can help with *The Waste Land* (what Pound said about *Hugh Selwyn Mauberly*, that it was an attempt to condense the James novel, can be applied to *The Waste Land*), we are forced to admit that we need other reading skills as well.

One of the difficulties we face is the poem's perplexing collection of fragments. But there is coherence here, which works through the medium of the image. Students need a good concise definition of image (Perrine's "the representation through language of sense experience" from *Sound and Sense* works well [46]), and they need at least one class in which they explore the strengths and limitations of imagery by working on personal writing exercises. With this foundation, I have them catalog the water images of *The Waste Land*: "spring rain," "forgetful snow," "dry stone," "brown fog," "hot water at ten," the waters of Lower Thames Street, "dry sterile thunder," "a damp gust / Bringing rain," "the arid plain." Almost every line contains some reference to water or its opposite, drought, and even the weakest students have success finding many of these images. We discuss the importance of rain to farmers, the significance of water in baptism, and the meaning of the poem's title. The students grow more and more involved in the poem as they begin to see connections that images create among the fragments and as they gradually uncover themes that concern Eliot, themes such as literal and figurative fertility, love and the waste produced by its absence, the potential for order and collapse in a civilization unsure of ways to fertility and love.

Much of what we have learned involves appreciation of Eliot's method of juxtaposition within these patterns of imagery, but to appreciate more fully the poem's juxtapositions, it helps to recognize allusions and how they work.

I have each student explore a different allusion in some depth (for me to explain allusions in a lecture would be about as effective as explaining a joke), and then I have them share their discoveries with the class. In this way each student experiences the pleasure of recognizing the impact of one allusion on the poem as a whole, and all the students gain a sense of how allusions work in poetry.

The allusions in *The Waste Land* could provide a useful guide to designing a course that would feature the poem as a capstone text. Advanced placement courses, surveys of world literature, and junior and senior electives could be structured in this way. Such courses might include Ezekiel, Ecclesiastes, and Luke from the Bible; Vergil's *Aeneid*; Ovid's *Metamorphoses*; Augustine's *Confessions*; Buddha's Fire Sermon; selections from the *Upanishads*; Dante's *Inferno*; Kyd's *Spanish Tragedy*; Shakespeare's *Hamlet* or *Tempest*; Milton's *Paradise Lost*; Marvell's "To His Coy Mistress"; and Baudelaire's *Fleurs du mal*. Students completing such a course would be able to approach Eliot with some sophistication and would have become well read along the way. Eliot's poems could also be taught in surveys of major writers or in introductions to poetry, and an Eliot unit could easily be included in courses such as advanced placement. Such a unit could apply the techniques I have just discussed to a progression of poems such as "Preludes," *The Waste Land*, "The Journey of the Magi," and "East Coker." By demonstrating continuities within Eliot's work, the unit would enable students to study "Prufrock" and other poems on their own.

I hope that with these courses and methods in mind, we as high school teachers will have the courage to share with students our love for Eliot's powerful poetry and our conviction of his importance in the struggle to understand our times. Instead of restricting ourselves to "easy" literature, we should patiently and thoughtfully teach the skills our students need to appreciate the literature we ourselves value most.

ONE POEM AS AN APPROACH TO ALL

Teaching "The Love Song of J. Alfred Prufrock"

Cleanth Brooks

My concern in this discussion of "The Love Song of J. Alfred Prufrock" is with the lineaments of the poem itself: with its structure and meaning, and indeed with the way in which its literary shape determines its meaning. I do not hold with the newest fashion that regards poems as ultimately meaningless. Eliot's poem has a meaning, a meaning that can be expressed fully and precisely only through its structure, not through any paraphrase that I or any other teacher can frame. We can guide students in the reading process and can persuade them that some interpretations are more valid than others, but in the end they must appropriate the poem for themselves.

Students vary considerably in the help they need to understand a poem, depending on their maturity and sensitivity and also on their knowledge about the world set forth in the poem. Those acquainted with the novels of Henry James and Edith Wharton, for example, will already have some sense of the world that the speaker of Eliot's "Love Song" inhabits. In the following account of the poem, I have chosen to address the needs of students who lack such background and thus need considerable help.

"The Love Song of J. Alfred Prufrock" is one of Eliot's earliest poems and, if we are to believe his friends Conrad Aiken and Ezra Pound, the best of his early poems. It is a thoroughly achieved poem in its own right, but insofar as it foreshadows "Gerontion" and *The Waste Land*, it can be used to introduce students to Eliot's methods and themes. Like the later poems, "The Love Song" contains literary references and allusions that require special knowledge. Yet simply to possess the knowledge does not suffice. Students need to know what to do with such information, just how it bears on the main theme and what emotional weight it deserves to bear. Knowing, for example, which of the two New Testament Lazaruses is meant in line 94 or identifying the source of the phrase "works and days" (29) is not enough. Such knowledge, even if discovered through scholarly diligence, may result in nothing more than a heap of learned glosses on particular lines. The poem as a total experience is the important thing, and that must be the goal of any serious reader.

"The Love Song" is set in turn-of-the-century Boston. Most students will need to know something about Bostonian society at this time. The "world" in which Prufrock moves is one that, at least in its upper social levels, has become somewhat overrefined. Its people are highly self-conscious and mannered, even effete. Some of the more reflective spirits of this class feel that civilization has completely flowered, that it has fulfilled itself, and that its basic energies are now exhausted. Though Prufrock in some sense represents a whole culture, he is, as we shall find, a very special case. He recognizes his plight as typical of the plight of the culture itself. In the poem, this insight is nowhere stated but everywhere implied.

Students may be interested to know that in an early essay entitled "The Hawthorne Aspect," Eliot observed that "the society of Boston was and is quite uncivilized but refined beyond the point of civilization." (The essay is reprinted in Edmund Wilson's *Shock of Recognition*.) One might argue that such excessive "refinement" is the subject of Eliot's "Love Song." But how seriously can we take Eliot's statement? Did he write it in a pique of bad temper, or was he being playful? Or what could he have meant by his distinction between "civilized" and "refined"? Interesting questions, but understanding the poem does not depend on understanding Eliot's prose statement. If the poem does its proper job of dramatic rendition, we may reverse the matter and use the poem to interpret the essay.

The surname of the protagonist, as I learned long ago from Marshall McLuhan, is one found in Eliot's native city of St. Louis. "J. Alfred Prufrock" may or may not be a symbolic name, but it does fit the character as he develops in the poem: a man "deferential, glad to be of use, / Politic, cautious, and meticulous." The "love song" promised in the title, actually, never gets sung. Far from bursting into song, J. Alfred Prufrock finds it difficult even to speak. His "love song," then, is ironic. The epigraph of "The Love Song" may be troublesome to students. It is important, but its meaning will be easier to grasp if discussed a bit later, after students have been introduced to the protagonist.

Prufrock makes his entrance by inviting the reader, whom he seems to accept as inhabiting his own social world, to take a walk with him, a stroll that will take them both to an afternoon tea. The evening and the scene, as he describes them, are so powerfully shaped and colored by his emotions that they must be imagined to exist in good part in his mind. Consider his comparison of the evening to a "patient etherised upon a table." Students are quick to appreciate the difference in tonality between this simile and more traditional ones, such as William Collins's picture of evening as a nymph whose "dewy fingers" draw over the landscape the "gradual dusky veil" ("Ode to Evening"), or Wordsworth's conception of an evening that is as quiet as a "Nun / Breathless with adoration" ("It is a beauteous Evening, calm and free"). Prufrock's evening is also quiet, but its unnatural sleep suggests illness and the artificially induced sleep of a patient on the operating table. The shocking quality of Eliot's description is intended to reflect Prufrock's mental state. In Prufrock's mind, the very streets through which "you and I" pass reek of "insidious intent." Prufrock apparently believes that this intent is to bring him to an "overwhelming question." But the nature of the question is withheld. We are not to ask, at least not now, what it is. But presumably the journey itself will suggest what the question is. References to the question, a question that Prufrock evidently dreads to face, recur throughout the poem.

The reader's walk with Prufrock provides glimpses of two classes of society: the elegant but overrefined world in which people dress correctly and discuss the high arts and the very different shabbier part of the city. As seen by Prufrock, neither world is joyous; both lack purpose and energy. Neither the cultivated accents of ladies "who come and go / Talking of Michelangelo" nor the "muttering retreats / Of restless nights in one-night cheap hotels" hold out much promise. If the former seem bored and boring, the latter exude a sinister atmosphere. Eliot's presentation of the shabby district, with its sawdust restaurants and cheap hotels, and of the elegant district, with its overheated, overrefined drawing room, is significant, for "The Love Song" is not primarily about the plight of an individual person or a particular city but about the plight of an era and of Western civilization itself.

Prufrock, then, to some extent represents a social class but also a culture. In his crippling self-consciousness and his inability to make decisions, he suggests the spiritual blight that had set in upon his world. Eliot's epigraph supports this view, and this is a good place to bring it into our discussion. The Italian lines at the beginning of "The Love Song" are from canto 27 of Dante's *Inferno*. They relate that Dante, allowed to visit Hell in the company of Vergil, has come upon the spirit of Count Guido da Montefeltro, encased in a tonguelike flame. Dante asks Guido what he did to deserve this punishment. A proud man, still jealous of his reputation on earth, Guido answers that he will agree to tell Dante what his sin was, only because his confession will be to another damned soul, for he takes Dante to be another who can never return to earth. Guido's words (as John Ciardi translates them) are:

If I believed that my reply were made
   to one who could ever climb to the world again,
   this flame would shake no more. But since no shade
ever returned—if what I am told is true—
   from this blind world into the living light,
   without fear of dishonor I answer you.

The invitation to the reader, it now appears, may suggest a darker complicity: Prufrock evidently believes that anyone capable of truly understanding what he has to reveal on this afternoon will be a fellow sufferer, one who already knows something of his life among the living dead. Other readers will probably be unable to comprehend what he is talking about. Is Eliot, the poet, suggesting that "The Love Song" is a rather private poem, one that could be understood only by a few of his friends? We cannot say. But the assumption of complicity and fellow-suffering should be taken seriously. Eliot once twitted Ezra Pound for vividly describing in his *Cantos* a hell *for other people*, one filled with censors, bishops, international bankers, and munitions makers. In "The Love Song" Eliot has depicted a hell to which someone more or less like himself might be condemned. He avoids taking a holier-than-thou stance and at least can imagine himself as caught up in Prufrock's timidities and indecisions, his sense that life may be a meaningless charade.

We must be cautious, of course, in identifying Eliot with Prufrock. I suppose all authors put something of themselves into every character they create, but they also distance themselves from their characters. Eliot was not writing an autobiographical document, but he certainly knew the Prufrockian type, knew the society, and knew the zeitgeist of the period. This is all that we need to demand of a literary artist.

Let us return to the mind of Prufrock on this particular day when the evening sky is unnaturally quiet in a drug-induced sleep. We find him in line 12 still addressing the reader: "Let us go and make our visit." In line 13, we find ourselves in the mansion where the women guests are walking about discussing Michelangelo's art. The shift is abrupt. But then we remember that the method of progression is through Prufrock's consciousness. Why Michelangelo rather than some other celebrated artist? Because his art is strenuous, passionate, and heroic, and so sets off the vapidity of all the tea-table and cocktail chitchat. We glimpse (through the windows?) the fog settling around the building. Prufrock, with his fanciful mind, sees the fog as an animal frisking about and then going to sleep. Its muzzle suggests a dog, its movements a cat. But no matter. The fog outside is alive, as the people in the mansion are not.

Then apropos of nothing in particular, Prufrock begins to talk about time. Evidently it is on his mind; here and later he keeps reassuring himself that there will be time enough. For what? Presumably for nothing special. The reassurance is little more than the compulsive verbal twitch of a man who perpetually puts things off—especially decisions. In a brilliant play of words, rhyming *indecisions, visions,* and *revisions* (32–33), Eliot condenses Prufrock's whole habit of mind, and then, in the reference to "toast and tea," trivializes the whole matter.

The phrase "works and days of hands" will probably seem odd to students. It is an allusion to a poem by the Greek poet Hesiod, a sturdy Boeotian farmer, of the eighth century BC. His poem *The Works and Days*, a kind of manual and seasonal calendar describing the proper times for and the various methods of sowing, reaping, and other farming activities, really had to do with hard work and manual labor. But in Prufrock's world the hardest labor specifically mentioned is that of some servant's dropping a letter (from the morning mail?) on one's breakfast plate. The letter contains what Prufrock dreads, a question, or perhaps the question is simply treated figuratively as if it were a letter, a message of some kind.

Eliot ironically calls Prufrock's cogitations and reflections a love song. In *Works and Days*, Hesiod also refers to love or at least to choosing a bride. As translated by Richmond Lattimore, Hesiod declares:

> You are of age to marry a wife and bring her home with you when you are about thirty, not being many years short of that mark, nor going much over. That age is ripe for your marriage. Let your wife be full grown four years, and marry in the fifth. Better marry a maiden, so you can teach her good manners, and in particular marry one who lives close by you. Look her well over first. Don't marry what will make your neighbors laugh at you, for while there's nothing better a man can win him than a good wife, there nothing more dismal than a bad one.

How businesslike the old Greek is in his thoroughgoing practicality. In Hesiod's scheme of things, there are presumably no indecisions and revisions; the prospective husband knows just what he needs and wants.

Eliot was widely read in classical literature, and he may or may not have had this passage from *Works and Days* in mind. Without being dogmatic on this point, a teacher can suggest that Prufrock is getting past what Hesiod termed the flower of a man's life, and yet he has not chosen a bride and seems unlikely ever to get up the courage to do so. For one thing, he is uneasy in the company of women—it may be significant that the original title of the poem was "Prufrock among the Women"—and he is terrified of making a faux pas. In lines 37–39, the reiteration that there is time enough leads into a sharply etched account of Prufrock's intense self-consciousness

—his concern for his physical appearance, of course, but also for the impression he makes on others. He is acutely conscious of the conventions of his class, and yet he cannot break out of them.

In part, the problem is that Prufrock knows too much about his society. Suppose that he did try to establish a tone of intimacy with a particular woman. What if she dismissed his timid overture? He can imagine so well how she would do it. His knowledge of his society cripples him and prevents him from being spontaneous, impulsive, or even natural. The future is closed to him, closed because it has been trivialized. The world that he knows so well has squeezed the life out of the human enterprise. In fact, it has become no longer an "enterprise," an undertaking, a movement toward some end or goal. It has become a routine, a meaningless round.

Such, I take it, is the import of lines 49–72 and indeed of most of what follows in the poem. But there are some special considerations that call for attention, especially with lines 70–72. The people of Prufrock's class are isolated from the workaday world outside them. The ladies who talk of Michelangelo, in Prufrock's judgment, have no knowledge of or interest in the workaday world. If Prufrock told them that he had gone at dusk through "narrow streets / And watched the smoke that rises from the pipes / Of lonely men in shirt-sleeves, leaning out of windows," they would either stare blankly or ask, "Why ever did you do so?" At least, Prufrock is convinced that such would be their reaction. Lines 73–74 stress this breakdown in real communication. In longing to be a "pair of ragged claws," Prufrock ruefully regards his own thin skin and hypersensitivity. Had he been a crab, he would have been protected by an armor of bony shell and would have had no need of companionship. He now feels that the inability to establish serious relationships is absolute. The members of his society have sealed themselves off from any intercourse except the most conventional and trivial. In this world where heartfelt expressions of any kind are bad form, people are not fully alive. But, as Prufrock knows, he too is convention-bound, hyper–self-conscious, lacking in resolution and decision. Never easy on himself, he includes himself among the living dead.

The evening described in the first lines of the poem as "spread out against the sky," sleeping an etherized sleep, is in line 75 still sleeping. Somehow, it has got inside the mansion and, "[s]moothed by long fingers" (those of the elegant ladies in the rooms?), is now "[s]tretched on the floor." The evening itself is tired or else pretending to be ill or exhausted. So the somewhat sinister quality of the evening is maintained. In any case, its enervating character saps whatever may have been left of Prufrock's resolution to give utterance to his love song.

Prufrock speculates endlessly on what might happen if he tried to break through the sacrosanct conventions, but he lacks the strength to force "the moment to its crisis." What does he mean? What is it that needs to be said or done? We are not told, but Prufrock's admission to himself that he is no prophet hints of a need to make some honest declaration to these people, an assertion of their lifelessness. But he cannot be candid. He knows that a forthright assertion of what is woefully wrong with his society would be regarded as an outrageous breach of good manners—at the very least. The fate of a particular prophet, John the Baptist, comes to his mind (82). John had spoken of the need for people to change their ways and had paid for his temerity with his head. Prufrock is aware that he is up to nothing so heroic. Besides, a balding head brought in on a platter is somewhat ridiculous; it does not suggest tragic dignity. The allusion, of course, is to the story of Salome's dancing before King Herod and, when asked by Herod to name her reward, demanding at her mother's bidding the head of the prophet (Matt. 6.6–11). Earlier in the poem Prufrock had imagined himself as an insect, mounted for inspection, wriggling on a pin. That image now gives way to a worse: an actual decapitation.

"To have squeezed the universe into a ball" echoes Andrew Marvell's "Let us roll all our Strength and all / Our sweetness up into one Ball . . ." (from "To His Coy Mistress"). Marvell's lover is vital, charged with energy, pressing his suit with intellect as well as passion. Eliot's Prufrock is languid, world-weary, and unmanned by a sense of his own inadequacy. In Prufrock's remark, the figurative element is the same as in Marvell's, but the import is utterly different. Marvell's lover means to contract all possible pleasures into one powerful, concentrated pleasure that will sum them up. Prufrock suggests the reduction of all questions to one supreme question that demands an answer. What is this question? The meaning of life? The essential nature of reality?

Perhaps the nature of the "overwhelming question" is hinted at in the reference to Lazarus. There are two Lazaruses in the New Testament. One is the beggar who gladly would have gathered up the crumbs from under the rich man's table. At his death he is taken to Abraham's bosom (Luke 16.20–25). The other Lazarus is the man whom Jesus raised from the dead (John 11.1–44). Prufrock seems to have taken something from both accounts in asking, "Would it have been worth while, / . . . To say: 'I am Lazarus, come from the dead / Come back to tell you all, I shall tell you all.' " The Lazarus who was raised from the dead, having experienced both death and life, could speak with authority on the difference between the two states. But could Prufrock, even clad in that authority, convince the people around him that they are not really alive? That may be the primary reference, but Luke's account of the other Lazarus is also relevant here. When the rich man in hell asks Father Abraham to send the beggar Lazarus to tell the rich man's brothers what lies in store for them if they do not mend their ways,

Abraham tells him: "If they hear not Moses and the prophets, neither will they be persuaded, though one rose from the dead" (Luke 16.30). Even if the members of his society had ears to hear, the deferential Prufrock, in his correct morning coat and well-chosen necktie, would be incapable of delivering such an indictment. And he knows it.

The allusions to Shakespeare's *Hamlet* reinforce the impression that Prufrock is acutely aware of his unimportance. He is not Prince Hamlet (111). Considered in terms of that play, his would be a role more nearly like that of a fatuous Rosencrantz or a Guildenstern; perhaps a role even less dignified, that of the pompous and ridiculous Polonius. Prufrock is no hero, but unlike these secondary characters from Shakespeare, he has no self-delusion, and honesty of this sort has its value. It is Prufrock's only virtue, but it is rare in a confused and muddled age such as the poem suggests that our age is.

As the poem draws to its end, Prufrock becomes harder and harder on himself. He has already shown that he knows his Shakespeare, and so when he says, "I grow old . . . I grow old . . .," he is probably consciously echoing Shakespeare's Falstaff. But if so, this passage also sharpens the irony. Falstaff was a genial rogue who flouted the conventions; though truly an old man, he still possessed enormous vitality and a tremendous appetite for life. Falstaff was willing to accept almost any dare, whereas the languid Prufrock mocks himself by asking "Do I dare to eat a peach?" The decisions he is willing to make have to do with where to part his hair. It is amusing to note that, according to Conrad Aiken's *Ushant*, when Eliot returned to Harvard from Paris in 1911, he created a sensation with his Left Bank clothing and his hair parted behind.

At last Prufrock does leave the house for a walk along the seaside. Does he literally walk along the beach, or is this little excursion merely figurative—another event that occurs only in his mind? It really does not matter much to a reading of the poem. Throughout this poem, the outside world that prompts Prufrock's memories and reveries and the outside world as reshaped and colored by Prufrock's imagination are more or less indistinguishable. One melts into the other. Nevertheless, the lines that describe this real or imagined walk matter very much for the meaning of the poem. Whether the fresh sea air is actually blowing on his face or whether he merely imagines that he has entered into such a fresh and bracing atmosphere, the atmosphere of the poem is suddenly changed. There is a quickening of the senses that the sensitive reader at once feels.

No sooner does Prufrock come into this reinvigorating environment than he is saying, "I have heard the mermaids singing, each to each." Who are these mermaids? J. Alfred Prufrock is presumably too rational and too sophisticated to believe that these creatures of the folktales exist. Are they, then, merely figments of the imagination? Perhaps so; yet even so, they possess more living reality than the languid and overrefined women who have been walking about, "[t]alking of Michelangelo." The mermaids have a reality that the ladies among the teacups do not possess. These latter are not really alive but exist in a kind of half-way state between life and death.

Earlier I pointed out an obvious reference to the Greek poet Hesiod. In another of his poems, the *Theogony*, Hesiod relates that once he himself heard the nine Muses dancing and singing together. Is Eliot here making an oblique reference to Hesiod's experience? It is impossible to say certainly, but the ironic contrast between the ancient Greek's experience and the modern American's does make a point. Hesiod's Muses and Prufrock's mermaids sing to one another, but the Greek poet was able to profit from the Muses' inspiration—to write his poems—whereas Prufrock presumably does not. Though he can hear their singing, he cannot himself utter any love song.

Far more important, however, than this possibility of an echo of Hesiod is the contrast between these fabulous creatures of the imagination and the human beings sipping tea. The mermaids are more "real." Symbolic of supernatural energy and elemental power, they fairly surge with vitality as they ride the sea waves. Aphrodite, the Greek goddess of love and fertility, was fabled to have been born from the seafoam. Life itself, we are told, first began in the sea. Prufrock is aware that the fabulous and the mythical have a life that his fin de siècle world does not have. Unfortunately, he cannot attain to this source of power; the very conditions of his "civilized" existence render it unavailable to him.

The closing lines of the poem ironically sum up his situation. Prufrock feels the sea's attraction; for a moment, he shakes off his languor and has a vision of beauty linked with power. But "human voices" soon shut out the song of the mermaids, wake him from his dream of freedom and energy, and cause him to "drown." The truly suffocating element for Prufrock is the world in which he normally draws his breath. But as we have said, he does not blame others for his pusillanimity. He assumes responsibility for not having forced his way out of his enervating prison.

"The Love Song of J. Alfred Prufrock" implies a judgment on a whole culture and on Prufrock as its fair representative. That he recognizes and takes responsibility for his situation keeps us from despising him but does not cancel the judgment. Eliot's epigraph from Dante's *Inferno* not only supports this interpretation; it also implicates the reader in the blighted scene. Like Guido da Montefeltro, Prufrock, in giving an account of his plight, is addressing fellow sufferers. All of us, it is implied, are to some degree in the same situation.

Other aspects of the poem deserve attention. Students should try to see, for example, how the rhythm of the first dozen lines differs from that of the last half dozen. Probably the best way to experience this difference is to read the lines aloud, with attention to the emphases and pauses and the functions of the rhymes. The rhythms, of course, do not do the job alone. Replace them with nonsense syllables and the expressive rhythm will itself disappear along with the "right words." Yet what an adjunct to meaning the rhythm becomes in skillful hands.

Tone may require considerable attention. What tone does Prufrock take when he speaks of himself? Contemptuous? Dryly ironical? Sarcastic? Rueful? Or what? In a poem such as "The Love Song," in which the speaker is critically regarding himself and the very culture that has nurtured him, tone is very important. Alter the tone of voice and you alter what is said.

Most of all, imagery must be studied—that is, as contributing to the meaning, not merely embellishing it. The use of figurative language has always been the poet's great resource. Consider, for example, how concretely Prufrock's finicky fastidiousness is caught in the line "I have measured out my life with coffee spoons."

What I have set forth in these pages is to be considered an outline, a sort of map. Maps have their value. They may prevent our getting too badly confused or wholly lost. But a map is not a natural landscape or a cityscape. If we keep our eyes too closely glued to the map, we will not get the experience of our journey. We will not observe the houses or the trees, the rivers or the hills that we are passing. No account of a poem, call it an analysis or an explication or what you will, is a substitute for the poem itself. The student must read it and reread it.[1]

NOTE

[1]Special thanks are due to the editor, Jewel Spears Brooker, for expert help in shortening and so giving point to an otherwise overlong essay.

"Prufrock" as Key to Eliot's Poetry

Grover Smith

A strategy to identify the essence of Eliot beyond, as well as within, a single poem needs the right poem. To make "The Love Song of J. Alfred Prufrock" this poem, whether one is proposing to teach Eliot comprehensively or selectively, offers several advantages. "Prufrock" is familiar and is outstanding in interest and attractiveness; it comes near the beginning of the canon; it links in theme and technique with various other poems by Eliot; and, most useful, it anticipates certain equally familiar critical principles (two especially) that he was to declare. Those principles, though they only took shape ten years further on, in his most active period of critical theory, apply to "Prufrock" and other poems of the 1909–11 period because it was in these, as a practical exercise, that he discovered their necessity. In "Tradition and the Individual Talent" (1919) he set forth a kind of theory of mutual adaptation between the poet and the cultural past; in "The Metaphysical Poets" (1921) he pointed to certain distinguished cases of poetic excellence achieved through unity of thought and feeling. (These papers, reprinted in Eliot's *Selected Essays*, are extremely interesting to read and are of value to the teacher. The best introductory summary of Eliot's critical theories is still René Wellek's 1956 essay in the *Sewanee Review*.) Tradition in the poetry of Eliot represents the impact of the past on the thought-feeling unity of the achieved work of art—the old renewing itself in the fresh and original. The two principles thus combine into one. Each entails for critics a kind of pons asinorum; for tradition to Eliot meant adapting the past, not copying it, and the unity of thought and feeling meant a poetic formulation, not a discharge of personal philosophy and passion—though indeed these might be sources for poetic transformation. The principles work in "Prufrock" by giving technical significance to what happens there, and they can help a teacher open up the poem for students. They also provide standards and a vocabulary for treating "Prufrock" as a touchstone—not quite in Arnold's sense—for Eliot's subsequent development. With them, the teacher of "Prufrock" can introduce Eliot as poet and theorist together and prepare students for dealing with poems, similarly grounded, that lie ahead. And since in teaching Eliot one teaches tradition or nothing, in a more Arnoldian sense "Prufrock" may become a touchstone for the work of other poets, even for the genuineness of a poem.

The teaching of poetry calls for a certain restraint. Interpretation is next to falsification: therefore it has no value (unless sometimes comic value) for its own sake. Yet we must confess that we are all tainted with it. The only expiation is to devote ourselves as far as possible to letting the poem reveal its true nature as we read and teach it—its own point of view, not ours. Pedagogically one is probably unwise to begin with theory in teaching a poem, for theory demands from the student prior knowledge of the object. If one sets out by establishing that "Prufrock" is a monologue, or more privately a spoken reverie, and one gets the class to recognize through the grammar and syntax that the persona's "visit" on that foggy late afternoon takes place in time, not space, in his projective imagination, then the remaining essentials should prove easy to explore. Why Prufrock revolves in his mind, assisted by his memories, a program of action that should lead to an amorous declaration but cannot even commence can be answered only by reference to his character. Partly he gains definition through his rhetoric of vacillation and diffidence, which the members of the class who have read the poem aloud to themselves, at home, will know is confirmed by the ruefulness of his tone. An unhurried reading of selected strophes in class, however, may be used to question the proposition that he only suffers, that mere ennui and frustration are his only portion. Partly he emerges through a rhetorical effect quite other than rueful, namely, his invocation of a personal mythology of power, according to which he transitorily takes to himself, soon after the middle of the poem, exaggerative guises such as "ragged claws," a great saint's severed head "upon a platter," the mana of the resurrected Lazarus, and the grave perplexities of Hamlet, and at last locates himself in the chambers of "sea-girls." The ambivalence of these images of power— images that he both dodges and embraces, illustrates the transformations of thought and feeling, their interpenetration. One scenario for the teaching of "Prufrock" will therefore involve an analysis of the persona's rhetorical division into a comically pathetic self and a boastfully poetic one, two selves that coexist. And Eliot's 1921 theory of a fusion of thought and feeling can, perhaps uniquely, provide the right clue to what is going on. Theory enters the scene precisely on time, its presence required and its message respectfully attended.

As likely as not, that scenario will fail to work in the classroom because the rhetorical effect fails to be noted before some different question intervenes. Unless one is simply lecturing, a student may short-circuit the line of development by asking, for example, what the Italian poetry, the epigraph, at the beginning of "Prufrock" is *for*. This is a fair question and provides a useful topic, which will guide one to the character of the persona by a different way, but hardly through the unity of thought and feeling. Either the epigraph, from Dante's *Inferno* 27, or the references to John the Baptist, Lazarus, and Hamlet can prompt a general explanation of the role played in Eliot by tradition. More urgently, a student may pose a question, based on outside reading or a detective instinct, that challenges Eliot as unoriginal, plagiaristic, or inaccessibly highbrow. To concede the reasonableness of these charges is good tactics; one need only show afterward that, once laid open to inspection, tradition is as accessible as anything else and that the originality of Eliot's recourse to it, for source material or whatever, lies beyond cavil. Meanwhile, as most of our students have no familiarity with Dante, Shake-speare, or the Bible, access should benefit them. It can make no difference whether, at any early stage, one introduces the principle of the enduring tradition or that of the unity of thought and feeling; indeed one may need to discuss them together, as accident or opportunity may suggest. Some teachers may be uneasy with this amount of improvisation and may wish to control the sequence of topics more strictly. On occasion I might agree; but among possible experiments the least promising appears to be that of teach-ing the theoretical principles as a separate unit while actually teaching a poem. One says enough about them in naming, explaining, and applying them. In a course where they can compose a unit apart from the poetry, poetry by Eliot might be instanced to explain them.

With "Prufrock" I prefer any scenario that deals with the man's character first and leaves until later the consideration of style in relation to the past and to literary models or sources. The epigraph from Dante suggests itself as a source of Prufrock's character as well as of his situation. (In Eliot the sources always furnish some essential fiber of significance.) Most students will admit to some confusion over the "I-you" question: to whom really is Prufrock talking? One may cut the Gordian knot by replying that he is talking to himself; but his reasons are not altogether simple. They seem to be involved with the answer to another question: what is Prufrock representing himself as? It may be expedient in teaching to note, with the help of a translation, the possible parallel between Prufrock and Guido. In *Inferno* 27, Guido speaks the lines of the epigraph to the poet Dante, who has "dropped in" and who, in a kind of treachery, reports (in the very poem they occur in) the secrets that Guido says can never leak out, from those depths, to the world of the living. An indicated corollary of the Dantean parallel is that Prufrock's treacherous confidant ("you") is (as it were) the poet Eliot. Like Guido, moreover, Prufrock is hoist with his own petard: not knowing that he is a character in a poem, he blabs. It is Eliot, not he, who doubles Prufrock with Guido and who offers himself ("you") as a double of the Dante with whom Guido converses; but since Eliot does not play a further role in the monologue, Prufrock has only himself to talk to, "after all." My account—an interpretation, the reader is warned—postulates a joke in the manner of Laforgue, played on Prufrock by his author; Eliot would again double himself with Dante in *The Waste Land* (line 63) and in "Little Gidding" (pt. 2, line 44). Prufrock's ambivalent assimilation to Guido, Hamlet, and others specializes Eliot's practice, in poems at every period of the canon, of fabricating poetry by means of transformed source materials bearing traditional weight. The models for Prufrock's character besides Guido illustrate the composite impact of tradition. Since some of them, furthermore, also derive historically from Hamlet, they show multiple linkage at work in the composite. (On this chain effect or "genealogy" of sources, see Smith, *The Waste Land* 100–01, 126–27.)

A main source for Prufrock was Henry James's story "Crapy Cornelia," which I have briefly discussed elsewhere (*T. S. Eliot's Poetry and Plays* 15; the parallel was pointed out to me, in conversation almost forty years ago, by my then-colleague Richard Earl Amacher). In the middle-class would-be suitor White-Mason of "Crapy Cornelia," Eliot found a character that he endowed with certain pretensions to cultivation or dignity, as merited by Strether in *The Ambassadors* and overreached by the dithering Marcher in "The Beast in the Jungle." Besides manifesting a Jamesian mold, Prufrock seems to regard himself in a Jamesian light. Unlike other sentimental bachelors, from Charles Lamb's to Ik Marvel's, he introspects to break his way out, not wholly unsuccessfully. For at least he achieves a rhetoric of mythic grandeur, though of absurd components. The "mythical method" greeted by Eliot in writing of Joyce a dozen years later was already invented in "Prufrock." The important issue for this method, and for all Eliot's manipulations of received material, of tradition, consists in the changes made in the specific sources. The teacher of "Prufrock" may wish to press this point. It becomes ever more cardinal in the teaching of the Sweeney poems, of "Gerontion," of *The Waste Land*, and later work of Eliot. Prufrock is the first of Eliot's complex synthetics, his psychological lineaments along with his milieu being derived variously; and he seems too, as brought out, to feel that he is an artificial person, made by his tailor. He talks furthermore as if playing the part of a Henry James character, such is his mode of self-description. If so, he has obviously become entrapped in the role, so much so that he displays hardly any claim to natural as opposed to literary existence. Prufrock's artificiality results from literary artificiality and can with difficulty be separated from it. His effort to escape his role by finding his opposite does not deliver him from his antiheroic condition. An early text of the poem bore the title "Prufrock among the Women," perhaps in allusion to the least glorious stratagem of Achilles. The rhetoric with which Prufrock rehabilitates his vitality carries the general implication of heroic failure, death rather than triumph. Another model for him was the Hamlet of Jules Laforgue's *Moralités légendaires*, a very different personage from Shakespeare's, an alter ego of Yorick the fool and the living counterpart therefore of Death. Laforgue's Hamlet, in defiance of a really tender conscience, parades himself as antihero, antilover, and antinomian of a type that believes "anything is permitted" and hails the Unconscious as his liberator from the categorical imperative; in despair he plunges into cruelty. His nihilism resembles that of the unregenerate Raskolnikov in Dostoevsky's *Crime and Punishment*, another prototype of the solitary rebel for Eliot. (See John C. Pope's essays on Prufrock and Raskolnikov in *American Literature*.) Prufrock draws his urbanity from James, his bitterness and irony from Laforgue, his intensity from Dostoevsky; but the mixture is both unequal and innovative. Like the concoctions of mock epic, it leaves its originals undiminished but not quite the same—enhanced ever so slightly by feedback. Such is the possible reverse effect of Eliot's principle of tradition. In teaching, one can accordingly make "Prufrock" a touchstone for theory.

The unity of thought and feeling as a characterizing device brings singleness out of doubleness without blurring either. Prufrock is what he thinks in the course of the poem, but very little of his thought appears except as objective imagery, flashes of feeling. Before writing "The Metaphysical Poets," which speaks of "a direct sensuous apprehension of thought" and "a re-creation [hyphen mine] of thought into feeling," Eliot had ventured to term it "impossible . . . to draw any line between thinking and feeling" ("Prose and Verse" 9). Of course the two faculties work together: the thought apprehended by feeling is not eliminated by it. That no line can be drawn between them, moreover, does not imply that they are the same. Their difference becomes glaring when they do *not* work together, when in poetry they fail to combine or there is too much of either of them. Because "Prufrock" is a persona poem, the known interaction occurs at Prufrock's point of view, between his thinking and his feeling, and not in the poet's sphere of being. And it occurs constantly, but not in a constant form; one needs to keep students alert to the subtleties of the shift into feeling as the thought is phrased with overtones of irony, indifference, distaste, or desperation. Thus in the lines about the women and Michelangelo, used first as a focus for the proposed departure and later as a definition of the limits imposed by an arrival, the thought is stretched into more than one shape of feeling, dependent on connotations of the confined, the superficial, the pompous, the transient, the magnificent, the incongruous, which diversely collide. That it is not merely a thought is the main point. Up to the "lonely men" and "ragged claws" passages, Prufrock keeps reiterating his superiority to circumstances and then producing an imagery of his humiliation; but in the latter part of the poem the boasts take fanciful forms with imagery and are followed by more matter-of-fact observations. It is as if his mind were gradually convulsed with spasms of suffering and then were intermittently rallied with a mythology of self-esteem, only to succumb each time to more rational despair. The thought and feeling interact both in the reflective and in the fanciful utterances but are always shifting in intensity.

It is more important to get students to hear "Prufrock" than it is to get them to "follow" it. The teacher who does not manage to convey those apposite rhymes, those lovely cadences into the presentation of it misses a fine pedagogic exercise. But I do not know how to systematize that undertaking except by reading the poem aloud. Alas—because the unity of thought and feeling inheres in the delivery of the lines. It is possible, once again, to illustrate Eliot's recycling of tradition by citing from "Prufrock" a couplet that renews the past by transforming it, the couplet

> Arms that are braceleted and white and bare
> [But in the lamplight, downed with light brown hair!]

The contrast of coldness and warmth, artificiality and animal intimacy, sums up so much of the thematic essence of "Prufrock" that nothing more is called for. Yet behind these lines lurks a world of more solemn implication. If one can hear in them the line they primarily echo from John Donne's poem "The Relique,"

> A bracelet of bright haire about the bone,

and remember the significance of this emblem of passion and devotion (found also in "The Funerall"), the concentration of feeling in the couplet undergoes a heightening almost, even, to a sensation of physical pain, as intense as Donne's grim consciousness of love triumphant over charnel mortality. I do not say that Mr. Prufrock can hear this echo—though why not?—for he creates it, varying "bracelet" and chiming "white and bare" with "bright haire" and then near rhyming "downed" with "bone" and finally repeating the near rhyme and definitely rhyming, himself, with "light brown hair." And what is more he borrows from "The Funerall," which has "That subtile wreath of haire, which crowns my arme," a rhyme to prove his near rhyme a true one and adopts the essential word "arms" that denotes the objects of his attention and absorption and frustration. Perhaps it was Mr. Eliot that did and felt all this. He would often in the future raise voices from the grave (as one's students are pleased to discover), though none more comically sad and musical than Prufrock's own. In them nevertheless something from Prufrock would be blended, having in some manner joined a tradition perpetually to be enriched by his thought and feeling.

Hearing Eliot:
"The Hollow Men" as Exemplary Text

Graham Clarke

In the teaching of poetry, too little attention is given to hearing poems spoken aloud. To spend class time listening to a poet read is to spend it well: it suggests that performance is a chief aspect of poetry, and it offers a peculiar and immediate presence that cannot be conveyed in discussions of poems as written texts. I usually begin teaching "The Hollow Men" by inviting students to listen to Eliot read it. The very presence of his voice enacts, in its performance, the paradoxes, ambiguities, and gaps in meaning that are central to the experience of the poem.

The most obvious problem facing teachers of Eliot's poetry is the sheer difficulty of the written text. This difficulty, which is related to Eliot's consciousness of the complexities of language itself, is a primary subject of many of his poems. In his reading of "The Hollow Men," Eliot dramatizes the poetic process in which meaning is layered and held in ambiguity and enigma. That the gap between presence and absence, between statement and suggestion, can be immediately heard makes "The Hollow Men" an exemplary text. In its resonance of endless suggestiveness that is both hollow and dense, it gives an immediate experience of ambiguity. I am suggesting not that this effect can be explained, rather that it is the experience of heard difficulty that brings students into the res of the poetic. As the students listen, their problem with meaning becomes part of the meaning of the poem; it becomes the dramatized subject and can suggest the wider issues in which Eliot's poetry is situated. To hear Eliot's enactment of his struggle with words and meaning is to have the poem restored to its play as sound and to be reminded of the importance of sound in the complex that makes a poem worth reading in the first place.

This approach to "The Hollow Men," with its insistence on the ear rather than the eye, moves students away from the kind of interpretative exercises that tend to defuse Eliot's difficulty and dilute his subject. I do not wish to suggest that performance can replace analysis, but I do believe that more can be gained by pointing to the act of voicing than by giving explanations ("this means . . ."; "this is from Dante"). This approach also empowers students to advance, almost intuitively, to wider intellectual and critical considerations, for example, to Eliot's concept of the unified sensibility in which ideas are felt and sensations are perceived. Students can begin to realize the poem as an intellectual and emotional complex in which the allusions can be felt, in which the elements of the poem achieve substance through ambiguity.

With more traditional approaches, students are sometimes allowed to take refuge in notes and sources. Teachers discuss Conrad's *Heart of Darkness*, explain the context of the Gunpowder Plot, and then move into the allusions to Dante, the Bible, and nursery rhymes. Of course, allusions are central to the poem's density of effect, but they need to be placed amid the dramatic context that a hearing of the poem creates. The difference is between explaining an allusion to *Heart of Darkness* and inviting students into a verbal text whose center enacts that heart of darkness; it is a difference between describing states of being and presenting them. In this invitation into its verbal depths, the poem thus dramatizes the problem of meaning. Hovering between act and paralysis, the textual voice (voices) works (work) through a binary structure of promise and denial—a multiple effect of presence and absence, denial and affirmation. The series of voices in the poem acts out the condition to which it speaks, the darkness and hollowness of its states as both text and consciousness.

On a more specific level, the student can be encouraged to notice how much of the poem is itself about the act of speaking, of finding a language. "Hollow," as much emptiness as echo, reverberates through its hollowness and gains presence as it announces absence. Other words and other voices create a chorus of echoed sounds amid the mysterious: voices are "dry," voices "whisper," voices are "in the wind's singing" just as there are lips that "would kiss" and "[f]orm prayers to broken stone." All are placed against the larger perspective of lines such as in the "last of meeting places / We grope together / And avoid speech." And as with the voice so with the eye, for the poem speaks as much to a pattern of sight as it does to the voice. Thus, there are those who "cross" with "direct eyes" to "death's other kingdom"; there are "eyes I dare not meet"; and in section 4 we are left "sightless." In examples such as these the movement of meaning parallels that of the poem as a whole. The more we concentrate on these patterns (the references to sight and sound), the more the poem—committed to a speech it would avoid and looking for meaning out of "sightless" eyes—denies them significance. It thus denies us access to itself as a text, moving forward by moving back, affirming through its negations. As in other Eliotic texts, we have "Shape without form, shade without colour / Paralysed force, gesture without motion." This terrifying paralysis is a condition more accessible through the ear than through the eye, more meaningful as a human voice than as a written text.

Students might also be directed to section 5, in which the gap in fulfilled meaning (what the poem offers as "shadow") is realized once again through the way in which the words are voiced. "Between," for example, has a formal insistence, consistently coming down between the inception of meaning and its frustrated conclusion. The word "between" splits opposites and breaks into the interior space of the poem—the limbo, the stasis, the gaps in meaning in which the "desire" is enacted. Significantly the spatial dimension of this final section, the pattern of the lines on the page, creates the sense of a number of voices—as if separate groups on a stage come at us with sounds at once ceremonial and formal, innocent and empty. The oppositions in this final section can be read (heard) as a dramatized enactment of the poem articulating its own peculiar darkness. Encased within the patterns of song and prayer is a language of extremes fundamental to the act and the will to communicate—to make known what is unknowable. The voices speak to the wrestle with words and to our attempt to define a state always held between "conception" and "creation," "emotion" and "response," "desire" and "spasm."

The conclusion of "The Hollow Men" provides a special moment for hearing the problem at the center of the poem. These very quotable lines have unfortunately become part of the jargon of our age, but they can be reclaimed as part of a particular poetic experience. The "bang" in the closing line, for example, can be displaced in favor of the "whimper." Bang is an inhuman sound, mechanical, loud, obvious; whimper, in contrast, is a human sound that students can be invited to weigh carefully, a sound suggesting loneliness and fear. It has a powerful presence, and yet it invokes a pathetic deprivation; it stresses pain or suffering emanating as a cry, a suffused but intensely human sound.

As an exemplary text for the teaching of Eliot, then, "The Hollow Men" allows the philosophical, theological, cultural, and literary difficulties raised by Eliot's poetry to be centered in the student and to be given an immediate and felt dimension. It offers the student the experience of a daunting hollowness—a darkness that can enter the student as a state of ambiguity and struggle and on which a response to Eliot's other poems can be developed. Like Eliot's oeuvre, the poem refuses to be reduced to the sum of its parts. It provides a powerful rendering of paradox—of a consciousness and a voice held in the flux of language to which it is committed and yet which cannot ultimately render the meanings it promises. That is the poem's wider darkness—of the word as much as of the self—and that is the relation it dramatizes. The poem lives, so to speak, in its performance. It allows students to hear Eliot speaking to himself, to us, and to the word, the logos of his poetic perspective. In hearing Eliot's voice echoing their own experienced gap between an inner state and an outer stating, most students are deeply moved. The poem speaks to them and for them; it says what they cannot hope to say.

The Experience and the Meaning:
Ash-Wednesday

A. D. Moody

There were about twenty persons in the big room, sitting in a wide circle and giving me the feeling that they were at once welcoming and wary. There were women and men, most in their twenties, all casually dressed in styles that flowered in the late sixties. Through the tall windows was a roughly cut back wilderness, the ruin of what had been the spacious garden enclosing a London gentleman's residence in the plummy years of Victoria's reign. Not much furniture in the room: chairs and floor cushions, a threadbare carpet, nothing else. A chair was left empty for the visitor in the circle, center stage it seemed as I sat in it and was introduced by the staff member who had got me into this.

I was there because I taught literature, to talk about *Ash-Wednesday*. I was working on Eliot at the time, and that seemed as good a poem as any for a group of people who, by their own account, did not know much about poetry. This was not a class or any kind of teaching situation. They were not students. And my chair was not center stage—all points on a circle are equal. Moreover, it was their circle and their way of arranging themselves in this room.

They were drug addicts, who wanted not to be. That is a harrowing state, and an enterprise "[c]osting not less than everything" ("Little Gidding"). Their treatment was administered by themselves, as a group, in long sessions of encounter therapy and through a strictly enforced discipline of house rules. This community of young people, all more or less in extremis, were seeking the help they needed by learning to help each other to help themselves. The idea was, Only you can break your habit! But first the self that had formed the habit and been confirmed in the habit had to be recognized and faced up to. Seeing themselves in others was part of the process, an approach to self-knowledge, but letting others see into them was the harder part. Some had become addicts because there was something they could not cope with, because they needed to suppress the hurt, the anger, the inadequacy, the despair. For all of them, being an addict had become what they could not cope with. When we feel we have spoiled our own lives profoundly and irretrievably, the last thing we want to do is to face the fact. Yet that is what we most need to do. So these addicts tried to draw out those unfaceable feelings in one another. They defended themselves against the help with the savagery of self-hatred, and in the end, when they could stand it, were broken down and brought to live with themselves.

They were working with raw, primitive feelings, but really it was themselves they were dealing with, themselves in the raw. In their own way they were doing what Eliot said poetry should do for us when he wrote (in the closing paragraph of *The Use of Poetry and the Use of Criticism*), "It may make us . . . a little more aware of the deeper, unnamed feelings which form the substratum of our being, to which we rarely penetrate; for our lives are mostly a constant evasion of ourselves, and an evasion of the visible and sensible world" (155). In their way they probably knew more about poetry, and about Eliot's kind of poetry, than I did.

But poetry was my specialty, not theirs. I was their visitor of the week, offering a time-out from the sessions where they engaged with one another for real. This week it was to be this poem called *Ash-Wednesday*. It could just as well have been weaving or bookkeeping, beekeeping or hang gliding. I had become interested in poetry and in Eliot by the usual academic process, which is basically an intellectual process. (Academic and intellectual the addicts were not, though many of them were both educated and intelligent: they were quick to see through any clever remarks that were not backed up by experience.) Eliot's pre–*Waste Land* work—"Prufrock " and "Portrait of a Lady" and "Gerontion"—had been the first poetry that meant something to me. In my first year or so at university those poems articulated and dramatized my quite ordinarily banal and inarticulate adolescent moods. That the poetry was "difficult" gave the reassurance that to enjoy it was not to be "soft"; but it was the feeling, in the cadences and images, which possessed me and seemed to express me to myself. I first met "Prufrock" in a lecture. It was certainly a good one, since the lecturer was brilliant, but—or perhaps it should be *and*—I came away with nothing in my head but the poem itself. My experience then confirms Eliot's view that genuine poetry communicates before it is understood. Yet, of course, we do need to understand as well—to understand what we have experienced. Where we go wrong is in thinking we can understand poetry objectively, just out there on the page, when it needs to be understood in our response to it. That was where I went wrong, with every encouragement and reward.

In my MA year I was asked to write on "the music of *Four Quartets*." At that time, in the early fifties, the work was still relatively new, undigested, and not yet overlaid by exegesis. As an aspiring scholar I did my research and discovered the brown pamphlet "The Music of Poetry" (1942) in the library's special collection—later the essay would be collected in *On Poetry and Poets*. I also hunted out Helen Gardner's early essays on *Four Quartets* and the review-essays in *Scrutiny*. From these and other materials I worked out a theory and a scheme and proceeded to demonstrate how the *Quartets* conformed to it. The essay was well received, but I should have been told to tear it up and try again, only this time listening for the music of the poetry and finding it as I could with my ears and with the mind's ear.

That is the sort of thing I urge on my students now: ignore the jungle of criticism (including my own contribution to it) and concentrate on articulating the way in which the poetry articulates you. They do not believe me, of course. I can't mean it, since I am a teacher—it must be a trick to keep them from mastering my mystery. They are like that because the subtext of their education, if not the overt message, tells them that what counts is success in examinations and that nothing succeeds so well as a skillful recycling of some expert's view, while an honest effort to make their own sense of something is unlikely to impress. They have been educated to suppress their own experience and their gropings for the meaning of it and to go in instead for "scholarly research"—or, increasingly nowadays, for "theory," which has even less ground under it. (I should say that I can speak only from teaching in England and that things may well be otherwise in North America and elsewhere.) The sad consequence is that good students become able to discuss the meaning of a poem without its necessarily meaning anything at all to them. Not infrequently they then reach the cynical conclusion that it is all a meaningless game, poetry and criticism alike. Eliot was acutely aware of that possibility, and it made him doubt whether literature could or should be taught. He said, in *The Use of Poetry*, "I believe that the poet naturally prefers to write for as large and miscellaneous an audience as possible, and that it is the half-educated and ill-educated, rather than the uneducated, who stand in his way: I myself should like an audience which could neither read nor write" (152). That is asking not for unintelligent readers but for readers whose intelligence has not been interfered with. The primary use of intelligence is to be intelligent about our own immediate experience. But our systems of advanced education do little or nothing to develop intelligence in that way and do much to obstruct it. We who teach literature and who teach Eliot should bear in mind what he said in "The Frontiers of Criticism": "a good deal of the value of an interpretation is— that it should be my own interpretation . . . a valid interpretation, I believe, must be at the same time an interpretation of my own feelings when I read it" (*On Poetry* 114).

My group of addicts was as near as one is likely to get, in a country with compulsory education for all, to the sort of audience Eliot would have liked. They could read and write, of course, but concerning poetry they were as good as illiterate. I began by telling them that Eliot would have been happy to have them for an audience, and I gave a few dates and facts to locate Eliot and the poem. Then I asked if the term *Ash Wednesday* meant anything to them. They put together what they knew: something to do with Easter; Lent, the first day of; self-denial. One came up with the word *mortification*, and they took it apart, some trying to explain it, some objecting to it. "Is it religious, then, this poem?" I said, well, yes, in a way, but should I read some of it out?

I read the whole of the first part, from "Because I do not hope to turn again" through to "Pray for us now and at the hour of our death." So it was religious, with bits of prayers in it, like in church. But—"It made me think of Dick Whittington, at the start." Then, with several voices chipping in: There's a lot about giving up, and having nothing—there's a lot of sadness —but it doesn't feel sad, not really. Isn't he enjoying feeling sorry for himself? But isn't it a prayer? What difference does that make? It seemed the moment to move on to the second part. I told them that once when Eliot was asked what he meant by "Lady, three white leopards sat under a juniper tree," he answered, "I mean 'Lady, three white leopards sat under a juniper tree.' " This time the group had their idea of what was going on. It was like prayers again, with bits of the Bible, and it was all about giving up and dying and its being great to be dead. A death wish—no, more a dream of being dead, with all that light and those bones singing. It was a sort of love song too. One for the Beatles? Bits could be Dylan, almost. I reflected, who needs a disquisition on "the dream song and phantasmagoria"?

They were not so sure about the third part. It was like a bad dream— and a lovely dream. It was death again, was it, and then finding that garden he'd lost at the start? And love. We grappled with "strength beyond hope and despair," and I had the sense that a common nerve had been touched. Perhaps that made them question the section more sharply. When one said, "That's what it's all about when you come right down to it" the general feeling seemed to be that they knew that, though they might not put it that way. Would I read it again? I did, and then, after a moment's silence, I read part 4—"Who walked between the violet and the violet." They registered the hope and the dreaminess: it was surreal, clear colors and sharp lighting; a formal garden, like Hampton Court, flooded with white light—it was not like sunlight, and there were no shadows; a dream world, in which everything was all right again, and that was his bird by the fountain—only she wasn't speaking to him, but it did not seem to matter. They were not bothered by "Mary's colour" or "Sovegna vos," it seemed. No one asked, what does he mean, "While jewelled unicorns draw by the gilded hearse"? The poem had meant something to them, and they knew what it was, in their own terms. Their question was not, how do you interpret such an experience? but rather, what do you do about it?

It was as if they were able to take the poem literally—as a report on experience and not a fiction. They had no difficulty attuning to the kind of experience it was and entering into it. They knew all about wish-fulfilling dreams and hallucinations and lotos eating, and they knew those were not the answer but at the heart of the problem. So what was the poem up to, and what was I up to? Did I not know what they knew about the drug of dreams and the realities of seeing visions? Was I another innocent expert? They had been interested and engaged, but now they were cutting me out.

And time was getting on. I thought, Didn't the poem itself allow for their doubtfulness? and I read out from the last section the recognition of the persistence and the delusiveness of sensual desirousness. So Eliot did not think that dreams of bliss were the answer. They saw that but still were not satisfied. The poem had meant something to them, or to many of them, up to a point. They had made out a structure of feeling in it, which they could relate to their own experience. But then they were not convinced that the poem, or that I, really knew what it was like to go through that experience or how to get through it. Just how did this poem get from despair to that garden? And who wanted a garden, anyway!

Yes, so much does depend upon the interpretation of symbols and an understanding of the Christian way. But if I had tried to impose all that on them I would have lost them completely. Theirs was the valid interpretation for them, and my scholarship would have cruelly falsified it. But, again, perhaps the poem itself had more to give them. There was just enough time to read part 5 and for a few last words. Strangely, this part, which I had thought dispensable, seemed to appease their anxiety. They were not offended, as most readers in my experience are, by the apparent contempt for "those who walk in darkness . . . among noise and deny the voice." This had the bite of truth for them:

> Will the veiled sister between the slender
> Yew trees pray for those who offend her
> And are terrified and cannot surrender
> And affirm before the world and deny between the rocks
> In the last desert between the last blue rocks

Somehow that answered their need and answered to their experience, as no amount of explication could have done.

It was time for their tea break, which would be followed by a serious encounter session. They said, diffidently, that it had been better than they had expected and that they had got something out of it perhaps. And I tried to convey to them that it had been as good a discussion of literature as I had ever had. Of course, from another point of view, it had been a complete failure. I had left them knowing next to nothing about the poem, and they would have failed the simplest of exam questions about it. I had given them no understanding of the religious dimension and said nothing of the essential action of the poem, the transformation of the suffering soul through its attaining a Christian vision of suffering. But then, hadn't they got there in their own way? Eliot himself when young had argued—"in a paper on *The Interpretation of Primitive Ritual*," as he recorded in his introduction to *Savonarola*—that "the same ritual remaining practically unchanged may assume different meanings for different generations of performers; and the rite may have originated before 'meaning' meant anything at all" (viii). His later insistence, in "The Dry Salvages," on the interpretive function of Christian revelation was a development, not an abandonment of that view:

> We had the experience but missed the meaning,
> And approach to the meaning restores the experience
> In a different form, beyond any meaning
> We can assign to happiness.

The meaning can expand the experience but can never be a substitute for it. Those addicts had had the experience of *Ash-Wednesday*, though they may not have grasped Eliot's interpretation of their experience or my interpretation of the one or the other. But then the only interpretation they needed was their own, and they were working on that in their other sessions.

This account has been a "memorial reconstruction" of the event and should be taken with at least as much salt as the first Quarto of *Hamlet*. Memory works things over and synthesizes and simplifies. All that can be said for the veracity of my account is that it records how I have remembered the occasion. Others would remember it otherwise. Certainly, the twenty or so persons there did not all speak with one voice. The collective "they" is my fiction. And some were silent throughout, absent in their own thoughts or bored or baffled. It is only in my mind that they have been a model discussion group and a measure for more orthodox classes. But I would not expect any other group to be like that one, and every class must find its own way of reading a poem. The common factor in my good teaching experiences is that they all build on what the participants can see and feel for themselves. The sense we make of the text is what we can find in it and in ourselves there and then. Just the other week, a student coming to *The Waste Land* for the first time, unacquainted with the critiques but with a good ear for verse and an eye for imagery, reopened the whole poem for me. The only worthwhile meaning is the meaning of experience and of our own experience. We are all together in that circle.

TEACHING *THE WASTE LAND*

When Love Fails:
Reading *The Waste Land* with Undergraduates

Jewel Spears Brooker

Undeniably a complex and inexhaustible work, *The Waste Land* is also in many ways a simple poem with themes that are central in human experience and in Western literature. In presenting the poem to freshmen and sophomores, I focus on a single basic theme and move from that theme to more complex and more literary issues of structure and meaning. "When love fails, a waste land develops" is the form in which I express an idea that is basic to all Eliot's work from "Prufrock" to *The Elder Statesman*, a motif so clearly presented in *The Waste Land* that almost any student can pick it up, even on a first reading.

My presentation of *The Waste Land* requires three ninety-minute class periods. In the first, I introduce the theme of failed love and its consequences, lecture on the mythic backgrounds of the poem, and lead my students through a reading of the first seven lines of the poem and then of the epigraph, relating these passages to the theme and to the waste-land myth. In the second class, the students and I read together and discuss three passages of the poem that illustrate failed love and its consequences: the boudoir scene and the pub scene in "A Game of Chess" and the typist-clerk scene in "The Fire Sermon." In the final class period, we touch on other parts of the poem that are relevant to the theme, and we discuss why love has failed and how it can be recovered.

A crucial aspect of my approach to teaching literature involves the formulation of assignments that build common ground between me and the students. Even when they seem to be passive, when they are listening to a lecture or to the comments of their classmates, students can (and should) be active collaborators with the poet and with their teacher. To help students become my collaborators (and Eliot's), I have designed the following assignments to go with the three classroom sessions.

In preparation for our first class on *The Waste Land*, students read the poem and a handout that introduces them to the context of the poem, to its relation to the late nineteenth- and early twentieth-century crises in culture and religion. I have found that when cultural and religious backgrounds are emphasized in class, they can compete with or even overwhelm the poem itself. Yet the poem should not be taught apart from its cultural context. My handout solves this pedagogical problem; it discusses the collapse of Christianity as a cultural force, the collapse of a shared god concept capable of holding civilization together. In this handout, a version of which may be found in *College Literature* ("Second Coming"), I use Yeats's poem "The Second Coming" to introduce the idea of civilization's losing its center and falling apart. I then discuss *The Waste Land* as a picture of civilization with no moral, cultural, or religious center, no god concept. My students thus come to the first class on *The Waste Land* with an awareness that the poem consists of hundreds of fragments of the Western present, and of the Western past insofar as it had survived into the twentieth century.

The text of the poem is the focus of the second assignment. I have students reread the entire poem, dividing it into nuggets of narrative or drama or song. I require them to list these nuggets by line numbers and to label each with a descriptive phrase (e.g., pub scene or fortune-telling scene). And I tell them not to worry about how the fragments fit together. In doing so, I am deliberately planting the suspicion that the fragments might fit together in some less-than-obvious way, a suspicion that often leads the better students to think about the problem of unity. Also in preparation for this class, I ask students to pair off and practice reading aloud three special fragments: lines 77–138 and 139–72 in "A Game of Chess" and lines 215–56 in "The Fire Sermon." These are all scenes of love in the modern world that we will read together as illustrations of the statement "When love fails, a waste land develops." All three are dramatic, and all have obvious and traditional internal coherence.

For our concluding class on *The Waste Land*, students write an essay in which they identify and discuss scenes from the poem relevant to failed love and its consequences, or, to say it another way, passages suggestive of waste lands and the causes of waste lands. They may not use the fragments we have already examined in class (lines 1–7 of "The Burial of the Dead," the epigraph, "A Game of Chess," and the typist-clerk scene in "The Fire Sermon"). In completing this assignment, they come to their own understanding of how the poem works and how the fragments fit together, and they arrive in class prepared to share their insights and receptive to my attempt to pull things together. In my closing remarks, I usually refer to the mythic materials behind the poem, to the poem itself, and to the contemporary world, suggesting why, in Eliot's view, love has failed and how it can be recovered.

I want now to describe what we actually do in our three classes. My initial lecture focuses on the first seven lines of the poem and on the epigraph. Assuming that students have studied the handout and read the poem, I suggest that *The Waste Land*, though very complex, can be discussed in terms of a simple statement: "When love fails, a waste land develops." A few leading questions induce students to think about what *love* means and to consider the effects of love—fruitfulness, health, happiness, transcendence. Using the spring song from the prologue to *The Canterbury Tales*, I remind them of the association of spring with showers, with fruit, with small birds singing and young people falling in love. I also use Chaucer to suggest that the renewal of life in spring generates a longing for spiritual renewal, that April stimulates folk to go on pilgrimages, and, of course, that in April Christians celebrate the Resurrection of Christ and anticipate their own resurrections. From the meaning of *love*, we turn briefly to the meaning of *waste land*, which I define as a place in which life cannot exist or can exist only in a distorted way. I ask students for examples, because it is pedagogically useful for them to have a number of waste-land images in mind—not only deserts, but bombed landscapes, city slums, polluted lakes, and so forth.

I now turn directly to the startling variation on spring love with which Eliot begins his poem, "April is the cruellest month, breeding / Lilacs out of the dead land, mixing / Memory and desire, stirring / Dull roots with spring rain." The presence of April, warm rain, and lilacs reveals that Eliot is not referring to an actual waste land, that the waste land has to do with the perception of the speaker. Spring is experienced as cruel because it emphasizes by contrast the speaker's own spiritual lethargy; it calls forth memory, vague recollections of past love, and desire, intuitive longings for new life. The dull roots in winter's waste land breed lilacs, but the dull roots in the speaker are stirred to no purpose. Whispering promises that are not kept, April comes across as disturbing and ironic. And unlike Chaucer's pilgrims, the speaker has no shrine and no place to go for spiritual renewal. I point out that the title of part 1, "The Burial of the Dead," is an allusion to the funeral service in the *Book of Common Prayer*, a service in which the Resurrection of Christ on Easter is seen as the guarantee of human immortality. In view of the text that immediately follows this title—"April is the cruellest month"—the allusion to Christ as the first fruit of spring's new life is bitterly ironic.

Next, I discuss the epigraph of the poem, explaining that an epigraph, like a title, colors the entire poem. I show that the overarching reference to the Sibyl of Cumae, a divinity older than Christ, is consistent with the opening perception that spring is cruel. After reviewing the story of the Sibyl as given in the *Aeneid* and in the passage in the *Satryricon* that is behind Eliot's text, we discuss what April would mean to a being withered to the size of a cricket and imprisoned in a jar, a being who continues to age but cannot die. Further, we attend to the Sybil as a prophetess who knows, but cannot do anything with her knowledge, and we comment on other figures (e.g., Tiresias) whose knowledge survives their power. We discuss the implications of divinity being caught and displayed in a bottle for the amusement and the inspection of mortals. Students are fascinated with this image and have much to contribute about what such an inspection is bound to reveal: a withered body, a withered spirit, impotence on many levels.

From the Sibyl, I move to the withered prophet Tiresias, at the center of Eliot's poem, and to ancient myths about failed prophets and waste lands. To introduce the myth of the waste land, I use the description of blighted Thebes that appears in the opening scene of Sophocles's *Oedipus Rex*, a work all students in my college read in their first semester on campus. I tell the story of the Fisher King and his waste land and explain, briefly, that Eliot took his version of the myth from James Frazer and Jessie Weston. I then move on to my major subject—what we can learn about the relation of blighted love and waste lands by attending to the mythic backgrounds of Eliot's poem. The first point is that in myth, prosperity depends on inter-connectedness, and any failure to connect leads to disaster. Religion, according to Frazer, began with hard physical facts, such as the need to eat; and attempts to ensure the fertility of the earth and of animals led to the development of ceremonies involving human sexuality. I use examples from Frazer of sacred prostitution and sexual orgies devised as part of primitive agricultural engineering, emphasizing the fact that in myth, the fruitfulness of the land is inseparably linked to fruitfulness of human beings and animals. I point out that in both agricultural and sexual terms, a failure of connection results in a waste land. The latter point concerns the effects of love, that is, crops or children, but also, and of great importance, transcendence. From the sexual level, there is a move to the spiritual; in some mysterious way, lovers achieve self-transcendence or union. I show from the book of Genesis and various legends that in some myths, the spiritual fruit of transcendence actually precedes the physical fruit of children. Turning to the waste-land myths, I show that the relation between the king and the land is in certain ways analogous to the one between husband and wife, that the king achieves transcendence in his relation to his people, and that they achieve unity through their relation to him. I do not have space to set down each step in my argument, but I develop the point that in myth, health is related to a coexistence of physical fruits (crops, children) and spiritual fruit (self-transcendence, unity). The third point about love that I draw from the mythic materials is that in myth, horizontal love (or love between persons) and vertical love (or love between the human and the divine) are mutually contingent and interrelated. If human beings cannot love one another, they cannot love God. If they cannot love God, they cannot love one another. I illustrate this point from the gospel of John, from the waste-land myths, and from Samuel Taylor Coleridge's *Rime of the Ancient Mariner.* The moment love springs in the heart of Coleridge's old mariner, enabling him to bless the sea creatures, that very moment the curse begins to lift. By the time we finish this first class period, I have established the relation between love and fruitfulness, between lovelessness and waste, in the myths of Frazer and Weston, in the Bible, and in a few well-known works in the Western literary tradition.

The second class period again takes up the theme "When love fails, a waste land develops," this time focusing on three dramatic passages. We read them almost as reader's theater. Depending on my knowledge of the students and their reading abilities, I either invite certain students to be actors or ask for volunteers. For the boudoir scene in the first part of "A Game of Chess," two actors are needed: a female who is willing to play a nervous desperate woman and a male who is willing to play a bored reflective partner. For the pub scene, three roles must be filled: the nonstop gossip, the friend who is trapped in this nonconversation, and the bartender who interrupts them ("HURRY UP PLEASE ITS TIME"). For the encounter between the typist and the clerk in "The Fire Sermon," three roles must be filled: Tiresias, who speaks aside or from behind, and the lovers who eat and make love in silence. Simply setting up these reading situations is a valuable exercise for students, who are stimulated to interpret the scenes and to participate in the class presentation. My role is chiefly one of organizing the reading and encouraging discussion afterward. I ask a few leading questions about failed love and waste lands. My students are generally very enthusiastic in relating these scenes to the theme we have been emphasizing and to the mythic backgrounds. These discussion sessions almost always lead to interesting analogies and insights. Students are quick to notice in the boudoir scene the connection between narcissism and boredom and the special type of waste land that characterizes this failed love scene. In the pub scene, with the gossip talking about the marriage of Lil and Albert, students usually notice the coexistence of physical fruitfulness (five children) and spiritual sterility, of sex and waste. And students also have much to offer on the scene of the typist and the clerk. They never fail to note the relevance of "April is the cruellest month" to all these scenes, nor do they fail to note that sex does not produce transcendence or unity. They see the contrast between the symbolic importance of sex in the waste-land myths and in religion and the total desacralization of sex in the poem. To the first couple, sex is a way to kill time, analogous to a game of chess; to the second, it is a matter of appetite, analogous (for Albert and the gossip, but not for Lil) to a mutton chop; and to the typist, sex is analogous to a tedious memo ("Well now that's done: and I'm glad it's over.")

Students bring to our third class their own illustrative fragments, and we spend part of the period sharing these and relating them to failed love and to waste lands of various sorts. I occasionally ask a question or two, but I generally allow the students to lead. After they have heard my opening lecture on myth and love, read the poem three times, participated in our dramatization of the three scenes, and written a short paper on a fragment (or fragments) of their own choosing, most students have definite ideas on the poem, its relevance, its unity or lack of unity, and its value as a object of study. Most of them, even those who had never heard of Eliot before this course, have come to appreciate him and his achievement, and most, I have discovered, can quote parts of the poem. (I have often wondered whether these students actually memorize lines or simply remember them.) I reserve the last half hour of the period for a few concluding remarks on Eliot and the poem. Sometimes I use Eliot's essay on Baudelaire or the 1929 essay on Dante (both in *Selected Essays*) to say more about special ways in which love has failed in the modern world. Usually, I remind them that Eliot's fragments of failed love come from many times and places, that he is not simply contrasting an idyllic past with a sordid present. I often emphasize the inseparability of structure and meaning in the poem. Attending to the structure has the special value of suggesting that in taking fragments strewn on the surface of the poem and re-collecting them (both remembering where they come from and gathering them up again), we and our students are shoring up our ruins in a collaborative life-enhancing act.

The Waste Land as a Descent to the Underworld

Bernard F. Dick

The ideal student of *The Waste Land* encounters the poem in April, as is fitting, near the end of a two-semester course in world literature that has included the *Odyssey*, the *Aeneid*, and the *Inferno*. After a review of *Odyssey* 11 and *Aeneid* 6, covered in the first term, the student should be able to understand Eliot's poem as suggesting a journey through hell—a hell too often considered personal rather than archetypal. The student, who should be reminded that this approach is one of several possibilities, should also be able to derive a descent model from the ancient materials and apply it to *The Waste Land*. Such a model would include (a) an initiator who plays the dual role of character and mystagogue; (b) a quester who discovers an underworld in which the dead are grouped according to such categories as class, rank, common fate, and offense; (c) a location specific enough to enable the reader to envision the underworld as a place (Homer's grove of Persephone, Vergil's house of Hades, Dante's cavity within the earth, Eliot's unreal city); (d) a chronology explainable in clock time (Dante's twenty-four hours, Eliot's morning-to-evening span); and (e) a result measured by the quester's ability to apply the lesson learned in the other world to the quester's own life.

The Initiator

As a mortal, the quester is loath to visit the dead; even Odysseus is intimidated by the prospect. Thus someone endowed with supernatural powers (a sorceress, a priestess) must initiate the descent. As daughter of the Sun and aunt of Medea, Circe can speak to Odysseus in the language of the epic command, ordering him to journey to the land of the Cimmerians and consult with Tiresias about his homeward journey (*Odyssey* 10.505–40). As a priestess, the Sibyl can demand that Aeneas perform certain rituals before she can escort him through Hades (*Aeneid* 6.145–53). The initiator performs both a narrative and an ethical function; as an instrument of dramatic foreshadowing, the initiator prophesies events (Odysseus's next adventures, the wars in Latium) that come to pass later in the poem; as an instrument of destiny, the initiator sends the quester on a spiritual odyssey from which the quester returns better equipped for life.

While initiators are prophetically endowed, their sphere of activity is limited; ultimately, the quester must confront a higher power. At the beginning, however, the initiator is necessary; the quester can make no progress without one. Dante awakens in a dark wood, sluggish from sleep and far from the true way; Eliot's speaker, Tiresias, awakens from a winter of

109

inactivity and moral hibernation to the sound of spring—voices from the
past, snatches of conversation, and memories of sexual failure. Dante and
Tiresias require the same kind of direction that Odysseus and Aeneas received from Circe and the Sibyl, respectively. Dante finds it in Mary's
compassion, which is responsible for Beatrice's visit to Limbo to enlist Vergil's aid. Beatrice and Vergil, then, are coinitiators, performing the dual
function of prefiguration (Vergil's sketch in canto 11 of the sinners Dante
will meet in the last three circles, Beatrice's revelations in the *Purgatorio*
and *Paradiso*) and moral guidance.

Tiresias is less fortunate; he must settle for a clairvoyant with a bad cold.
In a waste land, those who should be preternaturally equipped to aid the
quester cannot because they are waste-landers themselves. Madame Sosostris is an anti-Circe, a bogus Sibyl, a false Beatrice, an unreliable initiator;
unlike the predictions of her classical counterparts, those of Madame Sosostris have no moral basis because they are only prefigurative. Her reading
of the tarot adumbrates the appearance of the other waste-landers (Belladonna, the Fisher King into whom Tiresias merges in part 3, Mr. Eugenides
as the one-eyed merchant carrying the legacy of sterility on his back, "crowds
of people" soon to be seen streaming across London Bridge) and introduces
major themes (Christ's absence from the waste land as symbolized by the
missing hanged-man card, water as bringer of death and giver of life). Madame Sosostris does little more than catalog (46–56)—something Circe, the
Sibyl, and Vergil also do; but unlike them, Madame Sosostris misleads the
quester. "Fear death by water," she warns, ignorant of water's salvific power.
Thus she gives Tiresias the card of the drowned Phoenician sailor for whom,
as one learns in part 4, there is no rebirth. Fortunately, she will be replaced
by another, in keeping with the descent tradition of lower yielding to higher.

If the initiator is female, she must yield to a male who will supplement
her prophecies and bring the quester to a higher level of knowledge. Circe
can predict Odysseus's immediate future; what she foretells in book 10 is
confirmed in books 11 (the trip to the underworld) and 12 (the final adventures). Circe, however, cannot narrate the details of Odysseus's last days;
Tiresias can, in addition to giving Odysseus an indication that the end is
near. As a priest-shade whose knowledge is deeper than Circe's, Tiresias
builds on her prophecies to give the quester a complete picture of his
remaining years. Although Aeneas is executing the will of his father, Anchises, who seeks a meeting with him in the underworld, the true initiator
is the Sibyl; yet she can only predict the trials awaiting Aeneas in Latium,
which constitute the last six books of the epic. Anchises, a shade dwelling
among the blessed in Elysium, can conjure up a pageant of Roman history
for his son, showing the role he and his descendants will play in it. Madame
Sosostris's prophetic powers serve a prefigurative, not a moral, end; later,

Eliot's Tiresias discovers a true prophet, Prajapati, who speaks through thunder, not through cards, and offers a way out of the waste land in the form of a real epic command (the tripartite give, sympathize, control) instead of the simple "fear death by water."

The transference of authority from female to male is more complex in Dante. Theoretically, Mary is responsible for Dante's journey, but she cannot descend to Limbo to engage Vergil; Beatrice can. Vergil cannot enter the Garden of Eden atop Mount Purgatory; thus Beatrice replaces him. Beatrice does not bring Dante to the vision of God; Bernard does.

Categories of the Dead

Arrangement by class or sin is not peculiar to Dante or his medieval predecessors. There is some categorical grouping in *Odyssey* 11 that, despite the interpolation at the end, can still be regarded as an attempt to impose order on the afterlife through systematic arrangement. Homer's arrangement is selective, limited to the famous and the infamous: heroines with unfortunate love lives, veterans of the Trojan War, and the damned (Orion, Tityus, Tantalus, Sisyphus) confined by themselves in Tartarus. The less renowned flit about making batlike sounds, having done nothing to merit special classification. Vergil's underworld is more elaborate and egalitarian; it consists of a threshold where the common cares of humankind dwell; the shore of Acheron where the unburied wander; a region beyond Acheron for the unjustly condemned, suicides, and children who died in infancy; the fields of mourning for unhappy lovers; the fields of heroes; Tartarus; Elysium.

The mythological hell is an inversion, a parody or antiimage of the real world, seen most clearly in the dead's living on in an underworld while the living continue in an upper world in homes built on foundations as opposed to a shell of a house or a conical cavity irrigated by subterranean rivers. The shade itself is a parody of the person it represents; it has only two dimensions, giving it the look of a cutout. In appropriating certain features of the mythological hell (Thames as Acheron, the Thames maidens as travesties of the hapless heroines in Homer and Vergil), Eliot produces an inversion of an inversion, especially when he turns Dantean. The sins that Dante considers major, fraud and malice, Eliot does not; conversely, apathy and lust, sins that Dante relegates to upper hell because of their universal and therefore less serious nature, Eliot considers the cardinal sins of the age. What were two sins in the *Inferno*—apathy and lust, punished in the vestibule and the second circle respectively—have been conflated in *The Waste Land*. Apathy has become amorality; lust, the misuse of sex. Their interrelatedness results in a new sin: disinterested desire, uninvolved passion.

There is only one circle in *The Waste Land* because there is only one sin, as is clear from the beginning when Tiresias sees the crowd flowing across London Bridge: "I had not thought death had undone so many," he exclaims, echoing the sentiments in canto 3 of the *Inferno* when Dante sees all the neutrals thronging the vestibule of Hell and realizes that they constitute the bulk of humanity. The crowd emits "sighs, short and infrequent" like the *sospiri* of the souls in Limbo (canto 4). Each member of the crowd "fixed his eyes before his feet" in the manner of the usurers who keep their eyes fixed on their moneybags (canto 17). The neutrals, the unbaptized, the usurers: in Dante's Hell, they are separate; in Eliot's hell, they are identical. They all belong to the undamned; never having exercised their unique gift of free will, they cannot even bring damnation on themselves. They simply *are*, pursuing an existence as empty as themselves. Since their existence is a mockery of life, their lovemaking is a mockery of sex; for Belladonna and her lover, passion has become boredom; for the clerk and the typist, it has become mechanical; for the Thames maidens, it has become lamentable.

Although Eliot has reduced all sin to one sin, he has not reduced all sinners to one sinner. While Homer, Vergil, and Dante group the dead in categories, Eliot goes further and arranges them in social classes. Eliot's is a class-conscious hell; while all commit the same anomalous sin, they do it differently, in accordance with the style, or lack of it, that characterizes their stations in life. Belladonna and Lil, the aristocrat and the slattern, spend their days amid the synthetic (Belladonna's cosmetics) and the barren (Lil's toothless mouth and exhausted womb). Yet Belladonna does it in a boudoir so elaborate that it makes the senses swoon; Lil, in one of those "thousand furnished rooms" described in the "Preludes" where hands raise "dingy shades" in the morning.

Belladonna and Lil are not the only ones who court death in life by cultivating sterility. Tiresias's friend Stetson mocks the spring planting by emulating Frazer's primitives and burying corpses in his garden as if they were year kings. Mrs. Porter and her daughter are not so anthropologically inclined, nor are they so upper-class. Yet they mock nature in their own way—by preventing conception through soda water, whose uses, as Eliot obviously knows, are not limited to footbaths. The Thames maidens, who belong to an even lower social stratum, should be the tutelary spirits of the great river; instead, they are whores who have made the Thames a river of woe, an Acheron. Ill used in the game of love, they recall the star-crossed heroines in the Homeric and Vergilian underworlds but have none of their counterparts' tragic grandeur.

Dante would have placed Mr. Eugenides, the sodomite who propositions Tiresias, in the seventh circle; but to Eliot, Mr. Eugenides is no different from the others who pervert the life-giving faculty. What differentiates him from the Thames maidens and the Porter duo is his merchant-class status.

Just as Belladonna is an anti-Cleopatra, -Dido, and -Francesca, Mr. Eugenides is an anti-Brunetto, roaming the seas (when he is not roaming around London) rather than a burning plain and speaking in demotic French that is no match for the French vernacular of Brunetto's *Tresor*. It is small wonder that Tiresias, who "foresuffered all," is so overcome by loathing of the flesh that he transports himself spiritually to the East.

Location

The other world is located not in some uncharted region but in a particular place, described in enough detail to make it real and even identifiable. Odysseus travels from Circe's island to the grove of Persephone in the land of the Cimmerians—from the northern Adriatic to the Black Sea, if Robert Graves (*The Greek Myths*) is correct. Vergil's underworld is also locatable; it is near Lake Avernus in Cumae.

While hell may have a specific location (in the vicinity of the Black Sea, in southern Italy, beneath Jerusalem), its boundaries are not fixed. Aeneas began his descent by entering a hellmouth in southern Italy; he ends it in Elysium, which the Romans identified with the Canary Islands or the unexplored Atlantic. There is an abrupt geographical transition at the end of the *Inferno* as Dante and Vergil climb down Satan's body; when they reach midpoint, Satan does a 180-degree turn, so that up and down are reversed, and instead of being in the Northern Hemisphere, they are in the Southern, where it is 7:30 a.m. instead of 7:30 p.m. Similarly, in *The Waste Land*, as the West falls to the hooded hordes, the setting, as if it were on a revolving stage, shifts to the banks of the Ganges. Like Dante, Eliot prepares the reader for the transition; as the grail chapel revolves, bats "crawled head downward down a blackened wall / And upside down in air were towers" (382–83).

Time

In the descent, time is subject to the same paradoxical laws as space. On the one hand, the descent occurs in a point of time; on the other, it is a voyage to a world where time as measured motion has no meaning. Still, the poet must maintain the fiction of clock time. Odysseus sails from Aeaea to the land of the Cimmerians and back in a day; both the Sibyl and Vergil remind their initiates that they must not waste time; by a hemispheric change, Dante reduces the trip through hell to a twenty-four-hour day, thus making the existential point that life can be hell. Eliot's Tiresias starts his descent at dawn, in the brown fog, and ends in the evening at the violet hour. The brown fog and the violet hour, Dante's *l'aere bruno* and *l'aere perso*, are the chronographic boundaries of the descent. Since Eliot inverts Dantean motifs and images, the brown fog, characteristic of the Good Friday evening when Dante and Vergil began their descent, has moved back to the morning where, in London, it would be more apt. Dante's lustful in the second circle are blown about in the perse air, perse being purplish black; hence Longfellow's translation of *perso* as "purple." To Eliot, *l'aere perso* signals the arrival of evening, a time of passionless sex as exemplified by the typist who copulates as mechanically as she strikes the keys.

Eliot has set a time limit to the descent, no doubt to make the same Dantean point: for waste-landers, each day is hell. Time, however, is more complex in Eliot than it is in Dante. Unlike Dante, who is recalling a past experience, Tiresias is remembering while he is descending. Tiresias is the voice of human consciousness; thus, it makes no difference whether some of the events are recalled or experienced during the descent. When memory is mixed with desire, past is mixed with future; out of this strange amalgam comes a present, not *the* present, but a continuum in which associations, feelings, and reflections have a simultaneous existence. Although Eliot's hell is bounded by the brown fog and the violet hour, within these limits is an unbounded present that neither reverts to the past nor anticipates the future; it is a present that is really eternity.

Knowledge

The poet of the descent is an impresario; Homer can create the illusion of a journey although Odysseus never leaves the trench from which the dead arise before him; Vergil has Aeneas traveling from Lake Avernus to somewhere in the Atlantic; Dante switches hemispheres, and Eliot changes continents. As West gives way to East in *The Waste Land*, the Thames yields to the Ganges where Tiresias is now fishing and asking a more overwhelming question than Prufrock's: "Shall I at least set my lands in order?" Tiresias may never be able to restore order to his community like Odysseus, found a race of kings like Aeneas, or experience beatitude like Dante. And if he does manage to set his lands in order, how will he do it? Through scraps of the past, Eastern mysticism, "a new start" as a Thames maiden would say, or a synthesis of East and West similar to Dante's synthesis of humanism and Christianity? If the ending fails to satisfy, it is because no descent to the underworld ever does. The descent does not result in perfect knowledge; it only increases the quester's awareness. At least the quester knows what must be done, and in a waste land that is not something to be dismissed. The descent, as Vergil noted, is easy; the return less so.

Structural Similarities in
The Waste Land and Early Film
Armin Paul Frank

When teaching survey courses in American or British poetry, I find that students feel at ease with Romantic and later nineteenth-century poets. The going usually gets rough when we approach the breakthrough of classical modernism. When confronted with Ezra Pound (*Hugh Selwyn Mauberley*) and the early T. S. Eliot, students sometimes exclaim, "But this is not poetry at all." Such reactions are similar to the ones that the (then) new poetry evoked among those critics of the teens and twenties who had been brought up on the verse of the "fireside" and "schoolroom" poets.

One reason students find Eliot's poetry hard to read is that it disappoints their expectations regarding coherence in poetic texts. From the point of view of most nineteenth-century poetry, Eliot's poetry can only be described negatively. It does not have the continuity—argumentatively, narratively, emotionally, rhetorically—that most earlier poetry had. The habits that work in reading, say, Wordsworth, do not work for Eliot. The reading experience simply contradicts the views of recent critics who align Eliot too simplistically with Romantic traditions.

One way of circumventing the structural difficulties is to suggest that students read some of Eliot's early poems, including *The Waste Land*, in the light of their experiences with film techniques. I have found that the initial problems called up by these poems tend to disappear when I enlist the students' moviegoing sensibilities. "Now for the first time *The Waste Land* begins to make sense," a student recently told me when I used this approach in a seminar on modern poetry.

In inviting other teachers to use this approach, I do not wish to suggest that *The Waste Land* or any other literary work is similar to a movie on the level of sense impressions. The two media certainly differ in the kind and range of constitutive physicality as well as in the kind of interpretive abilities they require of the reader or viewer. Nor do I wish to suggest that Eliot was influenced by film form. Eliot's early poetry is sometimes called "cinematic," but more properly, early cinema might be called Eliotic (or Poundean or Joycean). Eliot's innovations preceded those of Sergey Eisenstein, the pioneer director whose work I mention in this essay. If *The Waste Land* is cinematic, that illustrates a principle suggested in Eliot's essay "Tradition and the Individual Talent" (*Selected Essays*)—really new works (Eisenstein's films) modify earlier works (*The Waste Land*) in the tradition.

One way to begin a classroom discussion of form in poetry and in film is to refer to the principles used by the imagists. In 1915, soon after his involvement with the Fenollosa papers, Ezra Pound explained the imagist technique as an unwitting application of the "force of Chinese ideographs" to poetry (Stock 173). A typical imagist poem such as Pound's "In a Station of the Metro" ("The apparition of these faces in the crowd: / Petals, on a wet, black bough" [Pound, *Memoir* 89]) works by abruptly juxtaposing images from two realms that are normally regarded as incompatible, even contradictory: here, the subway and a flowering bough. Conventional poetic techniques of mediation such as simile and metaphor are eschewed. But by concentrating on minimal points of similarity behind the glaring contrast (the pale faces, the pale petals as color phenomena against a black background), the reader will discover surprising connections. Some of the poems (notably "Preludes") that Eliot wrote before meeting Pound are, in part, similarly structured.

In 1929 Sergey Eisenstein, in "The Cinematic Principle and the Ideogram," used the Chinese ideograph to explain some of his innovative techniques of structuring films (30). In *Battleship Potemkin* (1925), for instance, he combined shots of three sculpted lions in a park, each taken in a different phase of getting up from the ground, in such a way as to create the visual impression of a stone lion rising. He then inserted this sequence into a scene where it did not naturally belong, into a different "space-time continuum," the scene of the rebellion. This collision of independent takes suggests a new idea: the uprising is of such an elemental force that even a stone lion joins in. (Stills are shown in Eisenstein's *Film Form*, table 8.) That Eisenstein offers a somewhat different interpretation illustrates the high degree of indeterminacy that such techniques possess (56).

In a discussion of juxtaposition techniques in film (and other media), it is convenient to distinguish three structural principles and two modes. The structural principles are (1) *montage*, the juxtaposition of segments taken from the same space-time continuum; it achieves concentration and impressionistic intensification by the omission of segments from the "natural" course of events and by changes of perspective (the camera angle); one might think of a departure sequence consisting of juxtaposed shots of the signal going all clear, a puff of steam from the engine dome, huge wheels first spinning a bit, then catching, a handkerchief waving from a carriage window, and so on; (2) *collage* (as illustrated in the work of Max Ernst), the juxtaposition of incompatible, incongruous segments taken from different realms or continua and clashing when put together; the contrast suggests a deeper connection by dynamically and implicitly evoking a new experience or insight; some of what Eisenstein called "montage" and most of what Pound called "image" fall under this heading; (3) *assemblage*, where the fortuitous juxtaposition of incongruent segments does not produce a new unity. Assemblage is rarer in film and in literature than in the pictorial arts, though the "fragments . . . shored against my ruins" passage at the end of *The Waste Land* comes close.

The two modes, one "soft" and one "hard," are (1) the *cross-fade*, where a few of the traits of the material of one segment "softly" merge with similar traits of the second segment (for instance, similar shapes in movie cross-fades, similar sounds in radio cross-fades, similar linguistic features in literary cross-fades); the principle is similarity in contrast; (2) the *cut*, where no such merging occurs; this "hard" mode does not preclude the recognition of similarities on a deeper, spiritual level (imagination, ideation), as in the instance of the stone lion and the people "rising."

The three principles and the two modes combine to form six techniques for putting segments together. The technique most helpful in understanding *The Waste Land* is collage, in both modes. The film technique of *zooming in* is also anticipated in the structure of the poem. To illustrate the usefulness of bringing these techniques to bear on Eliot's poem, I offer a reading of the first forty-two lines, a reading that, because of space limitations, is more suggestive than analytical.

In the first forty-two lines of *The Waste Land*, I distinguish the following six segments, with the first three and the last three forming two subgroups.

1. Lines 1–7—root consciousness: strain of spring's awakening
2. Lines 8–18—Hofgarten, Munich: the uprooted nobility
3. Lines 19–30—desert: "roots that clutch"; Old Testament prophecy of fear
4. Lines 31–34—sailor's song from *Tristan and Isolde*: hopeful love
5. Lines 35–41—hyacinth garden: failure to commit oneself to human love
6. Line 42—end of *Tristan and Isolde*: love's despair

This division is based on textual features and takes into account A. D. Moody's idea of an encompassing structure, the idea of a parallel grouping of corresponding segments around the central hyacinth-garden vignette (*Thomas Stearns Eliot* 80–81). While I am grateful for this insight, I disagree with Moody on two counts. The encompassing structure is limited to "The Burial of the Dead," and even this section is less static, less spatial, than he says. To recognize the various ways in which the different segments are put together is to see in *The Waste Land* what Kenneth Burke refers to as "qualitative progression" (*Counter-Statement* 158–59).

The first segment introduces one of the poem's major themes: the growing pains involved in any revival. Here, the idea is put in natural terms by evoking the great effort it takes to stir winter-bound roots to seasonal life, to bring about the greening, as it were, of the "dead land," of the land laid waste. (The corresponding segment at the close of part 1, lines 69–76, which evokes the grosteque revival of the corpse that was planted last year, is an advance over the beginning of natural growth in springtime, since it evokes the fertility rites characteristic of various natural religions).

The transition to the second segment can be compared to a cross-fade using the collage principle, as becomes evident when one discerns the contrasts behind the apparent similarities of such lines as "Winter kept us warm, covering / Earth in forgetful snow" (5–6) and "Summer surprised us, coming over the Starnbergersee / With a shower of rain" (8–9). In the first place, each of the participle constructions in segment 1 has causal force; yet the one beginning in line 8 is temporal or circumstantial. Then, the pronoun "us," in line 5, includes the speaker among the roots hibernating under the warm snow cover and suggests a mythical root consciousness, whereas the "us" in line 8 refers to a different group, including a different speaker, an interlocutor ("Marie"), and other tourists in the Munich Hofgarten. Segment 2 is thus part of a completely different space-time continuum. The abrupt change of rhythm from a kind of verse whose "rhythmic constant" surfaces in the measured four-beat lines 4 and 7, in the first segment, to the lively, highly irregular conversational rhythm beginning in line 8 further indicates this transition to another segment.

The main speaker of segment 2 is Marie, who begins to narrate a childhood memory in line 13, "And when we were children. . . ." Despite the coordinating conjunction, the previous line, in German, should be assigned to a different speaker. The technique here is similar to the movie technique of zooming in: after first showing the Hofgarten café in a long shot (for a photo, see Hargrove, *Landscape as Symbol* 50), the "camera" zooms in on Marie and her interlocutor sitting at the table in the background, and, during the process of zooming, snippets of conversations going on at other tables fade in and out, including "Bin gar keine Russin, stamm' aus Litauen, echt deutsch." When Marie's table is up close, we begin to overhear her conversation in mid-sentence.

There are two reasons for assigning the German sentence to a speaker other than Marie. First, she has been identified, in the facsimile edition of *The Waste Land* (126), as the Bavarian Countess von Wallersee-Larisch, niece and confidante of the Austrian Empress Elizabeth, and the historical Marie had no connection whatsoever with Lithuania; but of course Eliot could easily have changed that. The second and more important reason is that Marie—though she fell into disgrace in 1889 when her cousin, Archduke Rudolf, successor to the Hapsburg crown, committed suicide—nevertheless represents the Austro-Hungarian nobility uprooted by the collapse, in 1918, of the Hapsburg Empire and that the anonymous woman from Lithuania (a country militarily contested by several nations for years after the end of World War I) was similarly uprooted after the collapse of the czarist empire. Read in this way, the reference to the breakdown of the old order—a theme recurring in the poem—is broadened, in segment 2, by the allusion to two of the three great monarchies that were destroyed by World War I. "And down we went" (line 16) takes on symbolic overtones.

The third segment, another new space-time continuum, a desert scene, is introduced by a clean movielike cut. Nevertheless, there is a subliminal connection between the painful memories of the uprooted nobility to the "roots that clutch," that hold on desperately to the soil in a desert made of "stony rubbish," a desert that connotes the destruction phase of the "Course of Empire." But the symbolic desert is devoid of life, and it is no wonder that a visionary voice announces "fear" to a wanderer who tries to cross it on his way east (lines 28–30), "fear in a handful of dust," fear in the face of death.

Thus, the first three segments complete a development from hopes for a revival, however painful, through failure to fear. The second group of three segments repeats this movement in the more limited scope of personal love. For brevity's sake, I discuss them conjointly and merely indicate the way in which segments 4 and 6, both quotations from the libretto of Richard Wagner's opera *Tristan und Isolde*, shade off meaning on segment 5, the hyacinth-garden vignette, which they are made to embrace in a collagelike composition.

Segment 4, from the sailor's song with which the opera opens, evokes his joyful expectation of a reunion with his beloved at the journey's end, just as King Mark looks forward to a happy marriage with Isolde, who sails on the same ship. Segment 6, by contrast, consists of words from the conclusion when, after the psychological and magical reversals that make up the plot, the dying Tristan learns that Isolde has not yet returned and that his love will end unfulfilled. The hyacinth-garden vignette, then, is embedded in two quotations that, within the work from which they are taken, mark the progression from a hopeful evocation of love's consummation to the recognition that love has come to naught. The same progression, I submit, characterizes the hyacinth-garden vignette itself, at the situational level. Very reticently, the hyacinth girl complains that what had clearly been understood, by herself and by others, as an opening gambit leading to a more intimate relationship—the gift of hyacinths that she had received from her partner a year ago—had not been followed up: the young man had failed to declare himself. (As any reader of Eliot knows, the theme of failed love abounds in his early poetry; its association with the garden motif, clear as it is in "La Figlia che Piange," is most evident in the unpublished "Entretien dans un Parc" (1911), where the hands of a young couple touch and hold on to each other and yet the young man does not speak, so that the poem ends in a psychological impasse. See Armin Paul Frank.)

In this second group of three segments, therefore, a reader aware of the collage principle can again recognize implicit connections that make for a qualitative progression, though the constructivist technique offers much interpretive leeway. Poems structured like *The Waste Land* give the reader much more freedom in constructing an interpretation. That is an important part of their challenge and their difficulty.

Freedom to construct is not the only difficulty, however. The quotations from *Tristan und Isolde*—an opera—are further connected by an allusive technique based on the données of opera as a medium that combines, even fuses, music with words. Introducing this consideration to students serves two purposes: it helps explain the "glue" (the range of associations) that holds this kind of collage together, and it suggests ways in which local collages, in *The Waste Land*, have a bearing on the overall structure and meaning of the poem.

The memorable tune to which "Frisch weht der Wind" is set recurs in Wagner's opera as the unmistakable leitmotif of the sea. In Eliot's poem, this musical allusion is as tenuous as it is significant. At short range, it reinforces the connection between segments 4 and 6 as the central part of the encompassing structure characteristic of "The Burial of the Dead," by tying in the musical allusion made by segment 4 with the dominant lexical item of segment 6, "desolate and empty the *sea.*" In addition, in view of the important part that the images of the sea and of a sea change play in the further progression of *The Waste Land*, this musical overtone also helps to integrate the Wagner quotations, over and above the meaning they contribute to their immediate context, into the entire poem, thus enriching the meaning of the whole. Together with a similarly remote graphic allusion, namely that to the Tarot card depicting the "man with three staves," who turns his back on the viewer and looks out on the sea, the musical leitmotif of the sea may be seen to point forward to the very conclusion when the "arid plain" has indeed been crossed and the "shore" has been reached (lines 424–25), the shore denoting the land bordering on a large body of water, the sea.

The comparison between form in poetry and form in film (also in painting and music) can thus be valuable in presenting *The Waste Land* in today's classrooms. It is not just a teaching gimmick aimed at the capabilities and limitations of contemporary students but an approach that is thoroughly justified on historical, scholarly grounds because of the near-simultaneous exploration of new structural principles in *The Waste Land* and in the other arts. This approach also enables the teacher to describe in positive terms what seems to be merely negative when viewed in the light of nineteenth-century poetry.

The Waste Land and Contemporary Art

Jacob Korg

The work of visual artists who were contemporary with Eliot has much to tell us about the formal aspects of *The Waste Land*. Early modern paintings exhibit many of the principles that motivated Eliot's treatment of his material. By showing slides or illustrations of these works while reading relevant passages of the poem aloud, the teacher can present the class with visible equivalents of the fragmentations, blendings, juxtapositions, and other departures from conventional form that characterize Eliot's poem.

Eliot's most immediate connection with the visual arts was through Ezra Pound and Wyndham Lewis, who in 1914 founded the movement they called vorticism as an English riposte to Italian futurism and French cubism. Through his friendship with Ottoline Morrell and his visits to Garsington Manor, Eliot also met Clive Bell and Roger Fry, two critics who represented an entirely different wing of modern art that nevertheless paralleled vorticism in encouraging abstraction and aesthetic detachment. Eliot's first publications (except for his Harvard juvenilia), "Preludes" and "Rhapsody on a Windy Night," appeared in the second number of the vorticist periodical, *Blast*, in July 1915. When *The Waste Land* first appeared in the *Dial*, its opening page faced a reproduction of Robert Delaunay's early cubist painting *St-Séverin*, as if to associate Eliot's revolutionary poem with the new art of the recent past.

One point that the teacher will probably want to make about *The Waste Land* is that, despite its excellent realistic passages, its general effect is something other than direct representation as that is conventionally understood. Almost any futurist, cubist, or vorticist work can be used to illustrate a comparable motive in the visual medium. All the modern art movements shared a critical view of conventional values, a sense that fundamental cultural changes were going on, and the belief that ordinary methods of expression were no longer adequate. The modern paintings can be used to show students that distortions of the visible field and the innovative poetic methods of *The Waste Land* both express this modern sensibility and convey similar messages about the world and the artist's response to it. The formal parallels can be interpreted as indications that Eliot shared with the painters the conviction that art must set aside the conventions of the recent past and find new forms of expression. The modern artists rejected realism as "illusionism," and *The Waste Land* often adopts a similar position in its depiction of figures, events, or ideas. This impression is created by such examples of analytic cubism as Pablo Picasso's portraits of Kahnweiler (1910) and Vollard (1909–10) and Georges Braque's *Pitcher and Violin* (1909–10), and it may be useful to ask the class why in paintings of this kind nonrepresentational forms occlude and distort naturalistic ones.

121

The discussion may very well generate comments resembling those made by critics about a vorticist work that Eliot is likely to have seen, the *Alcibiades* illustration from a portfolio of drawings by Wyndham Lewis for Shakespeare's *Timon of Athens* (reproduced in Hugh Kenner, *Pound Era* 235). It shows a space completely filled with a turbulent sea of shapes hovering between representation and geometrical abstraction in the midst of which a number of human faces and figures can, with some difficulty, be made out. These clashing and echoing forms are visible expressions of the relations among the figures and the forces that impact them—parallels, connections, conflicts, and radiations of power—but they are mainly controlled by the requirements of design. Lewis is less interested in representing objects or ideas than in using them to create an expressive conformation of lines, shapes, and shadings.

Ronald Bush has proposed that Lewis's *Timon* drawings may have inspired Pound to organize the *Cantos* through images that repeat and refer to one another, combining to give the impression that they are moving toward some unity that is never revealed (*Genesis* 48–49). A similar parallel can be drawn between the *Alcibiades* and *The Waste Land*. The poem's figures, settings, and events appear as fragments because their significance depends on their relation to the other images of the poem; these relations, like some of the nonrepresentational forms in Lewis's illustration, embody concepts developed within the poem itself. Once *The Waste Land* is read through with care, it is possible to go back and assemble some large unities out of its jungle of details. Such themes as the decadence of modern urban civilization and the sterility of life without faith and the images of the desert, the river, victimized women, and impotent or ineffective gods or kings emerge with some distinctness from the body of the poem, presenting a complex array of similarities and differences, like the echoic shapes in Lewis's design.

By rejecting the traditional notion that a painting depicts a scene as it appears at one particular moment, the modern artists gained a freedom that enabled them to develop an entirely new visual idiom. In the first, or analytic, phase of cubism, which occurred between 1909 and 1912, this process is motivated by two theoretical principles that modify the conventional ways of representing time and space. The first principle is simultaneity, and the second, the rejection of perspective. Simultaneity analyzes forms into parts that can only be seen from different angles of vision, sometimes merging the forms, sometimes presenting them as fragments or facets, sometimes displacing them to show the subject from a different point of view or in a different position. Perhaps the most famous example of this approach is Marcel Duchamp's *Nude Descending a Staircase* (1912), which presents all the stages of a temporal sequence at once. Perspective is rejected by arranging the surfaces of the objects or figures and the areas around them as a series of vertical planes, which are then brought together or tilted into each other. The class may well agree that such paintings seem fragmented, grotesque, and unintelligible if they are evaluated as representations of nature. But they may also agree that these methods of painting are comparable to those in a child's drawing or works of primitive art and, like them, represent departures from pictorial conventions. Students might then be guided to see that something memorable and expressive emerges when the artist perceives a subject as a design and, instead of merely copying it, emphasizes its formal, geometric properties. These motivations appear in the early cubist works of Picasso, Braque, Juan Gris, and others; natural forms are stylized in the direction of stable geometric ones and organized into visually significant patterns that stress the essentials of the object. The teacher can point out a comparable effect in the way in which synecdochic fragments in *The Waste Land* reduce scenes and objects to the features essential for the purposes of the poem. By recalling the Philomela myth through the "Twit twit twit" passage, Eliot strips it to its elemental savagery. Similarly, "The hot water at ten. / And if it rains, a closed car at four" schematically renders the life of privileged boredom.

The forms in cubist paintings typically avoid closure; each oblong, oval, or cylindrical shape is interrupted by some overlapping form, which is itself overlaid with another one, so that the distances they mark are interwoven to suggest a continuum. But because the overlapping forms also depict the subject of the painting, they have the effect of reconciling the separateness of individual forms with the continuity of space. Once students have been shown how cubist paintings break their space into successive planes and nonrepresentational volumes that overlap each other to form new shapes, they might be asked to select passages from Eliot's poem that seem disconnected but acquire significance when taken together. There is a good example of this effect in "What the Thunder Said," where three passages—the lines about the Passion (322–30), the speech from the desert (331–59), and the lines about the Ganges shore (369–400)—might be regarded as three planes in a cubist canvas, each marking a separate point in the space of the poem but containing fragmentary representational elements that can be joined through a kind of original syntax. Each is incomplete because, like the open forms in cubist paintings, it can approach closure only by collaborating with the others. The result is not the imitation of a natural form but a new form generated by the poem's internal relations. Perhaps the most perfect example of this effect is the list of decayed cities in lines 375–77:

Jerusalem Athens Alexandria
Vienna London
Unreal

The words are not grammatically connected, and the passage exhibits a neutral absence of specificity comparable to abstraction in a visual form; differences of time and grammatical function are set aside, achieving a flat immediacy comparable to the effects of simultaneity and of the abolition of perspective. I have found that when a group of students is asked to connect the city names with one another, the associations intersect in unprecedented and unpredictable ways, enacting the image that introduces the passage: "the city over the mountains / Cracks and reforms and bursts in the violet air." This image recalls paintings from the period of analytic cubism, and the procedure of making connections on the basis of free associations has a real correspondence with the way in which the cubist painter uses a subject to realize a design.

The fragmented and faceted appearance of paintings from this period reflects the antiperspectival principle that no one point of vision is adequate and that the model should be seen from varied angles if a more complete sense of it is to be conveyed. As a result, the painted form is composed of views that are incompatible with actual vision: the concealed back or bottom of an object is shown as part of what is logically visible, or the form is built up out of fragments of the object seen from slightly different positions. It is a useful exercise to ask a class to locate and reassemble these split or isolated fragments. The painter's procedure can then be shown to correspond with Eliot's method of treating his themes, not through unified narratives or descriptions, but by widely scattered instances or passing references that repeat and modify one another, as if one approach were inadequate and varied perceptions were necessary. Sterility, for example, is represented by the image of the desert, the impotence of the Fisher King, and the allusion to abortion in the pub monologue. Like the cubist painters, Eliot adopts multiple perspectives, approaching his subjects through realistic images, hallucination, association, memory, and so on using conceptual resources to achieve a more complete rendering than mere physical perception can offer.

In the book *These Fragments I Have Shored*, whose title acknowledges the primacy of Eliot's poem as a work that exploits discontinuity, Andrew M. Clearfield describes the poems of Guillaume Apollinaire's *Calligrammes* in language that applies perfectly to *The Waste Land*: "These works are characterized by an almost total lack of grammatical subordination, so that all sense of chronology, cause-and-effect, and focus is lost. There is no progression in such poems, and all events or objects are given equal rhetorical emphasis, just as in a Cubist painting all objects are crowded into the same plane" (73). In a painting of that kind, all the elements seem tilted forward and standing on edge, free of gravity, as if each were soliciting the viewer's attention or seeking to align itself with the surface of the canvas. Overlappings are often arranged as deliberate denials of logical perspective, so that forms that would normally be assigned to background and foreground aspire toward a flatness in which each would be equally close to the eye. As a result of Eliot's decision to follow Pound's advice and to reject long narrative sections and retain brief, abrupt effects like the "gists and piths" Pound admired in Chinese poetry, *The Waste Land* presents its materials in a similar way. Its images are sharply juxtaposed in enigmatic sequences, sometimes interrupting or repeating one another; few images recede or stand forward; there are few modulations or transitions between passages. Eliot, like the cubist painters, seems to reject conventional effects of emphasis, subordination, and depth, in order to allow each of the elements of his poem to participate fully in its design.

The extraordinary number of quotations, allusions, and parodic effects in *The Waste Land* corresponds to another cubist innovation, collage, a practice that quickly acquired both design possibilities and a philosophical program, making it one of the most widespread of modern art techniques. When Braque and Picasso began inserting bits of wallpaper, newsprint, concert programs, and similar products of the real world into their paintings, they achieved a variety of effects; collage might anchor the painting in reality, exploit textures or patterns of the external world, or create an impression of discontinuity as the real element invaded the space of the painting.

The principle of collage was transposed to literary use by Apollinaire and by Louis Aragon in the form of quotations, usually from conversation or popular language, which they inserted into their texts as a means of contradicting traditional notions of continuity and introducing an element of radical dissociation that rendered the work open and indeterminate. The quotations and the parodic insertions imitative of quotations in *The Waste Land* function in this way; they are intrusions from the external world, "found objects," which assert their reality within the space of the poem. They create an effect of discontinuity even when they are relevant to their contexts, because, like the papers pasted into a cubist canvas, they affirm beyond all else their own presence; the reader is free to connect them with the themes of the poem by using the associations they bring with them. In their relation to the rest of the poem, they enact the artist's problem of subordinating reality to the purpose of a work, for even when they seem most successfully integrated into one of Eliot's themes, they remain at least partially discontinuous with their contexts. The final lines of the poem, the "shored fragments," seem to defy unification; they acknowledge both the nobility of the cultural heritage they represent and the modern world's failure to assimilate it.

Modern paintings can bring both the spirit and the rhetorical innovations of Eliot's poem into the classroom in visible and unmistakable form. Eliot's purposes and ways of organizing the world do not, of course, correspond in all respects with those of modern painters, but the poem and the paintings share a basic aim that is well expressed in a comment of Ezra Pound's. "My brother artist," he wrote, "may, and probably does, disagree with me violently on all questions of morals, philosophy, religion, politics, economics; we are indissolubly united against all non-artists and half-artists by our sense of this fundamental community, this unending adventure towards arrangement, this search for the equations of eternity" (*Gaudier-Brzeska* 148).

The Waste Land as Gothic Fantasy:
Theology in Scary Pictures

Douglas Fowler

Albert Einstein once claimed that he had been able to discover some of the secrets of matter and energy because he never stopped trying to answer the questions little children ask. The wonderful naiveté in that claim should remind us by analogy that it is always important to continue to ask the simplest of questions about art and its creation, to recall ourselves to the first questions.

T. S. Eliot always wanted art to deliver up something beyond itself, and we must never forget that this great poet and essayist, so intimidatingly in command of much of our Western cultural achievement, desired with frank urgency to diagnose a deficiency in the human spirit. Eliot's intentions were spiritual, and an important if incomplete description of *The Waste Land* might be to call it a morally constructive sermon with edifying fright as its central mechanism—art for the soul's sake. Notice for example that Eliot's choice of the Buddha's Fire Sermon to furnish part of the allusive context of *The Waste Land*'s third movement brings before us an imperative of breathtaking simplicity: the heart must cast out its desire, its self-consciousness, its very appetite and identity in order to find its peace. In *The Idea of a Christian Society*, Eliot describes our civilization in a state of error, using familiar pulpit terms: "a wrong attitude towards nature implies, somewhere, a wrong attitude toward God, and the consequence is an inevitable doom" (47). Transmuted into poetic images and energies—Eliot's famous remarks on the objective correlative can really be said to point out the necessity of transforming captions into pictures—such urgent but featureless religious claims become the violent, terrifying texture of *The Waste Land*, a gothic experience of unrivaled power because we can see and feel the agony from the inside. Stephen Spender reminds us of a large simplicity about Eliot's verse when he points out that Eliot "is most a poet when he is describing extreme conditions, and the Dantesque circumference which is drawn about his work is of a consciousness always at the most extreme state of awareness of horror or boredom or glory" (52).

One of the subtlest falsifications we can inflict on Eliot's major poetry is to forget that we will make of his verse something more conventional and comfortable than he intended if we lose sight of the gothic and frightening content of its images and evocations. It is usually the sensational and lurid content of a writer's work that is reflexively diminished by our habit of regarding serious art as being intrinsically beyond violence and grotesquery for its own sake—or for ours. But of course the rhetorical shape of that sentence has already alerted you to the claim that we can best understand the black miracle of Eliot's creation if we experience his poems as an attempt to comprehend the ways of God—as theology. And not a theology of judicious commentary or learned discourse, either. In *The Waste Land*, Eliot's distress with the world is cast in terms of a horror unforgettably immediate, hopelessly sincere, and sometimes gothic to the point of freakishness; and one can feel everywhere in his work, but perhaps with especial urgency in this poem, the remarkable poignance of a consciousness that would find in its art not a mirror that simply reflects but a portal through which to escape. Speaking of Dante, Eliot makes one of those quietly offhand remarks that suggests with such moving eloquence his lifelong struggle to find within his imagination a way out of this "waste sad time": Dante's art, Eliot claims, is a "conscious attempt, as difficult and as hard as rebirth, to pass through the looking-glass into [another] world" that may even prove to be "larger and more solid than our own" (*Selected Essays* 236). But it is at least possible to achieve this "larger and more solid" kingdom, possible but terribly difficult, for, as Eliot grimly promises us in "Little Gidding," the *Paradiso* he finally achieved two decades after writing his *Inferno*, the effort to save ourselves will cost "not less than everything."

Thus *The Waste Land* is emphatically not just a work of art for art's sake, or just an elaborate elegy on the decline of the West, or simply an intimate psychiatric transcription—even though it of course includes all these dimensions. The marrow of the poem is concerned with the relation of humankind to a terrifying God, nothing less. In one sense it is the sort of poem a modern Dante might find himself writing—a guided tour down into a gallery of phantasmagorical horrors. But if the Eliot of the *Quartets* in the early 1940s will come to share Dante's conviction that those horrors are demonstrated to us solely for purposes of instruction and renewal, the Eliot of *The Waste Land* in 1922 is not so sure. He knows he is in the Inferno, only that. But the sense of a personal and immediate suffering behind Eliot's poem, quite unlike the theatrical artifice of Dante's work, is overwhelming—it is the Eliot of the twentieth century and not the Dante of the fourteenth who seems to be creating poetry out of a necessity as ancient as firelight playing on the wall of a cave and using some sort of half-formed Ur-language to try to convey to us his vision. To read *The Waste Land* with our most sensitive attention is to understand at a level beneath definition what Eliot meant when he claimed that "the poet is *older* than other human beings" (*Use of Poetry* 155).

Eliot's modernity was a matter of surface complication and narrative displacement, then, not substance. His organizing technique was in 1922 startlingly new, for, as Robert M. Adams put it, Eliot's approach was unsettling to readers schooled in Palgrave's *Golden Treasury*, adopting as it did a style "cutting off the horizontal decorative flow from image to image, in abrogating the familiar alliance of description and moral reflection" (139). But beneath a shell encrusted like a Fabergé Easter egg with allusions to anthropology and myth, readers discovered a description in small of the spiritual energies that invisibly organize the universe.

That *The Waste Land* is a contemporary *Inferno* is an equation of real significance, for it is important to see that both poems are theological fantasies that describe in harrowing images God's intentions for us and propose that the torture will cease at nothing less than a transformation of the soul. God, like gravity, is everywhere and sovereign and yet invisible, but he has chained us into nature to serve his purposes; we must desperately try to believe in that.

Eliot's theology is an eerie and personal one, and given to us not as rhetoric but as pictures—scary pictures. Nor is it the theology of the learned scholastic or the humanist-priest; it is the theology of the private vision, transcribed for us with alarming accuracy from inside the kingdom of nightmare. Biographically, we are not quite sure we have illuminated enough of the shadows that are gathered behind the genesis of Eliot's poem. Perhaps we never will. From evidence outside the poem we can infer some sort of sexual incapacity was involved in the failure of the poet's marriage to Vivien Haigh-Wood, and this private sexual catastrophe must have played a part, for example, in Eliot's choice of the myth of the Fisher King as one of his most crucial images of the human condition. More subtly if no less significantly, the poem can be read as an attempt to subdue the anguish Eliot felt at the loss of his beloved friend Jean Verdenal, the young French medical officer who died in the Gallipoli campaign and to whose memory Eliot had dedicated his first collection of poetry, *Prufrock and Other Observations*, in 1917.

Unlike Dante or Milton, Eliot could not use an elaborate supernatural machinery centuries in the assembly and frictionlessly familiar to every level of imagination he hoped to reach. If God were not really as dead as Nietzsche claimed, still the sensibilities Eliot hoped would sympathize with his poem could no longer be presumed to respond to dramatis personae and magic stories quarried out of the Book of Genesis and churchly fairy tales. The whole order of the world had died in the War of 1914–18, and its imaginative life had been mutilated forever by the explosion. The rational iron rails of expectation and attitude and shared meaning laid down so smugly for us in the previous centuries of European culture had been blown away in the catastrophe, and Eliot had to invent where his predecessors had merely to reanimate. This is a grave distinction. Thus the texture of *The Waste Land* of necessity became a concatenation of guesswork, improvisation, and hasty battlefield surgery. Private demons whisper from between the lines, and Ezra Pound's editorial blue pencil consigned once and for all into the outer darkness not only a shadow poem roughly equal in length to the published version we have before us but also any sort of syntax and connective clue that might be suspected of being soft on middlebrow expectation. And we must not forget that Eliot finished the poem in a Swiss sanatorium, evidently recovering his sanity by the act of offering up his poem as a substitute host for his personal demons to invest and feed on. *The Waste Land* could hardly help but be strange, even shocking, in appearance.

Eliot spoke of the writing of poetry as a kind of exorcism—and it is no accident that he chooses the language of theology to describe the processes of the artist. Poets, he claims, must work out their poems; this is not their joy, or their task, or even their obligation; it is their curse. For the poet "is haunted by a demon, a demon against which he feels powerless, because in its first manifestation it has no face, no name, nothing; and the words, the poem he makes, are a kind of form of exorcism of this demon" (*On Poetry* 107).

To teach *The Waste Land* is, then, to confront a challenge seemingly more daunting than that offered by almost any other work in the heritage. We are asked to comprehend a work of private but urgent theology and private but partially concealed autobiography, cast in a language and imagery invented ad hoc for this single occasion. It is an understatement to describe the poem as "allusive," for so many and varied are the cultural and theological referents that occur in microdot concentration throughout the verse that the editors of one of our most helpful teaching texts, *The Norton Anthology of English Literature* (ed. Abrams), have generated one hundred explanatory footnotes explicating the poem's 433 lines. The quantity and variety of erudition, arcana, quotation, and anthropology involved in glossing the poem sometimes seems less like a description of sources than an editorial assault on *The Guinness Book of World Records*.

And yet this very profusion of symbol and allusion and the near-hysterical eccentricity of style may well signify to us that Eliot intends to capture an experience, not provide an explanation. Instead of trying to manipulate every line and image into little cubes of "meaning," we can more sympathetically receive the poem if we understand it as an attempt to replicate primal dream stuff from our deepest consciousness, animated by energies from far below the bottom edge of the reasonable. The poem does have a method and a meaning, but it is anything but a paint-by-number kit of symbolic equivalencies. To teach poetry is too often to substitute fluorescent light for moonlight, to buy clarity of paraphrase at the expense of ineluctable beauty and magic rhythm. Eliot is no doubt giving us a clue to reading Eliot even as he gives us a clue to reading Dante: "It is really better, at the start [of reading the *Inferno*], not to know or care what [several of its symbolic identities] do mean. What we should consider is not so much the meaning of the images, but the reverse process, that which led a man having an idea to express it in images" (*Selected Essays* 204).

What is then Eliot's "idea," and how do his images embody it? To offer a useful simplification is the best first step in teaching anything, so one might begin discussing the poem by suggesting that certain images depict a world that has fallen away from God and finds that loss an agony. The epigraph from Petronius that frames the poem and is spoken by the Cumaean Sibyl —"I want to die"—sets out the poem's central dynamic: human consciousness chained into nature and helplessly, ceaselessly enduring the awareness of a better world now lost to it. But instead of an exquisitely structured *Inferno* where each torment is precisely that much more appropriate and awful than the one before it, Eliot's vision is a transcription of a human dream because sequential event, connective logic, and rhetorical cue have been stripped away, leaving the reader face-to-face with another person's nightmare. The last movement of the poem, "What the Thunder Said," begins with a highly charged example of Eliot's vision.

Eliot himself identified the theological underpulse of part 5 as deriving from the scriptural account of Jesus's visitation with the disciples on the road to Emmaus and from accounts of the Grail quest contained in Jesse L. Weston's *From Ritual to Romance*. What Eliot does not mention is that the first eight lines of the movement contain in microcosmic concentration nothing less than the trial and destruction of Jesus with a foreglimpse of his Resurrection—that is, that these lines retell, in reduced but perfect form, the central agon and miracle of the Christian faith: a human being must die a prolonged and horrific death sustained throughout only by the distant promise of Easter rebirth, "a reverberation / Of thunder of spring over distant mountains." Nowhere in the poem is the deathly sterility of the human situation made more vivid. The hallucinatory evocation of paradisal waterfall and the hermit thrush's "water-dripping song" that appear before the sun-tortured mind, encapsulating as these images do the suggestion of salvation and renewal, strike us as Eliot's poetic embodiment of Francesca's words to Dante: "The double grief of a lost bliss / is to recall its happy hour in pain" (lines 118–19; trans. Ciardi).

Lines 360–66 offer some of Eliot's subtlest gothic effects and most pointed theology. The "third who walks always beside you" evokes the eerie passage in Luke 24.13–34 where Cleopas and Simon on the road to Emmaus are visited by the spirit of Jesus and chastened for being "slow of heart to believe all that the prophets have spoken" about his certain Resurrection. Eliot's own notes indicate that the ghostly presence that hovers at the outside edge of human perception had its origin in the hallucinations of Antarctic explorers near death from exhaustion, but that secular image, which Eliot guesses that he borrowed from Ernest Shackleton's *South*, is really used to reinforce the supernatural visitation.

One of *The Waste Land*'s most powerful image patterns is that associated with the human corpse itself—the human remains before resurrection. It is almost as if Eliot were to concentrate on the flesh and bones of Jesus in the days *between* the Crucifixion and Easter. The effect is shocking, and Eliot meant it to be shocking. The corpse that Stetson "planted last year" and that may have "begun to sprout," the "withered stumps of time" that perhaps suggest human limbs sacrificed to the explosives of World War I, the rats dragging themselves over dishonored bones and the bones "cast in a little low dry garret, / Rattled by the rat's foot only, year to year," the bones of Phlebas "picked" by undersea currents—these images are set into the poem as deliberately as memento mori skulls into a medieval tomb, and for something of the same purpose: to shock the human soul into confronting its own mortality and the necessity of seeking salvation, moment by moment, breath by breath. *The Waste Land* began life as an account of one man's struggle with the demons of despair, the terrors of mortality. But genius is a gift for accuracy. Our century immediately recognized *The Waste Land* as its own portrait; the poem became its most significant metaphysical event, its master metaphor. It has remained its master metaphor for almost seven decades. Why?

If there is any single generalization that can be made to answer for the amazing durability of Eliot's metaphor, it is that *The Waste Land* has triumphed because, like all great religious art, it refuses to treat human life as a mechanical triviality and assumes that no matter what crimes we perform against our souls, our souls are important. The condition we fear far more deeply than an intended terror—a terror directed against us by an Inquisitor-God—is the state of meaninglessness. Meaninglessness is the special burden of our century. But Eliot's vision of the world implicitly and explicitly assumes we are not a random collection of molecules moving about in a dance of DNA—for it is one of the most stubborn vanities of the human imagination that the greatest crime we can conceive against ourselves would be to discover that there is simply nothing *out there*. *The Waste Land*, then, answers to our deepest anxiety. For all its modernity of structure, it remains a primitive spiritual drama, a theological poem of gothic images.

Tripartite Indo-European Patterns
in *The Waste Land*

William Harmon

As I once noted in an article in *PMLA*, three of T. S. Eliot's poems end with a triple repetition: *The Waste Land* with "Shantih" three times, likewise "Difficulties of a Statesman" with "RESIGN," and "Virginia" with "river." The fragmentary *Sweeney Agonistes* ends with three threesomes: "KNOCK" nine times, arrayed in three groups of three (two horizontal and one vertical). I then aligned some of Eliot's threesomes. From an Indian commentator, who was not dealing with Eliot or poetry at all, I culled the idea that the three evils described in Buddha's Fire Sermon (lust, anger, greed) could be matched up with the three thunder injunctions in the Brihadaranyaka Upanishad (control, sympathize, give) and with a special meaning assigned by a Sanskrit dictionary to a triple *Shantih*: "May the three evils be averted."

Although I was temporarily satisfied that I had discovered (or invented) something of the underlying structural and thematic symmetry of *The Waste Land*, I was left with some residual frustration, because I still could scarcely account for the power of the poem to reach, touch, and move so many thousands of readers who would hardly seem to possess the wherewithal to appreciate such sophistication. I began to think that the popular appeal of the poem—an unmistakable effect that I can observe whenever I have the privilege of introducing an undergraduate class to Eliot—may reside in its haunting rhythms, fine-tuned ironies, and myth-saturated symbols—subliminal, primordial, and even visceral things that communicate before a poem is understood. But I had to conclude, by and by, that the bewitching authority of rhythm, irony, symbol, and myth, all stored irresponsibly in that capacious pantechnicon called "Je ne sais quoi," was really little more than a procrastinator's tissue of sentimentality. Plenty of poems with all the right stuff in all the right places, after all, just fall flat (I am thinking of works by Conrad Aiken, Hilda Doolittle, Charles Olson, Ted Hughes, and many another), while other poems that seem to have none of the right stuff anywhere take up a place in the heart and mind, soon acquire permanent tenure, and refuse to budge. (Students can be helpful with examples of unlikely works that somehow catch on: the popular lullaby "Rockabye Baby," for instance, seems designed to frighten, not pacify.) It was at this point that I discovered the investigations of Georges Dumézil, and that has made all the difference. (For English-speaking readers, the best introduction and guide to Dumézil is C. Scott Littleton's *New Comparative Mythology*.)

Dumézil's studies, which have been appearing since the 1920s, have to do with the great and sometimes vexatious body of language, lore, and ideology preserved in the myths and legends of the diverse Indo-European peoples for several millennia. Dumézil's basic notion, derived from the sociology of Emile Durkheim, regards myth as an upward projection of secular social patterns, which myth serves to explain, justify, sanction, stabilize, and perpetuate. The most persistent pattern in the pagan lore of Indo-Europeans from India to Iceland traces three realms, which Dumézil calls "functions," and they typically appear in a set order and with set properties and qualities (colors, style of death, vices, virtues, punishments, and much else). None of the functions is simple, and each includes a number of human pursuits, from the first function, which is relatively limited, to the third function that, true to its hallmark of fertility, is almost unlimited in its abundance and diversity. The first function, Sovereignty, comprehends mastery over both nature (magic) and culture (law) and is situated commonly in such father-gods as Zeus, Jove, and Odin. The second function, Force, realized in forms uncultivated (brutality) as well as cultivated (chivalry), is the domain of the likes of Ares, Mars, and Tiu. The third function, Fecundity, includes a multiplicity of pursuits, all the way from biological reproduction (dignified as romantic love) to the cultivation of wealth in the abstract (economics). Table 1 (derived from the work of Dumézil, Littleton, and S. Radhakrishnan, as well as my own fancy), may help.

There are problems with this scheme. The Indo-Iranian and Greco-Roman orders cannot always be lined up neatly with the Germanic; Odin would seem to be the counterpart of Jove, but he is sometimes matched instead with Mercury (thus Odin's day, Wednesday, is Mercury's—e.g., *dies Mercurii, Mercredi*—in southwestern Europe), while Jove finds himself matched with Thor (and Thor's day is Jove's—*dies Jovis, Jeudi*). The second function tends to expand and ascend, so that its representatives take on features more

Table 1. Tripartite Patterns in Indo-European Ideology

	Function (Caste)		
	I. Sovereignty (Brahman)	II. Force (Kshatriya)	III. Fecundity (Vaisya)
Range (nature—culture)	Magic—law	Brutality—chivalry	Love—economics
Graeco-Roman deities	Zeus, Jove	Ares, Mars	Aphrodite, Venus, etc.
Colors	White, gold	Red, orange	Blue, green, brown, black
Death	Hanging	Burning	Drowning
Class of offspring*	Gods (*deva*)	Demons (*asura*)	Human beings (*manusya*)
Vices**	Lust (*kāma*)	Anger (*krodha*)	Greed (*lobha*)
Virtues*	Control (*dama*)	Sympathize (*dayā*)	Give (*dāna*)
Thunder*	Damyata	Dayadhvam	Datta

*Brihadaranyaka Upanishad.

**Implicit in the Upanishads and explicit in the Fire Sermon.

typical of priestly or legislative sovereignty than of military force (Hercules became something of an intercessor-demigod, virtually Christlike in being the son of God, in willingness to help humankind, and in his association with the sun's annual career; the Bhagavad Gita is addressed not to a priest but to Arjuna, a warrior-prince). None of these ostensible anomalies, however, can weaken our sense of the persistence and pervasiveness of the threefold lineaments of the ideology.

With *The Waste Land* in mind, we shall probably be struck by the congruence between the hierarchy of styles of death in the Indo-European model—hanging, burning, drowning—and those emphasized in the poem. But there are more and deeper connections, most striking in the moral parallels between the third and fifth sections of Eliot's poem. As we know, "What the Thunder Said" differs for three kinds of creature, and it is possible to construct a web of kinship uniting the triad of injunctions with other triads from the Indo-European font, as I have tried to do in my table. There may be some confusion about which commandment goes with which vice and about which vice goes with which class of creature (all creatures may be greedy, and "control" cures not only lust but greed and anger as well), but we can overcome such problems by understanding that human beings may be construed as combining godlike, demonic, and human qualities all at once. It is possible, moreover, to extrapolate the commandments centripetally to the gross anatomy of the individual specimen (head, arms, and loins) and centrifugally to the cosmic organization of the Olympian or Capitoline community of gods. The principal plane of the poem remains the human, and what looks mythic or divine is less a revelation of superhuman truth than an exaggeration of the human condition.

The scheme that I have suggested above can function as a world model based on certain postulates involving human anatomy, society, and history. *The Waste Land* seems deliberately to allude to such models, and it goes out of its way, in the title of its second section, to call up the Indo-European game of chess, the name of which, like the Iranian title *shah*, is derived from the same root as *kshatriya*. Other such models are the astrological zodiac, the fanciful tarot deck that Eliot concocted or distorted, and the names of days and months in the customary calendars of Indo-European peoples. (Here, again, students can suggest various symbolic world models.) It turns out that the structures and tonalities of *The Waste Land* vibrate, as it were, in harmony with one particular model that can be represented by a simple diagram:

These symbols represent, all at once, a set of highly charged relations, interfaces, or thresholds. Conventionally, the symbols are explained as the shield of Mars (with a spear sticking out) and the mirror of Venus; and we may recall that these two distillations of death and love—the second and third functions—are antitheses and also lovers. In biology, the symbols stand for male and female (the combination of which is found in no god and in only one human being—Tiresias). In astronomy, the symbols represent the second and fourth planets, precisely those whose orbits lie just inside and just outside that of the earth. In the calendar of months, these paired symbols could represent the tempestuous passage from the month of Mars (March) to that of Venus (April)—a boundary crossing that we have immemorially observed by a secular ritual of inversion and so-called practical jokes. April may not be the cruellest month really, but it does get under way with a foolish holiday that sanctions cruelty and folly. I believe that what we do on April Fool's Day—rather like what we do on Halloween and New Year's Eve, both of which fall at the end of a thirty-one-day month, with two consecutive odd-numbered days—amounts to a vestigial piece of superstition designed to ward off evil (an apotropaic gesture) by reducing ourselves to harmless clowns while the solemn world in the sky negotiates the messy transfer of power from Mars to Venus.

I calculate, then, that *The Waste Land* is set in the ideal Indo-European mind of Tiresias, who is blind and dead in hell but can still see—and suffer—all our past and future; in the City section of London, where churches, banks, and fish markets are still collocated (although the actual handling of seafood has been moved to Vauxhall, the old Billingsgate building remains); on the first day of April in 1921 or 1922. April 1 was a Friday in 1921 and a Saturday in 1922. Since the poem seems to be set on a weekday, 1921 is more probable. Besides, a Friday is most appropriate, because it permits us, subliminally and onomastically at any rate, to observe the inauguration of Venus's month on Venus's day (Frigg's day, *dies Veneris, Vendredi*). To the Indo-European racial mentality, no figure could be more compellingly lifelike, engaging, and representative than Tiresias, with a cross-section of his mind laid out dramatically in the City on the first of April. From this terrifically concentrated personage prodigiously laden with direct and indirect symbolic meanings richly underscored by parallels and emphasized by contrasts from a dozen tongues, literatures, and religions (almost all of them Indo-European), *The Waste Land* expands and reaches out to include virtually the whole world of practically any English-speaking reader, and the resulting power of the poem is unmatched by any other in this century.

The message of most Indo-European lore, from the earliest surviving inscriptions and prose Upanishads to *The Waste Land* and later works, hieratic and vulgar alike, is that the three great functions exist and coexist, with a certain organization and certain qualities, including inherent contradictions and points of strain (none more interesting than the frontier between Venus and Mars—which is where we live). The realms and claims of the functions have to be recognized, honored, and reconciled; and failure to do so leads sooner or later to confusion, calamity, and waste—personal, social, agricultural, military, political, and theological. The triadic doctrine expresses itself persistently in the form of a story about a family with three (or more) sons and one daughter, who is not the eldest child. These stories abound in primitive Indo-European lore, having to do with overtly superhuman figures or else transposed into human terms regarded as legend or history (historicized myth).

The same basic lineaments appear in the most sophisticated modern incarnations. In Faulkner's *Sound and the Fury* and Salinger's *Catcher in the Rye*, for example, we see a calamitous family (rather shadowy parents with three sons and one daughter) whose fortunes undergo vicissitudes and tragedies until, in a transcendent conclusion, we arrive at a pagan-Christian holiday (Easter or Christmas) signaled by the sacred totem animal, the horse (or a carousel effigy), moving in a circle counterclockwise. A similar pattern is found even in jokes (in pure, parodic, or varied form) and in *The Godfather, Dallas, My Three Sons*, the Ponderosa saga, and Frans G. Bengtsson's popular Swedish novel *The Long Ships*. (The jury is still out on *The Golden Girls*, a new series about three older women who seem to represent vacuous bossiness, cowardice, and menopausal lust, plus Sophia, the eighty-year-old mother of one of the "girls," a caricature of wisdom. Students freely suggest other examples.)

In Eliot's work, it is clear that *The Waste Land* follows archaic Indo-European patterns, of which Eliot would have been aware from his study of Sanskrit and Pali. The redounding presence and orchestration of these patterns account, I think, for much of the impact and influence of the poem. Thanks to Dumézil, we can appreciate much else about Eliot's poetry that may otherwise seem peevish, chaotic, anomalous, idiosyncratic, or personal—or merely "universal" in various overstrained patterns of symbols and hang-ups put forward by Frazer, Weston, Freud, Jung, or Frye. I have not the space to go into Eliot's lifelong devotion to avatars or parodies of Hercules (from Sweeney to Arjuna and Harcourt-Reilly), but I encourage others to consider Eliot's heroes in the light of what Dumézil has uncovered about the favorite half-human repository of second-function nobility.

Once in a while, having dallied too long *chez* Dumézil, I find myself ordering the notorious garlic-sapphires-mud passage in "Burnt Norton" according to Indo-European patterns: garlic is sacred to Mars, *sapphire* may mean "precious to the planet Saturn," fertile mud is associated with Venus. At such moments I turn to the nicely color-coded third and ultimate conclusion of Flann O'Brien's *At Swim-Two-Birds*, on the subject of "the dim thoughts that flit in a fool's head":

> Others will be subject to colors and will attach undue merit to articles that are red or green or white merely because they bear that hue. . . . Well-known, alas, is the case of the poor German who was very fond of three and who made each aspect of his life a thing of triads. He went home one evening and drank three cups of tea with three lumps of sugar in each cup, cut his jugular with a razor three times and scrawled with a dying hand on a picture of his wife, good-bye, good-bye, good-bye. (208)

Teaching *The Waste Land* in the Context of the 1920s

Nancy D. Hargrove

Teaching *The Waste Land* in the context of the 1920s offers a fresh and interdisciplinary view of the poem. I teach a course entitled American Literature of the 1920s, in which we first steep ourselves in the historical, social, and cultural milieu of that fascinating and complex decade and then go on to study in depth six major literary works of the period. We explore the ways in which these works reflect their times, noting similarities—and on occasion differences—in themes, techniques, images, and other significant elements. I begin with *The Waste Land*, which is the cornerstone of and key to the remainder of the course; it is followed by O'Neill, *The Hairy Ape* (1922) and *Desire under the Elms* (1924); Fitzgerald, *The Great Gatsby* (1925); Hemingway, *The Sun Also Rises* (1926); and Faulkner, *The Sound and the Fury* (1929). I have taught this course on the advanced undergraduate level, but with some alterations it would be suitable for a graduate seminar.

The three opening lectures present a wide-ranging overview of background material, using both traditional and revisionist interpretations. After noting that the decade is an extremely complex period full of changes and contradictions, I discuss World War I and its influence on the 1920s, giving handouts of Cummings's "my sweet old etcetera" and sections 4 and 5 of Pound's *Hugh Selwyn Mauberley* to illustrate the feeling of disillusionment occasioned by the war. Then I go on to the climate of the United States, pointing out that the populace wanted to forget about war, problems, and deprivation and enjoy a "normal" life of fun, riches, and relaxation. This leads naturally into a discussion of politics, economics (the boom economy and the age of business and industry), and prohibition. I spend some time on the life-style of the period, including the question of the "new morality," the additional freedoms for women, and the slight decline in religion. An aspect of the time that fascinates students is the great interest in entertainment: sports, radio and movies, sensational trials, the feats of Lindbergh, and fads and follies such as the craze for crossword puzzles and the advent of beauty contests. I touch briefly on one-hundred-percent Americanism and the "popularity" of prejudice and conclude with a discussion of music, art, and literature, emphasizing the dedication to experimentation and innovation in all three areas as well as the attitude of artists and intellectuals, who tended to disdain the values of average Americans (whom they labeled philistines or the booboisie) and who often became expatriates. Concerning the literature, I point out general characteristics and stress the amazing number of great literary works produced and the strong showing of all the genres.

For this part of the course, students are assigned to read Frederick Lewis Allen's *Only Yesterday* and portions of George E. Mowry's study *The Twen-*

ties: Fords, Flappers and Fanatics. In class I pass around a collection of postcards and photocopied pictures of 1920s material as well as the 1920s volume (which contains wonderful pictures) from the Time-Life series *This Fabulous Century.* Students are encouraged to offer comments and information from these sources or from their own fields of expertise; economics majors, for instance, often contribute valuable insights into the stock market crash or land speculation. Finally, to increase our knowledge of the period, I schedule various guest speakers throughout the semester to talk on art (a slide lecture with emphasis on surrealism), music (a lecture with tapes on jazz as well as classical and popular music), sports, film, women and fashions, economics, and the Harlem Renaissance.

Armed with this extensive background, we spend six class periods on Eliot's poem, exploring the ways in which it has grown out of its time and reflects contemporary issues, concerns, and climate. At the same time we discover themes, techniques, and images that we will encounter again and again in the succeeding works to be studied. As one student remarked, exuberantly if awkwardly mixing metaphors in an anonymous course evaluation at the semester's end, "Thorough discussion of *The Waste Land* triggered themes which then streamed throughout the remainder of the course."

Given the extraordinary richness and complexity of the poem, I begin with a discussion of how it reflects the decade's characteristic dedication to innovation both in subject matter and in style, perhaps best summed up in the resounding cry that echoed through the literary world of the 1920s, "Make it new!" Prime examples of innovation in subject matter are the use of the metropolis and, more especially, the frank treatment of sex. Numerous scenes of illicit sex include the encounter of the typist and the "young man carbuncular" and that of the vulgar Sweeney and the prostitute Mrs. Porter, the latter ironically presented with a bawdy song sung by World War I soldiers superimposed on a minor Renaissance poet's lines about the Greek myth of Actaeon and Diana. References to abortion and infidelity are found in the pub conversation of Lil's friend in section 2. This experimentation in subject matter, particularly in sexual concerns, is seen again in the torrid love scenes of *Desire under the Elms*, in Brett Ashley's casual and not so casual liaisons in *The Sun Also Rises*, and in Caddy's promiscuity and Quentin's incestuous inclinations in *The Sound and the Fury.*

Concerning experimentation in style, there are, of course, many elements to discuss. Having heard the guest lecture on surrealism in 1920s art, many students immediately point out the technique of collage, the combining of seemingly unrelated fragments into a unified work of art. The disjunctive form, the absence of transition, the coming abruptly into the middle of a conversation can all be illustrated in the first eighteen lines of the poem, while perhaps the best example of the combination of apparently disconnected fragments can be found in the closing passage. Also as a result of the art lecture, students may recognize section 5's nightmare technique (an influence of Freud, another important aspect of the 1920s) and the mixture of cultures and religions evidenced in the closing lines of section 3. Students majoring in communication or knowledgeable about films may comment on Eliot's use of cinematic techniques, especially that of scenes fading into each other (as the desert scene fades into the setting of the German resort at line 19) or, as Warren French points out, the technique "that intrigued many writers in the twenties . . . of following a general view of a landscape (usually—in those years—blighted) with a close-up view of one small group of people living in this land." To illustrate, French cites the two close-up shots of the upper-class couple and the woman in the pub in section 2, which are "representative of the society portrayed in the first section" (7). While looking at section 2, students invariably notice Eliot's experimentation with two vastly different styles, one elaborate and formal, the other colloquial and uneducated, and at some point in the discussion they mention the more obvious experiments with meter and rhyme, the obscure allusions to a wide range of works, and the use of seven languages. In studying the subsequent works, we see comparable technical experiments, for example, in Faulkner's use of time and narrative point of view, in O'Neill's use of dialects, and in Hemingway's use of sparse journalistic prose.

Next we look at how the themes of *The Waste Land* reflect the climate of the 1920s. Perhaps better than any other work of the decade, it captures the mood of disillusionment and despair that haunted not only the artists and writers but also the populace, stemming largely from the negative experience of the war. Indeed, the poem's major theme might be stated as the horror of a civilization whose rejection of human and divine love has left it physically, emotionally, morally, and spiritually sterile. Examples are legion in the poem's numerous bleak passages, from the famous opening section to the description of the melancholy wintry Thames River to the scene of swarms of "lost souls" going to dull jobs in the offices of the City. The reference in the desert passage of section 1 to "broken images" may suggest, among other things, the illusions, beliefs, and values shattered by World War I, while the meaninglessness of life is strikingly conveyed when the wealthy woman of section 2 cries out, "What shall we do to-morrow? / What shall we ever do?" Her frantic, desperate questions are echoed in many works of the postwar years; in *The Great Gatsby*, for example, Daisy asks, "What'll we do with ourselves this afternoon? and the day after that, and the next thirty years?" (118). The theme of disillusionment runs in a variety of forms through all the succeeding works studied: in the many losses in *The Sound and the Fury*; in disillusioned characters like Nick Carraway, Jake Barnes, and Yank; and in experiences without order or meaning like the fiesta in *The Sun Also Rises* or the colossal parties in *The Great Gatsby*.

Another important theme typical of the 1920s is the inability to love, to

establish significant or fulfilled human relationships. *The Waste Land* por-
trays a series of sterile or perverted human relationships both in and outside
marriage, the most memorable of which is the relationship of the young man
carbuncular and the typist who, as Northrop Frye puts it, "lets her body be
used like a public urinal" (52). After describing her in mechanical terminology
(another feature shared with surrealism), Eliot ironically describes their
copulation in the form of a Shakespearean sonnet (lines 235–48); although
students rarely notice the sonnet on their own, they are quick to realize its
significance. The absence of meaningful love is echoed not only in the sterile
relationships of Jake and Brett, Jay and Daisy, and Jason and Lorraine but
also, for example, in the loveless family life of the Compsons.

Other themes in *The Waste Land* representative of the 1920s are the
criticism of materialism and commercialism (best seen in the description of
the polluted Thames in the industrial quarter), the isolation of modern human
beings (best seen in the passage of the second command of the thunder),
and finally the more positive, but still very cautious, hope for salvation
implied at the poem's end. Although the works studied in this course have
predominantly pessimistic themes, students are intrigued to discover that,
like *The Waste Land*, most of them contain positive elements, however
overshadowed by the stronger negative tones; fruitful discussions of why
this should be so and what it may mean often develop.

We now look for images and symbols characteristic of the decade. The
most obvious, of course, is the waste-land image itself. Reflecting the stripped
battlefields of the war, as French suggests, as well as the blighted areas of
the modern urban and industrial scene (3), it is the predominant image in
1920s literature, expressing the feeling of sterility and waste that was prev-
alent at the time; students immediately recognize it later in the ash heaps
of *The Great Gatsby* and the rocky farmland of *Desire under the Elms*. The
city is another major image, suggesting sterility, chaos, and anonymity;
London in *The Waste Land* plays the same symbolic role as do New York
City in *The Hairy Ape* and *The Great Gatsby* and Paris in *The Sun Also
Rises*. While World War I, an image of the violence and senselessness of
the universe, appears in a somewhat understated manner in the poem through
references to Mylae, to the bawdy song sung by soldiers, and to Albert's
being demobbed, it is interesting for students to note its more extensive
use both in *The Great Gatsby* and in *The Sun Also Rises*; in the latter it is
the cause of Jake's impotence. Finally, the nightmare, an image of chaos
and terror found in section 5's vision of the destruction of modern civilization
by its "barbarian" values, will also be seen in various comparisons with human
experience in *The Sun Also Rises*.

A final element of 1920s literature illustrated in the poem is the focus on
the period itself. As Edward C. Wagenknecht notes, the 1920s was "a here-

and-now-minded" period (425); while to its writers the past seemed empty and the future hopeless, the present was disturbing and exciting. The references to taxis and closed cars, to women working at offices in the City and drinking in pubs, to the Metropole, with its unsavory reputation as a licentious pleasure spot for wealthy businessmen, illustrate this emphasis on the contemporary as do the allusions to Hermann Hesse's *Blick ins Chaos* and Jessie L. Weston's *From Ritual to Romance*, published in 1920, and to the crowds of City employees crossing London Bridge, a scene recorded in a 1920 photograph contained in the Eliot collection of Harvard's Houghton Library (for a reproduction, see sec. following p. 50 in Hargrove, *Landscape as Symbol*). Subsequent works reflect the period in their time settings (*The Great Gatsby* takes place in 1922, *The Sun Also Rises* in 1925, and *The Sound and the Fury* largely in 1928) as well as in such concrete details as descriptions of women's clothing and references to prohibition, the cotton market, and Babe Ruth.

For this portion of the course, students are encouraged to read the traditional critical works on Eliot as well as sections of French's book, *The Twenties: Fiction, Poetry, Drama*, which focuses on Eliot's poem. I also hand out study questions on *The Waste Land*, and I usually show Fritz Lang's 1926 silent movie *Metropolis* to give students a sense of the 1920s view of the city as dehumanizing machine. At the end of the course I host a party at my house to which the students come dressed as figures from the period or from the literature. There are usually numerous gangsters and flappers as well as various versions of Benjy Compson, complete with slipper, cushion, and bellowing voice. But my favorite is a Belgian student who came as Madame Sosostris and carried a crystal ball imprinted with the words "Fear Death by Water," in reality a round light fixture from her bathroom with letters glued on it.

The course has been popular with students for several reasons. It presents two very difficult, and often dreaded, works (*The Waste Land* and *The Sound and the Fury*) in an unusual and interesting way. Its interdisciplinary approach aids in attracting students from varied fields (I have had students majoring in fields as disparate as engineering, music, turf management, and accounting) and from minorities as well. The course is also appealing because it includes slides, pictures, tapes, and films (in addition to *Metropolis*, I show *The Great Gatsby*) and because it offers field trips to such places as Faulkner's home in Oxford, Mississippi, and, on one occasion, to Memphis to see *One Mo' Time*, a 1920s musical. From my own point of view, the study of *The Waste Land* as a period piece has been especially rewarding, providing me with a number of insights that are useful in more traditional literature courses.

TEACHING *FOUR QUARTETS*

On Teaching "Burnt Norton"

M. L. Rosenthal

Eliot's verse is embedded in so much commentary that we must remind ourselves to read it "e'en as folk o'the world." We don't need to kneel and pray first, or take Greek lessons, or pass examinations on John of the Cross or *The Golden Bough* or Helen Gardner's works or even *The Book of Common Prayer*. Of course, the more we know the better—no question—but teachers will be well advised to get right at a poem as best they can. This means a quick stocktaking of its physical structure to begin with and, especially, reading it aloud and asking a class to do so too—right around the room, a line or more each. Whatever the level, whether freshmen class or doctoral seminar, this elementary procedure is indispensable. The poem has to be heard and experienced in its own right.

Now, it's a lucky *and* well-trained reader who is "poetic" in the sense that a composer or instrumentalist is "musical." Such a reader can go over a poem silently, catching its rhythms and tonal shifts and varied intensities. But even someone with "absolute pitch" of this sort will discover unnoticed values or lapses by reading aloud and hearing others read aloud. For what is going on is a process conveyed by sound. All the senses, as well as imagination and states of feeling and awareness, are involved, but the foremost channel is the ear. That is to say, a poem is a work of art whose medium is its own language; also, it is a human expression whose bearing is revealed only by that same language. And language has to be *heard*, physically and in the mind's ear, just as does music. From the start it is important to accustom the student to this all too unfamiliar sense of a poem, instead of substituting prose abstractions or summaries of critics' interpretations and opinions.

I mentioned a quick stocktaking of a poem's physical structure. By this I mean something very simple indeed. Thus, we can easily elicit certain observations from a class. First, "Burnt Norton" is made up of five numbered parts of unequal length and varied form. Next, part 1 is a continuous verse unit divided into three sections by line breaks. (That is, its second and third sections each begin in mid-line, with the second part of the line dropped to mark a new turn of thought.) And the other parts—except for the brief ten-line part 4—each consist of separate verse units of uneven length and pattern.

This kind of elementary observation takes note of the visually obvious aspects of a poem's overall form. Even the least sophisticated, most fearful members of a class can be encouraged to speak up about them and thus begin to engage directly with the poem. As for the most sophisticated and fearless, they will be encouraged to let the poem steer them toward insight into its structure—that is, toward genuine receptivity. The point is that students are being headed, lightly and even playfully (I've sometimes called the game of noting the obvious "Idiot's Delight"), into thinking about organic form and, a bit further down the road, considering the artistic function of the characteristics noted.

I am not suggesting that the teacher oversimplify what is happening in the text: hardly the same thing as beginning simply. The teacher will certainly want to learn as much as possible about it, from Helen Gardner and others but especially from immersion in the poem's idiosyncratic process. The poem tries to use thought to "tease us out of thought," as Keats put it in pondering similar issues. Part 1 hovers over the yearning to find, within time, indications of immortal transcendence. It finds, amid exquisite gestures of humility and self-doubt, hints toward that end in the workings of memory, particularly the memory of a frustrated expectation. It ends in a burst of visionary imagery at once rapturous and psychologically alert to self-deception. Part 2 begins with a brilliant evocation of the interaction of earthbound reality with cosmic transcendence (repeating motifs of part 1 in a new, fatalistic key). It then advances into a lengthy discursive treatment of the poem's philosophical perspective before ending with some highly evocative images of moments of a kind of grace. Part 3 is a confrontation of dark despair and inability to summon up the remembered glow of such moments. Part 4 picks up from this desolate state and just barely turns toward its opposite in a succession of concise images and prayerful questions. It compresses the whole range of the poem's paradoxes into one singularly intense lyrical center. In the final part, the poet relates his artistic efforts and frustrations to the other motifs of "Burnt Norton" and ends the poem with an incantatory reprise of those motifs. At each stage, clearly, the teacher needs to think into the ways in which the poem's form and tonalities embody its changing emphases, and to suggest that the students explore the process in their own ways by raising questions and offering such insights as occur to them.

This larger enterprise is the fuller development of what began as the plain pleasure, almost therapeutic, of "Idiot's Delight." The real life of the poem (any poem) resides in its moment-by-moment unfolding, something we have no room here to follow through in detail. From here forward, therefore, I shall simply focus on two or three key passages that illustrate the process that makes the poem what it is. After all, in any case, reading the poem itself, and noticing what is going on in it, remain the main enterprise and "method." Thus, then, the first section of part 1:

> Time present and time past
> Are both perhaps present in time future,
> And time future contained in time past.
> If all time is eternally present
> All time is unredeemable.
> What might have been is an abstraction
> Remaining a perpetual possibility
> Only in a world of speculation.
> What might have been and what has been
> Point to one end, which is always present.
> Footfalls echo in the memory
> Down the passage which we did not take
> Towards the door we never opened
> Into the rose-garden. My words echo
> Thus, in your mind.

The first ten lines present a considerable challenge if read in a straight-forward tone. Ordinarily, the "normal" reading of a lyric poem will suggest its proper stresses and emotional coloration at once. Here, though, we are confronted by what appears rather drily logical prosaic language. One must take this fact into account at first reading and allow a class, and oneself, to speak the lines pedantically and, no doubt, haltingly, as an odd bit of rational discourse.

At the same time, certain counter-elements make themselves felt. There is an unusual amount of parallelism and other repetition, for instance—more than one would expect in flatly straightforward prose. (The words *time* and *present* are repeated a number of times, by themselves and combined with other repeated words. The sixth and ninth lines begin with the same clause:

"What might have been.") The parallelism, we should note, is ingeniously varied, with the repeated elements emerging at unexpected intervals. Then, too, one notices a certain awed gravity, implicit in the musing about time but deepened by words with religious connotations: *eternally, unredeemable, perpetual*. A second reading, after these observations, will bring us to approach the cadences and tones of prayer or incantation. Once we do so, and thereby become sensitized to recurrence of stresses within a worshipful context, another dimension of sound-patterning seems to come into the foreground: the ingenious four-to-five-stress control of lines that at first appeared to be irregular in length:

> Time present and time past
>
> Are both perhaps present in time future,
>
> And time future contained in time past.
>
> If all time is eternally present
>
> All time is unredeemable.

—Etc. I shall not insist that my stress placement is the only proper one in each instance; but the general pattern, with whatever exceptions, should be clear enough. Reading the first ten lines through, and thinking about their qualities as a passage to be read, profoundly change our initial impression of how they sound and what they express. The result is striking—like that of placing Japanese paper flowers in water and seeing them unfold vividly.

What we arrive at, finally,* is a reading of these opening lines as a kind of prayer: an act of obeisance to divine transcendence of time, already implicit within time. If we read with the intonation of the Lord's Prayer, ending each grammatical unit with a ritual or devout falling-off of emphasis, we shall have realized into the dominant tone of the poem that colors all the nostalgia, yearning, and visionary dimensions into which it will move.

It is interesting to note (to encourage the class to note) that the passage just discussed is not the whole of the first section of part 1. It is nevertheless the opening tonal movement of the poem, with its abstractions that take on the music of litany and the emotions of mystical readiness. But the question then arises: What is the connection between that passage and the next five lines, which complete the section?—

---

* i.e., "finally": i.e., "tentatively" or, as the poem puts it, "perhaps"; we should encourage students (and ourselves) to specify and even emphasize what we observe—BUT without breaking that butterfly.

> Footfalls echo in the memory
> Down the passage which we did not take
> Towards the door we never opened
> Into the rose-garden. My words echo
> Thus, in your mind.

The teacher should, if necessary, raise this question. It is preferable, though, that students raise it themselves: that is, that they take note of the significant shift in the two sentences just quoted. As a matter of teaching method, one needs to show students of literature, especially of poetry, how to watch for shifts of *affect* (the state—simple or complex—of feeling and awareness in a given passage, and also the degree of intensity in the language). In this instance, the poem moves from an initial affect of prayerfully devotional meditation to one of intimate memory of a longed-for, keenly imagined experience that never took place—a concrete, confessional instance of how "what might have been" remains "always present," both as a possibility fixed in past time and as a reality of the mind. The sudden introduction of this bittersweet non-memory that yet remains a memory is followed at once by a companionable jolt to the reader who, surely, has comparable "memories" of his or her own. The first section of part 1, then, ends on a note of almost intrusive insinuation couched as shared realization.

(A slight digression: We all can recall the fierce expectation in childhood of something promised but never actually attained. Little T. S. E., the poem seems to say, expected to be taken into the rose-garden, but it never happened. And then the poem reminds us that we too have been through the same sort of thing. Such disappointment is not limited to children, either. Pausing, therefore, over the way "my words" in the poem might "echo" in student-readers' minds could help them see something fundamental. Insofar as poetry is both art and human expression, it projects and shares felt awareness through the plastic medium of language. Here Eliot's poem superbly invites us to enter and contribute to its process by induced empathy.)

Getting the sound of the poem as right as one can, then, is the essential first step. It involves taking into account both natural speech as we ordinarily know it and the resources of language, tradition, and technique that a skilled poet can draw on. Isolating the basic affective units (which, I have just noted, evoke "the state—simple or complex—of feeling and awareness in a given passage" and also a particular "degree of intensity") follows hard on getting the sound right. The succession of these affective units constitutes the dynamics of the poem: its movements from one state of feeling and awareness at a certain pitch of intensity to the next, and also the units' interaction with one another throughout the poem, through echoes and contrasts and sudden torques and combined tonalities.

If the student can learn to recognize the affective shifts and to think about the whole poem as a dynamic relation among them, as well as to see how the poem's "technique" (rhyme, meter, etc.) feeds into that relation, the teaching job will in the main have been done. Take for instance the segue from the ending of the first section of part 1 to the very brief second one and then to the opening lines of the third:

> Footfalls echo in the memory
> Down the passage which we did not take
> Towards the door we never opened
> Into the rose-garden. My words echo
> Thus, in your mind.
>   But to what purpose
> Disturbing the dust on a bowl of rose-leaves
> I do not know.
>   Other echoes
> Inhabit the garden. Shall we follow?
> Quick, said the bird, find them, find them,
> Round the corner. Through the first gate,
> Into our first world, shall we follow
> The deception of the thrush? Into our first world.

The bittersweet evocation already discussed moves, as I have suggested, into a gently insistent pressure on the reader to add his or her own instances of the same sort—or, more literally, it assumes that is already happening. Then the one-sentence self-questioning that follows introduces, for the first time in the poem, a private note of uncertainty as to the value of the kind of memory and pondering that has up to now been so gravely summoned up. The image of "dust on a bowl of rose-leaves" suggests that we are dealing with long-repressed memories, neglected and well-nigh lost—as though they had not just been linked with an appreciation of transcendence within time. Thus the passage presents a faltering of vision and a wry self-doubting. Yet the next verse-paragraph assumes a plethora of seductive "echoes"—everyone's special memories, whether real or imagined—promising a miraculous recovery. "The bird" is a mystical bearer of promise that is nevertheless also associated with "deception" (just as the "bowl of rose-leaves" image brought a negative turn into the poem a moment earlier). It carries the first part of "Burnt Norton" into a visionary realm filled with images that, together, evoke a strangely mixed state, at once ecstatic and disillusioned, of imagined transcendence. The tone is both exalted and elegiac. This affect (which I cannot explore further here because of space) is a richly complex center of the poem.

I would wish to pause for a long time over the unfolding of part 1 if I
were teaching "Burnt Norton." The object would be to realize into the poem's
movement, and the way such effects as the echoing *o*'s—starting with the
word *echo* itself but picked up also in *opened* and *rose* and *know* and
follow—assist the associative presentation and create a matrix of sound that
reverberates with the resonances of those words and their contexts.

But let me, instead, dwell on a shorter passage, the remarkable opening
of part 2:

> Garlic and sapphires in the mud
> Clot the bedded axle-tree.
> The trilling wire in the blood
> Sings below inveterate scars
> Appeasing long forgotten wars.
> The dance along the artery
> The circulation of the lymph
> Are figured in the drift of stars
> Ascend to summer in the tree
> We move above the moving tree
> In light upon the figured leaf
> And hear upon the sodden floor
> Below, the boarhound and the boar
> Pursue their pattern as before
> But reconciled among the stars.

I shall make only a quick observation here, suggesting that what I have
to say merely points to characteristics of the passage that students might be
asked to discern. ("What do you notice about the syntax of this passage, and
its relation to the affect?") As the passage moves, conventional syntax dis-
solves into a syntax blurred by reverie. A self-induced mystical entrance-
ment, bolstered by hypnotic sound echoings, dominates the process. The
passage begins with two complete sentences, but thereafter the grammatical
units, like the images, collapse into one another, with no period until the
very end and only one bit of internal punctuation (absolutely necessary to
prevent syntactic disaster, but masterful in doing so with minimal fuss). The
form is an intricate pattern of repetitions, irregularly recurring but frequent
rhymes, and parallel phrasings, all contained within the densely concrete
four-stress lines. It provides a rich lingering within the powerful but unstable
vision of imagined ascent.

We may read many things into the passage, such as the assumption of an
infinitely varied yet consistent rhythmic design throughout the universe,
mirrored in the very form of the poem. We may detect something like a

distanced personal complaint: a trapped sense of being mired in our muddy, clotted earth and of being compounded, at best, of filth and exaltation. The passage seems to speak of "scars" from repressed internal struggles as well as from humanity's "forgotten wars" of historical and spiritual development.

"Ergo, *mes élèves*, what is the connection between the observations in the two preceding paragraphs? And in what sense is this passage an epitome of the whole poem?" Thus, *mes collègues*, might we address our *collégiens* (*-nes*) after such explorations as I have been suggesting. For it is important that they start over again on their own, and that they reexperience the particular resonances and dynamic relation of the poem according to their own lights. That process opens itself up unpredictably, through repeated reading and listening and submission to the instinct for empathy that leads to probing engagement. Its accuracy of sensitization can be enhanced by rejecting the notion of either definitive "interpretation" or a "subtext" more indicative than the actual lines and affective units of the poem. (Read the lines, not between the lines, where there is only blank space.) As a basic inductive exercise in strengthening responsiveness to the way the poem moves implicitly, one can always recommend (and illustrate) comparison with other poems of comparable external shape. Set "Burnt Norton" alongside any of the other *Quartets* or *The Waste Land* or *Ash-Wednesday* and compare, for instance, the two poems' initial tonal sets and the kinds of shifts of focus, feeling, and intensity that take place in successive units. It's best if the teacher can look at the poem as a poet might, feeling into its associative turns and breaks of continuity and following the sensual base of the phrasing and guiding rhythms. As Eliot keeps complaining throughout *Four Quartets*, we're dealing with things that won't hold still.

Four Quartets as Capstone Text in a Literature and Mysticism Course

John Gatta

For students trained to read in sequential units, few texts in the undergraduate canon are so initially intimidating as *Four Quartets*. True, the narrative dislocations of *The Waste Land* give similar cause for perplexity. But whereas the instructor of a period survey can at least begin to traverse *The Waste Land* by seizing on Eliot's familiar master image of cultural desolation, no such ground of recognition can be presumed for the later work. And while teachers can draw on a wealth of published commentary to explicate the literary sources of *Four Quartets*, undergraduate humankind cannot bear very much of this reality, either.

At the same time, few other poems in the canon can prove so magically evocative as the *Quartets*. Even some students dubious about the appeal of poetry in general can respond to its musicality once they feel permitted to do so. I have to remind myself that the obligation I sometimes feel to explain the enigma of Eliot's poem to my students is, in the main, a misbegotten creature of my own professional anxieties. The better task, I think, is simply to draw students toward an engagement with the mysteries the poem entertains.

A couple of central assumptions govern my approach to teaching this work. First, while I understand Eliot to be a modern master of Christian spirituality, I try to take seriously the critical commonplace that *Four Quartets* is more a poetry of reflection and search than of doctrinal apologetics, less an exercise of didacticism than an art of meditation. It follows that our classroom procedure for discussing the work should bear no small resemblance to a corporate process of meditation. Second, I share with students my conviction that *Four Quartets* is genuinely iconic. As numinously iconic literature, it invites us to look through it, not at it, toward the deeper reality it reflects.

For me a natural setting for applying such principles is the undergraduate course I have developed, Literature and Mysticism, in which a two-week study of *Four Quartets* provides the culminating experience to the twelve weeks we have spent exploring other writers and topics. An abbreviated account of this larger enterprise may be helpful, though some details would require adaptation to suit other contexts in which the *Quartets* is taught.

Beginning with the foundations of Western spirituality in biblical writings like John's Gospel, the course proceeds through an encounter with works such as the fourteenth-century *Cloud of Unknowing*, Julian of Norwich's *Revelations of Divine Love*, Dante's *Paradiso*, and brief selections from John of the Cross. By the time students reach *Four Quartets* at the end, they are intrigued to find all these writings enfolded together and can grasp what the works mean at a level of understanding beyond that yielded by a mere cataloging of allusions. Our usual schedule of topics looks like the following outline with several of the less overtly literary figures represented only in the form of brief anthology readings:

I. What is mysticism? Preliminary theories, definitions, and historical grounds of Western mysticism

II. Testimonies, epiphanies, and mountaintop episodes in Scripture
    A. Old Testament foundations
        1. Encounters of Moses and Elijah
        2. Visions of Jacob, Isaiah, and Ezekiel
        3. The Song of Songs
    B. New Testament foundations
        1. The Transfiguration and Pauline mysticism
        2. The Gospel according to John

III. Early Christian and medieval spirituality
    A. Seminal figures
        1. Augustine—first-person spiritual narrative
        2. Pseudo-Dionysus—negative ascent and the divine darkness
        3. Bernard of Clairvaux—the mystical marriage
        4. Bonaventura—the divine traces
        5. Saint Francis of Assisi—holy poverty and praises of the creatures
    B. Fourteenth-century English mystical tradition
        1. *The Cloud of Unknowing*
        2. Julian of Norwich, *Revelations of Divine Love*
    C. Dante's *Paradiso*

IV. Sixteenth-century Spanish masters; seventeenth- and eighteenth-century abandonment of the will
    A. John of the Cross
    B. Jean-Pierre de Caussade

V. Practical mysticism in nineteenth-century America
    A. Henry Thoreau, *Walden*
    B. Walt Whitman, *Leaves of Grass*

VI. Jewish mystical traditions [brief overview with one or two Hasidic tales]

VII. Three modern contemplatives
    A. Simone Weil
    B. Pierre Teilhard de Chardin
    C. Thomas Merton

VIII. Contemporary renewals of the tradition in fiction, poetry, and personal narrative
    A. J. R. R. Tolkien, "Leaf by Niggle"
    B. Annie Dillard, *Pilgrim at Tinker Creek*
    C. T. S. Eliot, *Four Quartets*

My first aim in the course is simply to show students that there is a long-standing tradition of Western spirituality, impressive in its richness and variety. The fine anthology edited by Walter Capps and Wendy Wright, *Silent Fire: An Invitation to Western Mysticism*, helps serve this end. Second, I try to explore with students ways in which the mystic's quest for God is rendered incarnate in literature, as a vehicle of spiritual search.

Beyond these major aims there are a few themes I underscore throughout our sessions. One is that the mystical way is integrative in several senses, as I argue in "Spheric and Silent Music," so that the *via negativa* and *via affirmativa* are more complementary than may first appear. Or, as Eliot suggests through Heraclitus, the way up and the way down converge in the dynamic stillness of God. The doctrine of the Incarnation is therefore a central focus of Christian mysticism—not merely on its more evidently "positive" face in the sanction of physical images but also in its "negative" aspect of Christ's affliction and self-emptying.

As a further corollary of my stress on the mystic's yearning for wholeness and unity, I argue that authentic Western mysticism is more characteristically described as a corporate vision, rooted in history and the communion of saints, than as a Plotinian "flight of the alone to the Alone." Here our later observations in class about Eliot's sense of place and about the memorable concreteness of his spirituality in the *Quartets* build on our earlier study of works like Dante's *Paradiso*. We also think about how the integrative project of mysticism involves cultivating the human faculties of intellect as well as those of the affections and will. In Western spirituality, at least, "intellectual mysticism" is by no means a contradiction in terms.

Finally, my course tries to reinforce the point that authentic mysticism is not to be confused with gnostic elitism. Most of the spiritual masters downplay the importance of privileged charismatic phenomena and ecstatic feeling; they affirm instead that the mystical way is a lifelong journey in faith, discipline, and love that is open in some version to all. Its fruit is less an otherworldly knowledge than a transfigured vision of the ordinary. And as Saint John of the Cross observes, the main "secret" pursued by contemplatives is that which is hidden from oneself, in the inmost center of one's being, rather than from others.

But when it comes to the particular case, some students always want to know whether Mr. Eliot, a man all too evidently sinful and self-absorbed, was a true mystic and saint. Probably not, I answer, in the sense of having reached the unitive summit of mystical experience during this mortal life. If "most of us," as Eliot admits in "The Dry Salvages," come no closer to hearing the silent music of contemplation than the snatches we catch now and then in an "unattended / Moment" of natural beatitude, the poet places himself squarely in the company of most of us.

Yet there is little doubt that by 1935 Eliot had committed himself to the path of spiritual discipline, that in *Four Quartets* he sought to envision artistically the full course and culmination of this way, and that even as a young man he had brooded over epiphanic moments in a manner that helped shape his entire imaginative career. In singling out those few elements of biography or of circumstance of composition most relevant to what goes on in class, I look for instruction from Helen Gardner (*Composition*), Lyndall Gordon, and Peter Ackroyd; and in reflecting on the textual interplay between Eliot's art and the broader tradition of contemplative spirituality, I find stimulus in the volumes by Grover Smith (*T. S. Eliot's Poetry*), Harry Blamires, Eloise Hay, and John Booty. But I play down any big bang theory of how the *Quartets* came to be, any suggestion that the work's meaning and motivation can be traced to a single episode of mystical euphoria. Though the epiphanic occasions mattered to Eliot, I see his mysticism associated largely with his conscious, bookish study of the contemplative tradition and his deliberate attempt to live out its existential demands that he knew ultimately cost "not less than everything" ("Little Gidding").

We spend much of our class time, as I have suggested, confronting Eliot's text through something of a corporate meditation. The collective aspect seems immediately justified by the poet's invocation of first-person plural pronouns in the first section of "Burnt Norton." But there is nothing extraordinary or cultish about our procedure, although the tone differs from that produced by the more competitive give-and-take of typical class discussion. We simply dwell together on a key word or image until it yields up some of its accumulated emotive, intellective, and spiritual wealth. Brief account has to be taken of what is happening in each section of each quartet, but I restrict line-by-line analysis in favor of a meditative inquiry that ends up seeming at once more minute and more comprehensive. Naturally, we attend to Eliot's echoes both within and outside the text; we also, to vary the metaphor, try to look through and beyond the poet's individual words and figures.

Once students begin to trace the interplay of congruences and polarities, they inevitably summon up some surprises—to them and to me. Yet the typical range of meditative topoi I propose is an unoriginal mélange of things elemental and ordinary. Thus we take up Eliot's images of light, darkness, and music, following the musical motif from its several songs as temporal sound through its less audible presence as spheric harmony to its ultimate stillness as beatific union. We look into gardens and paradises, flowers and other plants, ladders, dances, wheels, rivers, and the sea. We meditate on birds—thrush, kingfisher, petrel, and the dove of "Little Gidding." And as classic meditative technique advises, we ponder words: words like *word, way, still, end, union, communion, one,* and *pattern.*

If I have to isolate a single image or verbal sign that might focus the "pattern" of spirituality sustained through all four *Quartets*, I am lately inclined to name the biblical account of the Transfiguration. As rendered by the synoptic gospel writers (e.g., Matt. 17), Jesus becomes transfigured with light, appearing with Moses and Elijah amid a bright cloud, high on a mountaintop in Galilee. At this "point of intersection of the timeless / With time" ("Dry Salvages"), Christ stands revealed before his privileged disciples as what Paul calls elsewhere "the image [Greek *eikon*] of the invisible God" (Col. 1.15). Analogously, the artistic icon at once discloses divinity and negates its own essence behind a cloud of unknowing; it unites the affirmative way and negative way with a force I try to demonstrate early in the term by bringing to class a Russian icon of the Transfiguration. Yet for all the white radiance surrounding the Transfiguration theophany, its placement in the gospel narratives just before Jesus's descent to Jerusalem and Crucifixion identifies it as a glory in affliction comparable to the "showings" of divine love at the heart of Christ's Passion that were received centuries later by Julian of Norwich.

While the *Quartets* does not announce the paradigm of Transfiguration as overtly as it does the Christian doctrine of Incarnation, the Transfiguration nonetheless defines, I think, how a human subject might apprehend Incarnation, how objectified doctrine translates into personal spirituality. As such, its reflection is everywhere apparent in *Four Quartets*, rendering diaphanous the pattern of experience and understanding that begins with the illumination and children's laughter of the rose-garden episode and ends with the unific conjunction of fire and rose. Like the disparate poems constituting the *Quartets*, individual moments of experience reveal for Eliot a retrospective unity—an iconic glimpse of a transfigured world. In its spiral progression the work moves not so much to the knowledge of an antique order as toward a proleptic vision of things "renewed, transfigured, in another pattern" by which we might "arrive where we started / And know the place for the first time" ("Little Gidding").

Risks attend any such classroom commitment to examining the spirituality of *Four Quartets* seriously in its own, largely Christian terms. The teacher must beware of lapsing into authorial hagiography or doctrinal apologetics, particularly on a pluralistic campus. Still, a work like the *Quartets* affords plenty of common dialogical ground for believers to meet with skeptics and deconstructionists. It fosters experimental probings and discourages dogmatism; it highlights the *via negativa* experience of vacancy and the virtue of humility and omits mindless ecstasy and born-again optimism. And even at a decidedly secular institution like the University of Connecticut, which lacks a department of religion, today's undergraduates show a great hunger to investigate questions touching the spirituality of art and the art of spirituality. Instead of receiving the full exposure to Eliot's writings as personal and literary artifacts—an exposure they can find elsewhere in our departmental curriculum—students in this course view his artistry in subordination to the centuries-old contemplative tradition it sustains. Yet given the poet's own more familiar statements about literary tradition and the individual talent, I like to think Eliot would approve.

Eliot, Einstein, and the East

Marilyn R. Chandler

Four Quartets is arguably the most difficult poem in the Eliot canon to teach undergraduates, compounding as it does the poetic allusiveness and complexity of *The Waste Land* with metaphysical abstractions that demand acquaintance with a variety of religious traditions, considerable grounding in the history of ideas, and some notion of "higher consciousness." But difficult does not mean inaccessible.

One way to make the poem accessible is to use it as an instrument for understanding the deep congruities among various areas of modern thought. Assuming some prior introduction to modernism and its attempts to redescribe reality, one can build on that basis by demonstrating how *Four Quartets* not only embodies quintessentially "modern" characteristics but also recapitulates some of the most ancient recorded beliefs about the nature of reality and human experience. Moreover, in its attempt to arrive at a new descriptive paradigm, it parallels similar efforts at synthesis in other fields of inquiry, among them modern physics.

Finding a connection among Eliot's poetics, Einstein's physics, and the teachings of the ancient Eastern religions can awaken in students a much needed awareness of three facts: (1) that reality is larger than language, (2) that our descriptions shape and limit our perceptions, and (3) that the same questions underlie every discipline: how things exist, how things happen, and what part we play in changing or controlling them. Students who live in a culture where knowledge is increasingly fragmented, a culture that values poetry rather less than science, might well find it revitalizing to study one of the great poems of this century in the light of those deep unities.

The simplest way to present these congruencies is to point out that the poet, the philosophers, and the physicists are all seeking ways to formulate a comprehensive description of reality that would resolve disturbing contradictions. Underlying that quest is a common belief in certain axiomatic principles.

Ultimate simplicity   A pervasive uniformity underlies the complexity of natural phenomena. This conviction impelled Einstein's lifelong search for a "unified field theory"—a quest he describes in these words:

> . . . we are seeking for the simplest possible system of thought which will bind together the observed facts. By the "simplest" system we do not mean the one which the student will have the least trouble in assimilating, but the one which contains the fewest possible mutually independent postulates or axioms; since the content of these logical, mutually independent axioms represents that remainder which is not comprehended. (113)

Fritjof Capra describes Eastern thought in similar terms:

> The most important characteristic of the Eastern world view . . . is the awareness of the unity and mutual interrelation of all things and events, the experience of all phenomena in the world as manifestations of a basic oneness. All things are seen as interdependent and inseparable parts of this cosmic whole; as different manifestations of the same ultimate reality. (130)

This notion is central to *Four Quartets*; in its kaleidoscopic turnings, the poem both enacts and describes diversity within unity, leading finally to the ideal expressed at the end of "Little Gidding": "A condition of complete simplicity / (Costing not less than everything)."

Paradox or the convergence of opposites   The polarities we describe as opposites are interdependent, not mutually exclusive. Capra sums up the application of this notion in modern physics in this way:

> . . . the framework of opposite concepts, derived from our everyday experience, is too narrow for the world of subatomic particles. Relativity theory is crucial for the description of this world, and in the "relativistic" framework the classical concepts are transcended by going to a higher dimension, the four-dimensional space-time. Space and time themselves are two concepts which had seemed entirely different, but have been unified in relativistic physics. (149–50)

Likewise the distinctions between wave and particle and between matter and energy may be understood as continua rather than simply as mutually exclusive states. Chuang Tzu similarly describes the Tao as beyond conventional notions of opposition: "The 'this' is also 'that.' The 'that' is also 'this.' . . . That the 'that' and the 'this' cease to be opposites is the very essence of Tao" (Fung Yu-Lan 112). Compare this with the pervasive paradoxical formulations in *Four Quartets*—"And where you are is where you are not" ("East Coker"); "What we call the beginning is often the end"; "history is a pattern of timeless moments" ("Little Gidding")—leading insistently to the insight that our notions of opposition derive from our limited frame of reference but that our vision can be enlarged to a point where opposites can be comprehended as parts of a whole—interdependent and simultaneous phenomena.

The limitations of language   Language is based on experience ordered to a three-dimensional frame of reference. A great part of human experience and natural phenomena lies outside what can readily be described in available language. Acknowledging this difficulty, Einstein writes, "It is existence and reality that one wishes to comprehend. But one shrinks from the use of such words, for one soon gets into difficulties when one has to explain what is really meant by 'reality' and by 'comprehend' . . ." (112–13). Werner Heisenberg states the problem even more broadly: "The problems of language here are really serious. We wish to speak in some way about the structure of atoms. . . . But we cannot speak about atoms in ordinary language" (Capra 45). Suzuki, writing about Eastern thought, describes the issue similarly: "We have to use language to communicate our inner experience which in its very nature transcends linguistics" (Capra 45). The poetic language and structure of the *Tao Te Ching* are remarkably similar to those of *Four Quartets* (see Chung-yuan for a translation and commentary). There is, of course, a reason for this: the multivalence and cryptic quality of "poetic" language resembles the Zen koan—a form of statement devised to force one beyond conventional logic and syntax. In many respects poetic language approximates mathematical formulation, which at its higher levels becomes increasingly untranslatable into ordinary language. *Four Quartets* addresses the problem of language both directly and indirectly. In "Burnt Norton" 5, "East Coker" 2, "The Dry Salvages" 5, and "Little Gidding" 5, the limitations of language are explicitly considered. Moreover, the shifting forms of statement in the poems represent an attempt to get beyond ordinary discourse to express a vision of reality that cannot be contained or conveyed except by analogy, metaphor, paradox, and simultaneous appeal to the rational and nonrational faculties. Through these means we finally grasp the truth that understanding involves the whole being, a truth expressed in the maxim "The Tao that can be spoken is not the Tao."

The close relation of the physical to the metaphysical   The way to the spiritual is through the material. Einstein claims that "a conviction, akin to religious feeling, of the rationality or intelligibility of the world lies behind all scientific work of a higher order. This firm belief, a belief bound up with deep feeling, in a superior mind that reveals itself in the world of experience, represents my conception of God" (11). Eastern mysticism, Capra points out, is also empirical; the objects of the mystic's observation include both the physical world and consciousness itself. "Thus," he concludes, "the mystic and the physicist arrive at the same conclusion. . . . The harmony between their views confirms the ancient Indian wisdom that Brahman, the ultimate reality without, is identical to Atman, the reality within" (305). This conviction finds an exact parallel in the incarnational emphasis in *Four Quartets*: the way to those things that are beyond the material world is through the material world. Our cosmic insights begin with "[g]arlic and sapphires in the mud." And "only in time can the moment in the rose-garden . . . [b]e remembered"—the way to the invisible is through the visible.

These are only a few of the common denominators that allow Eliot's poetics to be understood as an analogue to other efforts to describe reality. Indeed, this way of presenting the poems can easily be extended to include analogies with shifting perspectives in theology, psychology, art, and music as well. The value of such an approach is apparent the moment one student awakens to the deeply hopeful vision of pattern, unity, and purpose that *Four Quartets* conveys.

TEACHING THE PLAYS

Reluctant Saints and Modern Shamans: Teaching Eliot's Christian Comedies

Carol H. Smith

Because T. S. Eliot's plays are often seen as puzzling and cryptic anomalies in the career of an acclaimed poet and critic, they raise problems for the teacher of modern poetry. They are commonly either ignored or treated as an appendix to Eliot's main poetic achievements. This perception of his plays as secondary plagued Eliot himself during his lifetime, despite their popularity and his many assertions regarding the importance of drama both for his time—a formless age—and for his own poetic development. When we recognize the degree of Eliot's engagement in his career as playwright—how much energy he put into translating his spiritual experience into a dramatic formula that would accommodate his views of the historical and anthropological roots of drama and at the same time ensure the involvement of West End theater audiences—we get some sense of the significance of this omission in our presentation of Eliot.

The fact is that Eliot, except for the hiatus between 1924, when he wrote the *Sweeney Agonistes* fragments, and 1934, when he agreed to write the choruses for *The Rock*, steadily pursued his own program of dramatic education and experimentation throughout his long career. Moreover, there is clear evidence that he regarded as one of his most important accomplishments the development of a conversational dramatic poetry that would attract lay audiences to poetic drama. That Eliot saw the possibility of a viable poetic drama for the twentieth century as an issue of political as well as

162

literary significance demonstrates the side of the poet that is most often missing in the classroom—the strength of his commitment to find a more positive role for the modern church and the persistence of his efforts to create a public art that could move secular audiences to understand spiritual experience. Thus, to add Eliot's plays to the teaching canon of his work requires nothing less than a rethinking of his entire development, but the reward is a more accurate picture of his career and a more enjoyable experience for students.

Before this change is likely to occur, however, teachers must be persuaded of the importance of drama to Eliot and of its relation to his religious and poetic growth. I would like to make that case before I describe my own classroom use of Eliot's plays. We are all familiar with the evolution of his personal philosophy. It can be traced in his critical writings and in his poetry—a movement from despair at the disorder of the natural world to acceptance of a supernatural order that could give meaning and unity to the world's apparent chaos. His literary judgments and tastes reflected this same search for order and form. His endorsement of classicism, for example, was an effort to require of art a form that could order experience, just as a religious interpretation of existence could order and make sense of nature. As his religious commitment grew, Eliot's view of the function of art changed until finally he saw as its purpose the microcosmic reflection of divine order.

Drama represented to Eliot a literary form with a special mission. The playwright could, he believed, create an artistically ordered world within the play and at the same time unite all levels of the audience in a communal experience. Most important of all, drama could re-create for the modern viewer what Eliot, building on the myth criticism that grew out of Frazer's work, believed to be at the heart of both drama and religion—the secular death and spiritual rebirth of the hero. The dramatic theme of all his plays, therefore, was the plight of the individual who perceives the order of God but who, forced to exist in the secular world, must somehow come to terms with both realms.

To complement this conception of drama, Eliot attempted to develop a special verse form, one that would be rhythmic and colloquial yet hint at spiritual meanings beneath. He shared with other writers of the modern tradition a belief that literary form and structure itself could conceal the artist's controlling hand and that myth could provide an underlying meaning for works that appeared to portray only the surface of contemporary life. This double allegiance to form and to contemporary life is discussed in general terms by Cleanth Brooks in "*The Waste Land*: Critique of the Myth" (136–72) and in more technical terms by Jewel Spears Brooker in "The Case of the Missing Abstraction: Eliot, Frazer, and Modernism."

As I argue in *T. S. Eliot's Dramatic Theory and Practice*, throughout his essays Eliot gives evidence of having followed with special interest the work of one group of Frazer's followers, the Cambridge school of classical anthropology, which studied the origins of Greek drama. They believed that classical drama was based on ancient ritual, on the primitive celebrations marking the cycles of the earth's productiveness. According to these scholars, tragedy was centered in the agon between good and evil or summer and winter, and comedy in the phallic ceremonies described by Aristotle that represented the marriage of the risen god to the earth mother, necessary for the renewal of all life in the spring.

The significance of these ideas for Eliot can be seen in *Sweeney Agonistes*, Eliot's first dramatic experiment. In it he planned to create a new kind of comedy for the jazz age, but he achieved a comedy so black that he found it impossible to complete. *Sweeney Agonistes* marks an important point in Eliot's poetic career, after *The Waste Land* (1922) but before *Ash-Wednesday* (1930), and shows a picture of Eliot in his period of spiritual despair that is very different from the one we are accustomed to. The almost effete passivity of the personae of the surrounding poems is missing here, and instead we see as hero Sweeney, a character Eliot had used in several earlier poems to represent the natural human being.

In teaching *Sweeney Agonistes*, I have found that students are at first mystified and then fascinated by these two short dramatic fragments. I include the Sweeney poems in this reading assignment to show how Eliot reused themes and characters from his earlier poems and how he faced the challenge of letting Sweeney speak. These fragments are packed with arresting scenes of prostitutes telling fortunes, a tale of murder, and syncopated patter songs lifted from Gilbert and Sullivan and the English music hall performances Eliot enjoyed. I lecture (briefly!) on Frazer's ideas and on the current status of *The Golden Bough* in classical anthropology. The flattening of character into caricature and the use of drumbeats to accent the verse were techniques Eliot adapted from Francis Cornford's and Gilbert Murray's writings on the origins of comedy. He was impressed with Cornford's theory that the ritual drama had provided comedy with its stock masks and that beneath the late and impermanent separation of the ritual drama into tragedy and comedy was the one essential ingredient of all drama—rhythm. Eliot came to see rhythm as the element necessary for catharsis and to see stylization as essential to achieve the balanced relation of the parts to the whole in art. This material is especially interesting to students who have not studied the backgrounds of modernism before, for they begin to see the influence of these ideas on the work of other modernist writers they have studied.

The play's title and the epigraphs from Saint John of the Cross and Orestes are good illustrations of Eliot's use of allusion and myth, ones that are not so familiar as those in *The Waste Land* or "Prufrock" and are thus more challenging to students. I use this opportunity to demonstrate how the mythical method works in another context, and students can see that the title and the epigraphs provide clues that the play is a modern "agon" of a man plunged into the purgatorial experience by the murder of his mistress. Eliot's matching of the party world of postwar London with Saint John's statement, "Hence the soul cannot be possessed of the divine union, until it has divested itself of the love of created beings," produces one of Eliot's favorite effects. The mystic's truth about the need to separate one's self from human love before divine love can be attained takes on the macabre literal meaning of Sweeney's, and every man's, need to "do a girl in":

> Any man has to, needs to, wants to
> Once in a lifetime, do a girl in.

His tale of the murderer's destruction of the victim's body in a Lysol bath makes grotesquely real the dissolution of the bonds of human love. In a climate of feminism (and in a class where the professor is a woman), teaching this play is a special challenge, but it does provide an opportunity to air openly debates on Eliot's attitudes toward politics and gender. I try to emphasize the play's symbolic meanings but allow myself to be persuaded that the work's surface "plot" *is* sexist.

Reading scenes in class is an effective way to get students to hear the many rhythmic effects of Eliot's verse. *Sweeney Agonistes* is short enough to read in its entirety, and when read accompanied by the drumbeats Eliot specified to accent the syncopated rhythm (there are always willing students to do this "part"), it makes a memorable class. It also leads into a discussion of the rhythmic effects in Eliot's other poems and prosody in general. After this session students listen in a new way to Eliot's use of voice and stress.

When we turn to *Murder in the Cathedral*, students can see the more ambitious agenda for drama that Eliot developed in the ten years after *Sweeney Agonistes*. When he returned to drama, his acceptance of Anglo-Catholicism lay behind him, and he began to see the possibilities of applying his dramatic ideals to the social goals of the embattled modern church. In accepting the task of writing the choruses for *The Rock* and a commissioned religious drama for the Canterbury Festival, Eliot could hardly have anticipated their tremendous success and his public role as spokesperson for the Christian community.

We discuss in class the historical background of the play, but our main focus is on Eliot's shift of theme. What interested him now was not the private torment of the dark night of the soul but the more public effects of a saint—the effects of Thomas's actions on his people and on his king. The struggles of the flesh have given way to the saint's struggle with pride. When

Thomas recognizes that his final victory is actually surrender to God's will, willingly rejecting the role of actor for the role of sufferer of God's action, he has achieved the saint's vision.

Even though Eliot has cast the saint's struggle in a stylized twelfth-century setting, it is clear to students that he used Thomas Becket's conflict with Henry II to dramatize the dangers to the contemporary church from both the totalitarian right and the communist left. The part of the play that typically arouses the most discussion is the final appearance of the knights. Eliot intentionally breaks the formality of the ritual language and allows the knights to address the audience in the prose of modern political debate. The knights defend their murder of Thomas according to the best modern logic, insisting that they were disinterested, that violence was the only way to secure social justice, and that Thomas's death should ultimately be judged "suicide while of unsound mind." The modernity of the language and argumentation emphasizes the secular judgment on martyrdom, but in the context of this religious drama the knights' comments are intended to be seen as blasphemy. Students react to this attack on modern secularism in a variety of ways, but it never fails to provoke a lively discussion.

Most of my students would vote *The Cocktail Party* (1949) Eliot's most successful play. After reading *Sweeney Agonistes* and *Murder in the Cathedral*, they are delighted by the wit of transplanting the saint's journey into the dramatic world of romantic comedy. They recognize in Celia Coplestone another of Eliot's reluctant saints, whose problems with loving drive her to seek the help of one of Eliot's most successful comic creations, Sir Henry Harcourt-Reilly, the God-like, gin-drinking psychiatrist. Her path is paralleled by the spiritual maladies of the Chamberlaynes, who also consult Sir Henry about their unhappy marriage. We discuss in class the way the play is structured to match the two Christian paths, the negative way and the affirmative way, and the solutions Sir Henry offers Celia and the Chamberlaynes. We also talk in more general terms about how the elements of surprise and unexpected juxtaposition work in comedy and how Eliot extends the meaning of comedy to include the "happy ending" of the martyr's horrible death and the Chamberlaynes' acceptance of their role as witnesses. After the discussion of this play, students often express admiration for the way Eliot has used the possibilities of comedy to win over his audience to a view of experience that is both difficult to understand and difficult to accept.

Perhaps because of the difficulty of persuading modern audiences of the presence of divinity in everyday life, Eliot presents in his last comedies an ordered and seamless dramatic surface that contains a fable that can be read on two levels, allowing the play's imagery to carry the deeper meanings. In *The Confidential Clerk* (1953), he chose the dramatic conventions of farce or "high comedy" and exploited for his own purposes the age-old themes of the abandoned child, the dishonest nurse, mistaken identities, and the search for one's true parentage.

Eliot's Greek source for this play, the *Ion* of Euripides, deals with the abandoned child of the princess of Athens, who has been raped by Apollo, and the god's attempt to rescue his divine offspring and restore him to his royal birthright. Much of the comedy of Eliot's play concerns the misdirected attempts of Sir Claude and Lady Elizabeth to establish ties of paternity with Colby, Sir Claude's new confidential clerk, while they ignore the claims of their true but "mislaid" children of earlier affairs. Both Sir Claude and Lady Elizabeth have developed substitutes for religion that make everyday life bearable, Sir Claude in his private escape into the world of art and Lady Elizabeth in her dabbling in occult religion or "mind control," and each tries to make Colby into his or her own image by persuading him to deny his own "musical" longings and to relegate music to a part-time escape. Only Eggerson, the god figure disguised as Sir Claude's retiring confidential clerk, sees Colby's true identity as a person of religious commitment. The climaxing reversal and recognition scene toward which the whole comic action builds occurs when Sir Claude and Lady Elizabeth discover their true children and relinquish their claims on Colby, who finds himself to be the child of his heavenly Father.

Since the tradition of classical comedy is unfamiliar to most students, we spend some time in class discussing Eliot's source and the conventions of farce, especially the mechanisms of surprise and discovery and comic reversal. I often assign Oscar Wilde's play *The Importance of Being Earnest*, which was the model for the performance style of the play's first production, to provide an example of high comedy used to explore the question of identity. We continue to read scenes aloud in class so that students can experience directly Eliot's more conversational late verse style. Students can see how Eliot used the theme of the foundling child to express the search for a spiritual relationship with god as father, and they find delightful his use of Mrs. Guzzard, Euripides's Pallas Athene transformed into a modern fairy godmother, as the dishonest nurse who holds the key to everyone's true identity. They also see how Eliot has used the imagery of the garden and Colby's music to carry the double meanings of Christian experience. This context provides a valuable opportunity to talk about Eliot's use of these motifs from his earliest poetry to his last plays. His insistence in this late comedy (as well as in the garden imagery of his last play, *The Elder Statesman*) that the garden of religious experience must not be isolated from the rest of life shows the distance Eliot has traveled on his own religious journey. Colby's choice of Eggerson's garden of work and prayer and his wish to share it with someone express the Vergilian ideal of the integration of the spiritual and the material in a Christian community, the same impulse that is behind much of Eliot's social writing during the last part of his career.

In exploring the full range of Eliot's Christian comedy, students can trace his progress in a form that is both approachable and audible to them. Moreover, in studying the plays they experience directly his effort to bring drama back to its religious origins. Students are, in fact, an interesting test of Eliot's goal, for in one sense they represent the secular audience he chose to address. While few students share Eliot's religious perspective, most come to understand more fully both the private agony of the mystic path and the Vergilian hope for Christian community and to applaud Eliot's long struggle to communicate with a secular world.

An Unnatural Eloquence: Eliot's Plays in the Course on Modern Drama

Katherine E. Kelly

It is the rare survey or anthology of modern drama that contains a play by T. S. Eliot. And yet these plays, together with Eliot's essays on the drama, offer students a valuable record of the competing claims of naturalism and poetic stylization on the modern stage. The radical style shifts in the work of Ibsen, Strindberg, and Shaw, as well as the tension between poetic depth and banal surface language in Chekhov, Beckett, and Pinter, can be anatomized for the student with the help of Eliot's dramatic theory and practice. The poet's ambitious program for drama was most eloquent in defining the limits of naturalism and in pointing to its alternative in a theater of poetic intensity with roots in ancient ritual. Eliot's turn toward the theater signaled his growth as a writer. No longer satisfied with the range of his lyric voice, he wanted his plays to reach an audience wider than that of his poetry. And this desire to extend his audience led him, as it had led G. B. Shaw and Oscar Wilde before him, toward popular dramatic forms with proven appeal.

Students may find it helpful to divide Eliot's plays into three stages, each unified by a central concept described in his essays and illustrated in the plays themselves. First came his preoccupation with rhythm in *Sweeney Agonistes: Fragments of an Aristophanic Melodrama*. Eliot defined *rhythm* generally and specifically to mean both the most primitive of human impulses toward mimesis and the syncopating lyrics of jazz and comic cross talk popular in the British music halls. The second stage of Eliot's drama is bound up with his conversion to Anglicanism and the related notion of a dramatic poetry that would move spectators much like the prayers and rites of the Anglican church were designed to move them. *Murder in the Cathedral* is Eliot's experiment in liturgical drama. In his third and final stage of development, Eliot shifted his emphasis from liturgy toward a carefully adapted naturalism in *The Family Reunion, The Cocktail Party, The Confidential Clerk*, and *The Elder Statesman*. When viewed in these stages, Eliot's plays can offer students a blueprint of the conflict between verisimilitude and ritualized stylization that defines the two poles of modern drama.

Eliot's deep admiration for the great music hall artist Marie Lloyd helped inspire *Sweeney Agonistes*, first published in the *New Criterion* of 1926–27 under the title *Wanna Go Home, Baby?* and next appearing under its present title in 1932. We can only speculate why Eliot left the play unfinished (the ending he wrote for Hallie Flanagan's Vassar production can be found in Flanagan 83–84), but his description of it as "fragments" should warn students that the poem does not present a fully developed and integrated plot but consists rather of two closely related dramatic scenes with accompanying songs. In *Sweeney* Eliot was trying to objectify the themes of human isolation, suffering, and spiritual yearning that he had developed in his lyric voice as author of *The Waste Land*. But to accomplish this, he needed a universal dramatic form and a modern idiom that would speak immediately to a diverse audience. He found his form in ancient art and ritual and his idiom in the comic turns and jazz lyrics played in the British music halls. Much of the action and imagery of the play's two fragments is indebted to Francis M. Cornford's *Origin of Attic Comedy*, while the syncopation of dialogue and choral songs, as well as the comic treatment of serious themes, shows the direct influence of the music hall on Eliot's dramatic rhythm. This same influence shaped the duologues in Samuel Beckett's *Waiting for Godot*, another farce on metaphysical themes. Students might appreciate an example of how Eliot used his esoteric sources in writing his first play. It may surprise (and relieve) them to recognize that the action in "Fragment of a Prologue" loosely corresponds to Cornford's description of the first movement in the three-part comic ritual underlying Aristophanes's comedies (C. Smith 63, 67).

In the first two dark fragments of *Sweeney*, Eliot uses his ancient sources to stage an ironical encounter of mutually uncomprehending characters speaking to each other from different levels of moral awareness. Students will notice that these levels recur in all Eliot's plays and are his chief means of distinguishing between characters. As a bold experiment in combining serious theme with farcical treatment, *Sweeney* is only partially successful. But Eliot's linking of popular form with mythic action allied him with several of his contemporaries—G. B. Shaw, W. B. Yeats, Jean Giraudoux, Jean Anouilh, and Bertolt Brecht—who were also interested in creating an alternative to dramatic naturalism. Just how far Eliot wanted *Sweeney* to move from the conventions of the naturalistic theater is clear in his letter to Hallie Flanagan where he calls for a production style following Yeats's and Pound's borrowing of stylized elements from religious Japanese Noh drama:

> The action should be stylised as in the Noh drama—see Ezra Pound's book and Yeats' preface and notes to *The Hawk's Well*. Characters *ought* to wear masks; the ones wearing old masks ought to give the impression of being young . . . (actors) and vice versa. . . . I had intended the whole play to be accompanied by light drum taps to accentuate the beats (esp. the chorus, which ought to have a noise like a street drill). (Flanagan 83).

This insistence on the rhythm of drumbeats may remind students of Eugene O'Neill's 1920 stage success, *Emperor Jones*, which anticipated Eliot's reliance on musical and scenic effects in rendering intelligible the most basic of human drives.

When next Eliot turned to write for the stage, he had declared his conversion to Anglicanism and had merged his interest in dramatic poetry with a commitment to Christian belief. It is no surprise, then, that he reversed his early interest in colloquial and primitive rhythm by attempting a dramatic poetry of high seriousness. By the time he had written *Murder in the Cathedral* in 1935, Eliot had discovered the second of what he called the "three voices of poetry":

> The first is the voice of the poet talking to himself. . . . The second is the voice of the poet addressing an audience. . . . The third is the voice of the poet when he attempts to create a dramatic character speaking in verse; when he is saying, not what he would say in his own person, but only what he can say within the limits of one imaginary character addressing another imaginary character. (*On Poetry* 96)

The striking feature of this play for students of the modern drama is its attempt to ascend to the heights of tragedy by adapting a martyr's story to poetic patterns reminiscent of prayer and chant.

The play's choral speeches offer the strongest evidence of Eliot's new experiment in liturgical dramatic verse. The stately beauty of the choral poetry and the startling intensity of its imagery blanket, but do not bury, the poet's earlier preoccupation with ritual sacrifice. As Becket is killed, we hear the Chorus asking, "Can I look again at the day and its common things, and see them all smeared with blood, through a curtain of falling blood?" (*Complete Poems* 214). Eliot wanted in his liturgical play to "concentrate on death and martyrdom" (*On Poetry* 86). The central subject is still blood, but here the victim and the occasion of his ritual sacrifice are clearer than the suggestions of murder in the *Sweeney* fragments. A host of modern playwrights share this dramatic territory with Eliot, among them Federico García Lorca, whose 1933 *Blood Wedding* is a poetic treatment of the *Sweeney* themes of sexual passion, violence, and sacrifice, and G. B. Shaw, whose *Saint Joan* probably provided the model for Becket's prose sermon and for the Knights' startlingly colloquial speeches following the archbishop's murder (G. Smith, *Eliot's Poetry* 194–95).

But despite its success as a play in its own right, independent of the Canterbury Festival for which it was written, Eliot was impatient with its limits, calling *Murder in the Cathedral* a "deadend" in his search for a dramatic language that would bring poetry into the theater (*On Poetry* 84). This search culminated in the third stage of his playwrighting, whose centerpiece was *The Cocktail Party*, first performed at the Edinburgh Festival in August 1949, under the label "a comedy." As a comedy, this piece both unites Eliot's earlier preoccupation with popular forms and liturgical stylization and reconciles these with an emerging interest in natural-seeming speech and action, the sort of playing style that could appeal to a broad spectrum of theatergoers. The formal and thematic preoccupations central to Eliot's earlier plays coalesce in this most popular of his dramatic works: characterization is based on subtly suggested levels of spiritual awareness, with the guardians Alex, Julia, and Sir Henry the most aware, and the filmmaker Peter the least; the theme of ritual sacrifice and communion takes the Christian form of Celia's reported murder by crucifixion; and the milieu is undeniably modern, set in affluent living rooms and offices with the characters speaking dialogue at once idiomatic and rigorously precise. In choosing as his central theme the struggle of the Chamberlaynes to live honestly and vitally as a married couple, Eliot was building on a long established tradition on the modern stage. Beginning with Ibsen's *Doll House*, and continuing through Strindberg's *Ghost Sonata*, Chekhov's *Uncle Vanya*, Shaw's *Man and Superman*, O'Neill's *Long Day's Journey into Night*, Williams's *Streetcar Named Desire*, and Albee's *Who's Afraid of Virginia Woolf?*, to name only a few, the disappointments of marriage have taken a central place in twentieth-century drama. When writing this piece, Eliot drew particularly on Noel Coward's drawing-room comedy, best exemplified by plays such as *Blithe Spirit*, *Hay Fever*, and *Private Lives*, whose urbane characters speak a cultivated English and have the leisure necessary to permit their indulgence in witty analyses of themselves, their historical moment, and one another. But Eliot's intense interest in his characters' spiritual salvation finally distinguishes his marriage play sharply from those preceding it.

Many of the techniques present in his earlier work operate here as well, but to quieter effect. As before, we discover that his characters play double roles—the guardians are both real seeming, even comically meddlesome friends and spiritual arrangers. The play's ostensibly secular theme is doubled by a larger sacred design—the reconciling of the Chamberlaynes' marriage is a metaphor for the unifying of the entire Christian community. Language also operates on two levels—the guardians' apparently banal party talk is code for a nearly inexpressible spiritual communication among them. Eliot manages these levels more delicately, less overtly than he had before, largely through his increased control of dramatic irony. As the spectators begin to understand during act 2 that the characters they had taken to be conventional, affluent types are doubling as spiritual guardians, they must backtrack and reinterpret the events of act 1. By encouraging spectators to assess and reassess the events and language of the opening act, Eliot engages them in probing the deceptively Noel Coward–like surface of the play, which in turn has the effect of drawing the audience into the characters' search for salvation. Harold Pinter's comedies of menace, such as *Old Times* and *No Man's Land*, similarly use a deceptively innocent surface language to suggest another level of communication occurring among characters. But this second level in Pinter is savagely hostile and devoid of the influence of Christian grace. Tom Stoppard's more benevolent comedies, particularly his recent marriage play *The Real Thing*, while secular, come closer to Eliot's tone and use of dramatic irony in fixing the spectator's critical attention on the events unfolding on stage.

Only during the libation scenes at the ends of acts 2 and 3, and even then in a context carefully deflected by comedy, does Eliot resort to the stylized liturgical rhythms and ritual gestures so prominent in *Murder in the Cathedral*. And only in the indirectly reported incident of Celia's sacrificial murder does he come close to stating outright the overarching Christian design of the play: one must choose a path to salvation, either by denying human relationships (Celia's way) or by affirming them through love and marriage (the Chamberlaynes' way) (C. Smith 162–63). Eliot has come a long way since his preoccupation with rhythm in *Sweeney Agonistes*, his explicit reliance on liturgical forms in *Murder in the Cathedral*, and his development of levels of awareness in all his works preceding this comedy. Turning toward naturalism seemed to have helped Eliot achieve a greater compression of language and gesture that kept his work just within the boundaries of realism acceptable to a mass audience. In his development from the rhythmically stylized *Sweeney* to the liturgically formal *Murder in the Cathedral* and finally to the quasi-naturalistic comedy *The Cocktail Party*, Eliot recapitulated the journeys taken by the great writers for the modern stage, most of whose works oscillated between the two poles of naturalism and stylization as their materials and creative interests drove them first one way, then the other.

Precisely because Eliot eventually positioned his drama at the difficult junction of poetry and naturalism, it offers students an unusually clear look at these two tensions in the modern theater—the pull toward verisimilitude on the one hand and stylization on the other. Those students wishing to try other approaches to reading the plays might look for thematic parallels between Eliot's plays and those of other playwrights—O'Neill, Pirandello, Pinter, and Shepard—in their uses of implied and expressed stage violence, of the strengths and failures of language as an expressive and evocative instrument, and, finally, of the adequacy of myth and ritual as paradigms for dramatic art.

On Teaching *Murder in the Cathedral*

Linda Wyman

Whether I am teaching *Murder in the Cathedral* to students trying to satisfy their humanities requirement, to English majors, or to graduate students, the particular things that I do in class derive from my understanding of the kind of play it is. Taking my lead from R. S. Crane's discussion of the plot of action, the plot of character, and so on (52), I have arrived at the concept of the "plot of diction," and I understand the plot of *Murder in the Cathedral* to be of this kind. That is, while we are shown a change in the situation of the protagonist (Thomas is killed) and a change in his thought and feeling (Thomas comes to understand the nature of martyrdom), we are shown, in the total design of the language, a meaning more comprehensive than that encompassed by the protagonist alone, so that our final attention is directed to a complex of meanings (the nature of martyrdom), of which all that we have learned about the protagonist is a part. (For a fuller exploration of this idea see Wyman). In Eliot's play, it is not enough to say that the words cannot be separated from what happens: to a very great extent, the words *are* what happens. That is why it is not enough when reading *Murder* to watch Thomas make perfect his will and then to watch him die, for these events do not encompass the play. The design of the play is revealed gradually, and the reader must come to understand it gradually—as Thomas, and then the Women of Canterbury, come to understand "the design of God."

"The design of God" and the design of the play are made clear in the interlude, in which Thomas preaches his Christmas sermon. Structurally and thematically, the sermon is the pivot of *Murder*. It deals with the mystery, the fundamental paradoxes, of Christianity, and because it is fully dramatic, it enables that mystery dramatically to inform the totality of the play. Everything that happens in part 1 leads up to these lines, and everything that is to happen in part 2 follows from them. The sermon expresses orthodox Christian doctrine, but it is not "merely" doctrinal: the words have dramatic meaning because before the fourth temptation Thomas would not have been able to say them.

What Thomas says in the Christmas sermon has been prepared for from the first lines of the play. Class time is well spent in giving close attention to the play's opening chorus. This speech is no mere mood setter; it begins the dramatic action. Whether or not students are familiar with the conventions of the dramatic chorus, the teacher must alert them to the necessity for attending to the Women of Canterbury. I suggest that this be accomplished by informing students that in Greek *martyr* means "witness." One of the few things that the Women know is that they "are forced to bear witness." Thomas is to be killed, and the Women are to witness his murder;

martyr, then, is a word that conjoins the murdered one and the witnesses to his murder. As it happens, to note that *witness* encompasses and fulfills *martyr* is to note the central fact of Eliot's play.

Having made the point about the meaning of *martyr*, I would read the opening chorus aloud, perhaps listing certain words on the chalkboard in an effort to implant them in students' minds:

wait	wait
witness	saints and martyrs
witness	martyrs and saints
Saints	wait
martyrs and saints	witness
wait	

Leaving those words on the board as the play is discussed will serve as a reminder that the Women—"forced," as they say, "to bear witness"—never leave the stage. Furthermore, if students have to think about a question such as "How does the Women's use of the passive voice correspond to the sense of what they are saying?" they may have yet another way to begin to see how the language of this play truly embodies its action. Then as they consider the speeches of the Three Priests, students might profitably look for similarities in the language of the Priests and the Women. Such exercises as those I have mentioned equip students to see that the second chorus builds on, intensifies, particularizes, and extends the meaning of the first (and so on throughout the play).

Once students have been helped to hear the words of the play and to analyze its language, they will be well prepared for Thomas's first appearance. They will be able to see, for instance, that his use of such words as *action*, *suffering*, and *pattern* is not merely coincidental. When Thomas says of the Women, "They speak better than they know" (*Complete Plays* 17), students may begin to suspect that this statement is also true of Thomas. Thomas's command "Watch" directs attention once more to the Women (and to the words on the chalkboard), who, as it soon becomes clear, are to be witnesses to Becket's temptation.

In the temptation scene Thomas is characterized by unusually concise and allusive—that is, poetic—means, but he is far from being an unbodied abstraction. He returns to England fully anticipating his martyrdom and fully anticipating that temptation is to precede it. Close attention to the language of the tempters' speeches may reinforce the effort to help students hear the play's verse, especially its rhymed verse, and such attention may serve the additional pedagogical purpose of modeling for students some of the ways that verse contributes to meaning in this work. For example, if students are helped to hear the rhythms of the First Tempter's speech ("Old Tom, gay Tom, Becket of London") and the series of weakly stressed end words (*ceremony, acrimony, gravity, levity*), they may well realize that the First Tempter is not presented as a formidable foe. At the same time, students who can hear, and attend to, Eliot's language may perceive several correspondences in the speech of Thomas and the tempters that, taken together, would seem to be subtle indications that the first three tempters are not completely out of touch with the archbishop. Thomas and the tempters share metaphors of the seasons, shadow, and substance, for instance. Furthermore, Eliot gives the First Tempter lines that rhyme with Thomas's: *turns, spurns; master, faster; late, fate.* Similarly, Eliot binds one of Thomas's end words with rhymes from the Second Tempter's lines: *madness, sadness, gladness.* Since rhyme is not the norm for this play, the presence of a sort of interlocking rhyme asserts itself and suggests that Thomas is tempted more seriously than his words alone reveal. For the most part, however, students will rightly conclude that the first three tempters do talk of "seasons that are past," and Thomas withstands their temptations.

When the Fourth Tempter gives Thomas a vision of "pilgrims, standing in line / Before the glittering jewelled shrine," the archbishop must answer, "I have thought of these things" (26). Moments later he realizes the main thing that he must realize in this play: "The last temptation is the greatest treason; / To do the right deed for the wrong reason" (30). It is at this point that teachers may profitably invoke their students' common sense, their elementary logic, and their knowledge of conventional drama. If the play is a "character drama," it should end here; there will be no further developments in Thomas's character. That it does not end now suggests that the play is about something beyond Thomas—as indeed the Women's being "forced to bear witness" has suggested from the beginning. Although Thomas's final speech in part 1 has several properties of a soliloquy, there are no soliloquies in this play, nor, one thinks, could there be any. Every speech is "witnessed." The last lines of Thomas's speech explicitly indicate that Thomas is aware of his witnesses (and that he includes the audience among them).

Direct address is, at any rate, the mode of the next scene, the interlude—the Christmas sermon. When students identify the words that Thomas could not have preached in, say, his Christmas sermon of the preceding year, they will have hit on the idea of which this entire drama is an enactment: "A martyrdom is always the design of God, for His love of men, to warn them and to lead them, to bring them back to His ways" (33). If at this point I ask students, "What has to happen next in the play?" they answer that Thomas must be killed. And if I ask them what has to happen after that, they tell me that someone must be "brought back." In understanding the

Christmas sermon as a dramatic speech, then, they come to understand both the structure and the meaning of the play. They see that, in the terms of this play, a martyrdom is not complete when one submits one's will to God; if this were true, *Murder* could conceivably end with part 1. Nor, by further implication, is a martyrdom complete when one who has submitted one's will to God is killed; if this were true, the play could end with the death of Thomas. Contemplating the Christmas sermon as a dramatic speech leads students to anticipate what will happen in part 2—leads them to understand that without the "bringing back," the murder is simply a killing, not a martyrdom; it leads them to see that logically and dramatically the "murder" requires the "cathedral."

Students do not have to be told that Eliot tries in several ways to ensure that *Murder* will reach beyond the year 1170, beyond the stage, into what one might call the "active," as opposed to the "contemplative," consciousness of the audience. Having saturated themselves in the language of the play, students easily recognize that Eliot periodically departs from its characteristic diction, meter, and tone in order to extend it in time, to make it simultaneously historical, contemporary, and timeless. However much students may enjoy the knights' preeminently "sensible" and "modern" argument, a pause to recollect the proposition on which this play is built—the definition of martyrdom given in the Christmas sermon—will lead students to expect to see the knights' argument demolished. (When I have asked students, "Who, logically, should have the last words in this play?" I have never failed to hear them answer, "The Women.")

Thomas indicates in the Christmas sermon that he understands his martyrdom to be on behalf of the Women of Canterbury. Gradually, painfully, and certainly, the Women themselves come to understand it in this way. Rather than merely comment on their experience, the choruses that they speak show it happening. Far from being respites from the action, the choruses in *Murder* are the heart of it. Because I believe that it is important to help students reach this conclusion on their own, I ask them (for homework or classwork, singly or in groups) to trace in the final chorus the allusions to and transformations of the other choruses. They thus can see for themselves how the last chorus provides a record of the Women's "witnessing" Thomas's martyrdom and of the effect of this event on their lives. Students are likely to see, for instance, that the force of the first line ("We praise Thee, O God, for Thy glory displayed in all the creatures of the earth") depends on one's having heard the "death-bringers" chorus. That the same women who delineated in that speech the horror of "grey necks twisting, rat tails twining" (41) can recognize God's glory "displayed in all the creatures of the earth" is in itself a striking instance of change.

The concluding chorus—part *Alleluia*, part *Miserere*—both describes and *is* the result of Thomas's martyrdom, expressing the ultimate and saving perceptions at which the Women have arrived. Its full power resides in its being an extraordinary *dramatic* speech; it could not have been uttered by the bewildered women who stood in front of the cathedral at the beginning of part 1. When the Women proclaim, ". . . Thy glory is declared even in that which denies Thee; the darkness declares the glory of light," they summarize all that they have learned. Only when they can say, "Blessed Thomas, pray for us" is Thomas's martyrdom validated, made complete. And because the play enacts a certain proposition about the nature of martyrdom, it too is completed with this line.

While I do not attempt to secularize *Murder in the Cathedral*, I do introduce the play in broadly human, rather than specifically religious, terms, being confident that the spiritual dimension of the play will make its own presence known. Fundamentally, I rely on my faith in the ability of students to have an aesthetic experience, and I help them to read the play as the work of art it is. For twenty-eight years, I have seen them stunned, dazzled, and finally elated, as I always am, by the experience of reading it.

The Alchemy of Humor
in *The Cocktail Party*

Ann P. Brady

> The only wisdom we can hope to acquire
> Is the wisdom of humility: humility is endless.
> "East Coker" 2

By appending the words *A Comedy* to the title of *The Cocktail Party*, T. S. Eliot invites his audience to associate his play with a traditional genre and to attend to the ways in which his comedy differs from its predecessors. Like the audience who flocked to see *The Cocktail Party* at the Edinburgh Festival in 1949, students expect to see a comedy of manners. The Nobel laureate gives them a delightful one, but wrapped in its trappings is a divine comedy of salvation. In a 1938 letter to Ezra Pound, Eliot had whimsically stated his theory of getting across serious religious ideas to an audience unprepared for them: ". . . IF you can keep the bloody audience's attention engaged, then you can perform any monkey tricks you like when they ain't looking, and it's what you do behind the audience's back, so to speak, that makes your play IMMORTAL for a while" ("Five Points"). In *The Cocktail Party*, Eliot keeps his audience engaged with sophisticated living-room comedy while Old Possum performs his "monkey tricks" of bringing his characters to personal and communal salvation through their transhumanization by truth and love. The method is humor, whose alchemy transforms humiliation into humility, judgment into mercy.

The world of comedy is the world of humility, where people do not fall, because they are already on the ground (*humus*) where they belong. It is a world of reality where one comes to see the self in relation to the rest of the world, where one is free to celebrate the ordinary. To enter this world, one must relinquish the primacy of self, the loss of which is often accomplished through a comedic "fall" from eminence and experienced as humiliation, but eventually accepted as a descent to truth, to humility. The comedic struggle is not the unredeemed and unredeemable agon of the tragic vision, nor is it the mere provider of ridicule for the satirist; it is the struggle toward accommodation turning into affection and, possibly, love. In Eliot's play, the dynamic characters (those who move from ignorance to illumination) are lost in a world of illusions where everyone has false expectations of everyone else, sees others only in relation to the self. Edward and Lavinia thus try to escape the prison of their marriage by snaring Celia and Peter, respectively, into adulterous relationships born of blindness and selfishness and ending in disillusion. To move from tragic illusion to comic vision, they will suffer a sea change directed by those already residing in the world of comedy.

Thus the static characters—the guardians Julia and Alex, with the psychiatrist Sir Henry Harcourt-Reilly—can set these lost characters moving toward personal fulfillment in their separate vocations.

Comedy has always celebrated the ordinary, the finite, the human; and Eliot's comedy uses the most ordinary, unlikely, unelevated persons as agents of salvation. With encouragement, students can come to see that the chief mover is Julia. An apparent scatterbrain with imperfect vision, she cannot manage to keep up with her eyeglasses, which are of no use to her anyway because of a missing lens. She is in the tradition of the wise fool, the blind seer, a tradition the teacher can help students recognize. Alex, her chief agent and cohort in the process of directing and nurturing others, is a world-hopping diplomat and a bungling cook whose efforts to feed his friends provide part of the humor and part of the symbolism. Their chief activator in the salvific process, Sir Henry Harcourt-Reilly, is a psychiatrist with outrageous methods, who attends parties uninvited, drinks gin freely, sends false telegrams, and sings songs about "One-eyed Reilly" in sophisticated Mayfair parlors.

A good way to launch students' exploration of the play is to discuss its overall three-act structure. Act 1 reveals the need for the intervention of the guardians in the lives of Lavinia, Edward, Celia, and Peter: each is self-deluded and incapable of self-direction. Act 2 shows the guardians plying their trade; they have got Edward, Lavinia, and Celia separately to the physician's office where each chooses a course of action that will lead to their true destinies. Act 3 provides a glimpse of the results of those choices: Celia had consummated the heroic kind of love she had sought; Lavinia and Edward are living ordinary lives transformed by affectionate, accepting love; Peter, undeceived at last about himself, sets out to seek his own destiny, under the guardianship of Alex, who, of course, has "connections—even in California" (*Complete Plays* 195).

By far the longest and most complicated act is the first, and students benefit from seeing how carefully Eliot has laid out the dramatic pattern. Basically, it presents a humorless life (Edward's) that humor (in the persons of Julia and Alex) continually hovers over, baits, and tries to break into with illumination. Edward, after the breakup of the party, has three conversations, each in the form of a revelation without any illumination. In the first, with the Unidentified Guest, Edward reveals that Lavinia has left him and is informed in turn that the mysterious guest can get her back if her husband wishes it. Edward finds, much to his surprise, that he does. In the second interview, the equally humorless Peter reveals his illusory attachment to Celia and ironically asks Edward's help in furthering this relationship. These two conversations build up to the third, where Edward unwittingly reveals to Celia that the man she has been in love with is a creature of her imagination. These interviews are continually broken into by Julia or Alex, who will not leave Edward alone. They weave act 1 into a kind of fool's liturgy by which everyone will eventually be transformed.

In act 1 the Unidentified Guest gives Edward the disconcertingly droll advice, "Resign yourself to be the fool you are" (135). Edward, in turn, peevishly says to Peter, "I don't know why I should be taking all this trouble / To protect you from the fool you are" (143). Unlike Edward and Peter, who find it humiliating to be considered fools, Celia, on the verge of finding her true vocation, tells Sir Henry Harcourt-Reilly in act 2, "I don't mind at all having been a fool" (187). It seems that an ability to accept the self as foolish marks the characters' release from falsehood and self-deception. It is the comic vision—the vision of Julia and Alex, who do not take themselves too seriously and will not allow others to persist in doing so.

Julia firmly establishes herself as one who cannot maintain a conversation. She seems never to listen to or know what anyone is saying. No story of hers ever gets finished. After several pages of script held together by her continually interrupted story about Lady Klootz and the wedding cake, Julia responds to a final urging to get on with the tale with "What Lady Klootz?" and "Wedding cake? I wasn't at her wedding" (130). Careful reading of any sequence involving Julia will yield delightful touches. After needling Edward about the absent Lavinia and her sick aunt, Julia abruptly says, with her typical logic, "Well, we won't probe into it" (129). Students should be set to study the pattern of interruptions and the significance of their timing in moving the action toward salvation in laughter.

Julia is the fool of this Mayfair society, yet her power is recognized. Peter confides to Edward, "I'm rather afraid of Julia Shuttlethwaite" (139). Teasing Edward about his inept fabrication about Lavinia's absence, Celia wisely notes, "You should have been prepared with something better, for Julia" (146). Lavinia several times comments on Julia's uncanny sense of truth and sums it up to Edward: "Nothing less than the truth could deceive Julia" (164). We see just how formidable Julia's spiritual authority is in act 2 when she informs the great psychiatrist, "Henry, you simply do not understand innocence" (193). She shows power and purpose to the wavering Sir Henry—"We must always take risks. / That is our destiny" (192)—and finally admonishes him, "You must accept your limitations" (193). Act 1, scene 2 ends with Celia's recognition of Julia as her guardian; act 1, scene 3 ends with Lavinia's bitter observation to her husband, "I am unable to make you laugh" (170). Lavinia sees that in losing her own humor in the humorlessness of Edward, she has lost the means of saving their marriage. Laughter is the key to redemption. The characters gain it back as they place themselves under the direction of Julia, who sees with a comic vision. The contrasting paralleling of the ends of these two scenes is significant: Celia's realization foreshadows Lavinia's gradual perception of where her salvation lies.

Conrad Hyers, in *The Comic Vision and the Christian Faith*, describes the transforming power of humor in a way that corresponds perfectly with the vision created by Eliot in this play:

> There is . . . an intimate relationship between humor and compassion. Instead of moving only in the direction of a laughter at others and their faults and foibles or supposed inferiorities, humor moves toward a laughter that accepts others in spite of their differences. Since it is not grounded in a nervous insecurity, it does not need to be self-protective and self-assertive. It is therefore capable of becoming, in the purest sense, the humor of love. The element of judgment in humor (its prophetic, iconoclastic function) passes over into mercy.   (37)

Seeing oneself in relation to the rest of the world evokes laughter. It places the self in proper perspective by releasing one from the prison of self-importance. The characters in *The Cocktail Party* are released into this liberating vision of reality. The play ends in communion, reciprocal love, and concern for Peter, who has still to make the discovery. In a sense, Peter is where the students are themselves.

PARTICIPANTS IN SURVEY OF ELIOT INSTRUCTORS

The following scholars and teachers generously participated in the survey of pedagogical approaches that preceded preparation of this volume on T. S. Eliot's poetry and plays. Without their assistance, this book would not have been possible.

Charles Altieri, University of Washington; William Arrowsmith, Boston University; Robert W. Ayers, Georgetown University; Michael L. Baumann, California State University, Chico; Michael Beehler, Montana State University; Joseph Bentley, University of South Florida; Bernard Bergonzi, University of Warwick; Russell A. Berman, Stanford University; William Blissett, University of Toronto; Mildred Meyer Boaz, Millikin University; E. P. Bollier, Tulane University; George Bornstein, University of Michigan; Ann P. Brady, Gustavus Adolphus College; Cleanth Brooks, Yale University (Emeritus); Ronald Bush, California Institute of Technology; Daniel Cahill, University of Northern Iowa; Charles A. Carpenter, State University of New York, Binghamton; Marilyn R. Chandler, Mills College; Graham Clarke, University of Kent, England; Dianne R. Costanzo, Loyola University; Laura Niesen DeAbruña, Ithaca College; Bernard F. Dick, Fairleigh Dickinson University; Margaret Dickie, University of Illinois; Robert F. Fleissner, Central State University, Ohio; Douglas Fowler, Florida State University; Armin Paul Frank, Georg-August-Universität Göttingen; John Gatta, University of Connecticut; William A. Geiger, Jr., Whittier College; Lyndall Gordon, Oxford University; Michael Grant, University of Kent, England; Jeanne Gunner, University of California, Los Angeles; Leo Hamalian, City College, City University of New York; Nancy D. Hargrove, Mississippi State University; William Harmon, University of North Carolina; Gregory Jay, University of South Carolina; Judith Johnston, Rider College; Cleo McNelly Kearns, University of Strathclyde, Scotland; Katherine E. Kelly, Texas A & M University; James B. King, Hillsdale College; Jacob Korg, University of Washington; Thomas M. Leitch, University of Delaware; A. Walton Litz, Princeton University; Jean MacIntyre, University of Alberta; Marc Manganaro, University of Hawaii, Manoa; S. Louise McCreery, California Lutheran College; Rex McGuinn, Phillips Exeter Academy; David G. Mead, Corpus Christi State University; James E. Miller, Jr., University of Chicago; A. D. Moody, University of York, England; Jonathan Morse, University of Hawaii, Manoa; James Olney, Louisiana State University; Rose Orlich, Morehead State University; Jeffrey Perl, Columbia University; Sidney Poger, University of Vermont; William C. Pratt, Miami University, Ohio; Peter Quartermain, University of British Columbia; Allen Walker Read, New York, NY; John Rees, Kansas State University; J. P. Riquelme, Southern Methodist University; Audrey T. Rogers, Pennsylvania State University; M. L. Rosenthal, New York University; Ronald Schuchard,

Emory University; Nathan Scott, Jr., University of Virginia; Linda M. Shires, Syracuse University; William H. Shurr, University of Tennessee; K. M. Sibbald, McGill University; Carol H. Smith, Rutgers University; Grover Smith, Duke University; John J. Soldo, Brooklyn, NY; Derek Soles, Camosun College, Canada; James Spenko, State University of New York, Oswego; David Spurr, University of Illinois, Chicago; P. S. Sri, University of Alberta; Richard Sullivan, Rutgers University; James Torrens, SJ, University of Santa Clara; Lewis Turco, State University of New York, Oswego; Paula Uruburu, Hofstra University; George T. Wright, University of Minnesota; Glenn P. Wright, Eastern Illinois University; Linda Wyman, Lincoln University, Missouri.

WORKS CITED

Writings of T. S. Eliot

Collected Plays. London: Faber, 1962.

Collected Poems 1909–1962. London: Faber, 1963.

The Complete Plays of T. S. Eliot. New York: Harcourt, 1969.

The Complete Poems and Plays 1909–1950. New York: Harcourt, 1952.

To Criticize the Critic and Other Writings. London: Faber, 1965.

Elizabethan Essays. London: Faber, 1934.

"Five Points on Dramatic Writing." *Townsman* 1.3 (1938): 10.

Four Quartets. New York: Harcourt, 1943, 1968.

The Idea of a Christian Society. New York: Harcourt, 1940.

Introduction. *Savonarola: A Dramatic Poem.* By Charlotte Eliot. London: Cobden-Sanderson, [1926]. vii–xii.

Knowledge and Experience in the Philosophy of F. H. Bradley. New York: Farrar, 1964.

Letters of T. S. Eliot: Vol. 1, 1898–1922. Ed. Valerie Eliot. New York, Harcourt, 1988.

"London Letter." *Dial* 71.4 (1921): 452–55.

Old Possum's Book of Practical Cats. London: Faber, 1939.

On Poetry and Poets. London: Faber, 1957.

Poems Written in Early Youth. London: Faber, 1967.

"Prose and Verse." *Chapbook* 22 (1921): 3–10.

The Sacred Wood. New York: Knopf, 1921.

Selected Essays. New York: Harcourt, 1950.

Selected Poems. London: Penguin, 1948. New York: Harcourt, 1967.

Selected Prose of T. S. Eliot. Ed. Frank Kermode. New York: Harcourt, 1975.

The Use of Poetry and the Use of Criticism. London: Faber, 1933.

The Waste Land: *A Facsimile and Transcript of the Original Drafts Including the Annotations of Ezra Pound.* Ed. Valerie Eliot. New York: Harcourt, 1971.

The Waste Land *and Other Poems.* London: Faber, 1940. New York: Harcourt, 1955.

Books and Articles

Abrams, M. H. *A Glossary of Literary Terms*. 4th ed. New York: Holt, 1981.

———, gen. ed. *The Norton Anthology of English Literature*. 5th ed. 2 vols. New York: Norton, 1986.

———. "Structure and Style in the Greater Romantic Lyric." *Romanticism and Consciousness: Essays in Criticism*. Ed. Harold Bloom. New York: Norton, 1970.

Ackroyd, Peter. *T. S. Eliot: A Life*. New York: Simon, 1984.

Adams, Robert M. "Precipitating Eliot." *Eliot in His Time*. Ed. A. Walton Litz. Princeton: Princeton UP, 1973. 129–53.

Allen, Frederick Lewis. *Only Yesterday*. New York: Harper, 1931.

ApIvor, Denis. "Setting 'The Hollow Men' to Music." Braybrooke 89–91.

Aristotle. *The Works of Aristotle*. Ed. J. A. Smith and W. D. Ross. Oxford: Clarendon, 1910–31.

Augustine. *Confessions*. Trans. Edward B. Pusey. New York: Dutton, 1953.

———. *On Christian Doctrine*. Trans. D. W. Robertson, Jr. Indianapolis: Bobbs, 1958.

Baym, Nina, et al., eds. *The Norton Anthology of American Literature*. 2nd ed. 2 vols. New York: Norton, 1985.

Beehler, Michael. "T. S. Eliot." *Modern American Critics*. Ed. Gregory Jay. 63 vols. to date. *Dictionary of Literary Biography*. Detroit: Gale, 1987. 63: 98–122.

———. *T. S. Eliot, Wallace Stevens, and the Discourses of Difference*. Baton Rouge: Louisiana State UP, 1987.

Behr, Caroline. *T. S. Eliot: A Chronology of His Life and Works*. London: Macmillan, 1983.

Bell, Michael, ed. *The Context of English Literature: 1900–1930*. New York: Holmes, 1980.

Bergonzi, Bernard. *T. S. Eliot*. New York: Macmillan, 1972.

———, ed. *T. S. Eliot: Four Quartets*. Casebook Series. London: Macmillan, 1969.

Blackmur, R. P. *The Double Agent*. New York: Arrow, 1935.

Blamires, Harry. *Word Unheard: A Guide through Eliot's Four Quartets*. London: Methuen, 1969.

Blast. Nos. 1 (1914) and 2 (1915). Rpt. Santa Barbara: Black Sparrow, 1981.

Bloom, Harold, ed. *T. S. Eliot*. New York: Chelsea, 1985.

Boaz, Mildred Meyer. "Aesthetic Alliances in Poetry and Music: T. S. Eliot's *Four Quartets* and String Quartets by Béla Bartók." *Journal of Aesthetic Education* 13.3 (1979): 31–49.

———. "Musical and Poetic Analogues in T. S. Eliot's *The Waste Land* and Igor Stravinsky's *The Rite of Spring*." *Centennial Review* 24 (1980): 218–31.

Boethius. *The Consolation of Philosophy*. Trans. Richard H. Green. Indianapolis: Bobbs, 1962.

Bolgan, Anne C. *What the Thunder Really Said: A Retrospective Essay on the Making of* The Waste Land. Montreal: McGill-Queen's UP, 1973.

Booty, John. *Meditating on* Four Quartets. Cambridge: Cowley, 1983.

Bornstein, George. *Transformations of Romanticism in Yeats, Eliot, and Stevens*. Chicago: U of Chicago P, 1976.

Bradbrook, Muriel C. "Growing Up with T. S. Eliot." *Dictionary of Literary Biography Yearbook: 1988*. Detroit: Gale, 1989.

Bradbury, Malcolm, and James McFarlane, eds. *Modernism: 1890–1930*. Pelican Guides to European Literature. New York: Viking-Penguin, 1976.

Bradley, F. H. *Appearance and Reality: A Metaphysical Essay*. 2nd ed. Oxford: Clarendon, 1930.

———. *Essays on Truth and Reality*. Oxford: Clarendon, 1914.

Braque, Georges. *Pitcher and Violin* (1909–10). Kunstmuseum, Basle.

Braybrooke, Neville, ed. *T. S. Eliot: A Symposium for His Seventieth Birthday*. 1958. London: Garnstone, 1970.

Brooker, Jewel Spears. "The Case of the Missing Abstraction: Eliot, Frazer, and Modernism." *Massachusetts Review* 25 (1984): 539–52.

———. "F. H. Bradley's Doctrine of Experience in T. S. Eliot's *The Waste Land* and *Four Quartets*." *Modern Philology* 77 (1979): 146–57.

———. "The Second Coming and *The Waste Land*: Capstones of the Western Civilization Course." *College Literature* 13 (1986): 240–53.

———. "The Structure of Eliot's 'Gerontion': An Interpretation Based on Bradley's Doctrine of the Systematic Nature of Truth." *ELH* 46 (1979): 314–40.

———. "T. S. Eliot." *American Poets, 1880–1945: First Series*. Ed. Peter Quartermain. 45 vols. to date. *Dictionary of Literary Biography*. Detroit: Gale, 1986. 45: 150–81.

———. "T. S. Eliot: A Centennial Tribute." *Dictionary of Literary Biography Yearbook: 1988*. Detroit: Gale, 1989.

Brooks, Cleanth. *Modern Poetry and the Tradition*. 1939. Chapel Hill: U of North Carolina P, 1965.

Browne, E. Martin. *The Making of T. S. Eliot's Plays*. London: Cambridge UP, 1969.

Burke, Kenneth. *Counter-Statement*. New York: Harcourt, 1931.

———. "On Musicality in Verse." *Philosophy of Literary Form*. 1941. New York: Vintage, 1957. 296–304.

Bush, Ronald. *The Genesis of Ezra Pound's* Cantos. Princeton: Princeton UP, 1976.

———. *T. S. Eliot: A Study in Character and Style*. New York: Oxford UP, 1984.

Canary, Robert H. *T. S. Eliot: The Poet and His Critics*. Chicago: American Library Assn., 1982.

Capps, Walter, and Wendy Wright, eds. *Silent Fire: An Invitation to Western Mysticism.* New York: Harper, 1978.

Capra, Fritjof. *The Tao of Physics.* Berkeley: Shambhala, 1975.

Chung-yuan, Chang. *Tao: A New Way of Thinking.* New York: Harper, 1975.

Clark, David R., ed. Murder in the Cathedral: *A Collection of Critical Essays.* Twentieth-Century Interpretations. Englewood Cliffs: Prentice, 1971.

Clearfield, Andrew M. *These Fragments I Have Shored: Collage and Montage in Early Modernist Poetry.* Ann Arbor: UMI Research P, 1948.

The Cloud of Unknowing. Ed. James Walsh. Classics of Western Spirituality. Mahwah: Paulist, 1981.

Cornford, Francis M. *The Origin of Attic Comedy.* London: Edward Arnold, 1914.

Cox, C. B., and Arnold P. Hinchliffe, eds. *T. S. Eliot:* The Waste Land. Casebook Series. London: Macmillan, 1969.

Crane, R. S. *The Languages of Criticism and the Structure of Poetry.* Toronto: U of Toronto P, 1953.

Crawford, Robert. *The Savage and the City in the Work of T. S. Eliot.* Oxford: Clarendon, 1987.

Danielou, Jean. *The Bible and the Liturgy.* Notre Dame: U of Notre Dame P, 1956.

Dante Alighieri. *Divine Comedy.* Trans. Charles S. Singleton. 6 vols. Princeton: Princeton UP, 1970–75.

———. *Divine Comedy.* Trans. Dorothy L. Sayers. 3 vols. Baltimore: Penguin, 1949–62.

———. *Divine Comedy.* Trans. J. A. Carlyle, Thomas Okey, and P. H. Wicksteed. London: Dent, 1899–1901.

———. *Divine Comedy.* Trans. John Ciardi. New York: NAL, 1954, 1961, 1970.

Davidson, Harriet. *T. S. Eliot and Hermeneutics: Absence and Interpretation in* The Waste Land. Baton Rouge: Louisiana State UP, 1985.

Delaunay, Robert. *St. Séverin* (1909). Solomon R. Guggenheim Museum, New York.

Derrida, Jacques. *Of Grammatology.* Trans. G. C. Spivak. Baltimore: Johns Hopkins UP, 1976.

———. *Writing and Difference.* Trans. Alan Bass. Chicago: U of Chicago P, 1978.

Drew, Elizabeth. *T. S. Eliot: The Design of His Poetry.* London: Eyre, 1950.

Duchamp, Marcel. *Nude Descending a Staircase* (1912). Philadelphia Museum of Art.

Edwards, Michael. *Eliot / Language.* Isle of Skye, Scot.: Aquilia, 1975.

Einstein, Albert. *Essays in Science.* New York: Philosophical Library, 1934.

Eisenstein, Sergey. *Film Form: Essays in Film Theory.* Ed. and trans. Jay Leyda. New York: Harcourt, 1949.

Eliade, Mircea. *The Sacred and the Profane.* Trans. Willard Trask. New York: Harcourt, 1959.

Ellmann, Richard, and Charles Feidelson, Jr., eds. *The Modern Tradition: Backgrounds of Modern Literature.* New York: Oxford UP, 1965.

Ellmann, Richard, and Robert O'Clair, eds. *The Norton Anthology of Modern Poetry.* New York: Norton, 1973.

Fitzgerald, F. Scott. *The Great Gatsby.* New York: Scribner's, 1925.

Flanagan, Hallie. *Dynamo.* New York: Duell, 1943.

Ford, Boris, ed. *The Modern Age.* Pelican Guide to English Literature 7. Baltimore: Penguin, 1963.

Frank, Armin Paul. "The 'Personal Waste Land' Revisited: Or, What *Did* Happen in the Hyacinth Garden?" *Wirklichkeit und Dichtung: Studien zur englischen und amerikanischen Literatur.* Ed. Ulrich Halfmann, Kurt Müller, and Klaus Weiss. Berlin: Duncker, 1984. 289–304.

Frank, Joseph. "Spatial Form in Modern Literature." *The Widening Gyre: Crisis and Mastery in Modern Literature.* Rutgers: Rutgers UP, 1963. 3–62.

Frank, Mechthild, Armin Paul Frank, and K. P. S. Jochum, comps. *T. S. Eliot Criticism in English, 1916–1965: A Supplementary Bibliography.* Rpt. of *T. S. Eliot Review* 4.1, 2 (1977). Victoria, BC: Yeats Eliot Review, 1977.

Fraser, G. S. *The Modern Writer and His World.* 1953. Westport: Greenwood, 1965.

Frazer, James G. *The Golden Bough: A Study in Magic and Religion.* 1896. 3rd ed. 1911–14. Abridged ed. New York: Macmillan, 1963.

Freed, Lewis. *T. S. Eliot: The Critic as Philosopher.* West Lafayette: Purdue UP, 1979.

French, Warren, ed. *The Twenties: Fiction, Poetry, Drama.* Deland: Everett, 1975.

Frye, Northrop. *T. S. Eliot.* Edinburgh: Oliver, 1963.

Fung Yu-Lan. *A Short History of Chinese Philosophy.* New York: Macmillan, 1958.

Gallup, Donald. *T. S. Eliot: A Bibliography.* Rev. and extended ed. New York: Harcourt, 1969.

Gardner, Helen. *The Art of T. S. Eliot.* 1949. New York: Dutton, 1959.

———. *The Composition of* Four Quartets. New York: Oxford UP, 1978.

———. *T. S. Eliot and the English Poetic Tradition.* Nottingham: U of Nottingham P, 1966.

Gatta, John. "Spheric and Silent Music in Eliot's *Four Quartets.*" *Renascence* 32 (1980): 195–213.

Gibbon, Edward. *The Decline and Fall of the Roman Empire.* Vol. 2. New York: Random, 1932.

Gordon, Lyndall. *Eliot's Early Years.* New York: Oxford UP, 1977.

Grant, Michael, ed. *T. S. Eliot: The Critical Heritage.* 2 vols. Critical Heritage Series. London: Routledge, 1982.

Graves, Robert. *The Greek Myths.* 2 vols. Baltimore: Penguin, 1955.

Gray, Piers. *T. S. Eliot's Intellectual and Poetic Development: 1909–1922.* Atlantic Highlands: Humanities, 1982.

Guillaume de Lorris, and Jean de Meun. *Romance of the Rose.* Trans. Charles Dahlberg. Princeton: Princeton UP, 1971.

Hargrove, Nancy D. *Landscape as Symbol in the Poetry of T. S. Eliot.* Jackson: UP of Mississippi, 1978.

———. "T. S. Eliot." *Twentieth-Century American Dramatists: Part 1: A-J.* Ed. John MacNicholas. 7 vols. to date. *Dictionary of Literary Biography.* Detroit: Gale, 1981. 7: 151–72.

Harmon, William. "T. S. Eliot's Raids on the Inarticulate." *PMLA* 91 (1976): 450–59.

Hay, Eloise Knapp. *T. S. Eliot's Negative Way.* Cambridge: Harvard UP, 1982.

Headings, Philip R. *T. S. Eliot.* New York: Twayne, 1964.

Hesiod. *Hesiod* [*Works and Days, Theogony, Shield of Herakles*]. Trans. Richmond Lattimore. Ann Arbor: U of Michigan P, 1959.

Hoellering, George. "Filming *Murder in the Cathedral.*" *T. S. Eliot: A Symposium for His Seventieth Birthday.* Ed. Neville Braybrooke. 1958. London: Garnstone, 1970. 81–84.

Homer. *The Odyssey.* Trans. A. T. Murray. 2 vols. Cambridge: Harvard UP, 1953.

Howarth, Herbert. *Notes on Some Figures behind T. S. Eliot.* Boston: Houghton, 1964.

Howe, Irving, ed. *The Idea of the Modern in Literature and the Arts.* 1967. Rpt. as *Literary Modernism.* New York: Horizon, 1977.

Hulme, T. E. "Romanticism and Classicism." *Speculations: Essays on Humanism and the Philosophy of Art.* Ed. Herbert Read. London: Routledge, 1924. 111–40.

Hyers, Conrad. *The Comic Vision and the Christian Faith: A Celebration of Life and Laughter.* New York: Pilgrim, 1981.

Jay, Gregory. *T. S. Eliot and the Poetics of Literary History.* Baton Rouge: Louisiana State UP, 1983.

Jones, D. E. *The Plays of T. S. Eliot.* Toronto: U of Toronto P, 1960.

Julian of Norwich. *Revelations of Divine Love.* Ed. Roger L. Roberts. Treasures from the Spiritual Classics series. Wilton: Morehouse, 1982.

Kearns, Cleo McNelly. *T. S. Eliot and Indic Traditions: A Study in Poetry and Belief.* Cambridge: Cambridge UP, 1987.

Kenner, Hugh. *The Invisible Poet: T. S. Eliot.* New York: McDowell, 1959.

———. *The Pound Era.* Berkeley: U of California P, 1971.

———, ed. *T. S. Eliot: A Collection of Critical Essays.* Twentieth-Century Views. Englewood Cliffs: Prentice, 1962.

Kermode, Frank. *The Romantic Image.* London: Routledge, 1957.

Korg, Jacob. "Modern Art Techniques in *The Waste Land.*" *Journal of Aesthetics and Art Criticism* 18 (1960): 453–63.

Langbaum, Robert. *The Poetry of Experience: The Dramatic Monologue in Modern Literary Tradition.* New York: Random, 1957.

Leavis, Frank R. *New Bearings in English Poetry: A Study of the Contemporary Situation.* 1932. New York: Stewart, 1950.

Lendvai, Erno. *Béla Bartók: An Analysis of His Works*. London: Kahn, 1971.

Levin, Harry. "What Was Modernism?" *Refractions: Essays in Comparative Literature*. New York: Oxford UP, 1966. 271–95.

Littleton, C. Scott. *The New Comparative Mythology: An Anthropological Assessment of the Theories of Georges Dumézil*. 3rd ed. Berkeley: U of California P, 1982.

Litz, A. Walton, ed. *Eliot in His Time: Essays on the Fiftieth Anniversary of* The Waste Land. Princeton: Princeton UP, 1973.

Lobb, Edward. *T. S. Eliot and the Romantic Critical Tradition*. London: Routledge, 1981.

Ludwig, Richard M. "T. S. Eliot." *Sixteen Modern American Authors*. Ed. Jackson R. Bryer. New York: Norton, 1973. 181–222.

March, Richard, and Tambimuttu, comps. *T. S. Eliot*. Chicago: Regnery, 1949.

Margolis, John D. *T. S. Eliot's Intellectual Development: 1922–1939*. Chicago: U. of Chicago P, 1972.

Martin, Jay, ed. *A Collection of Critical Essays on* The Waste Land. Twentieth-Century Interpretations. Englewood Cliffs: Prentice, 1968.

Martin, Mildred, comp. *A Half-Century of Eliot Criticism: An Annotated Bibliography of Books and Articles in English, 1916–1965*. Lewisburg: Bucknell UP, 1972.

Matthiessen, F. O. *The Achievement of T. S. Eliot*. 1935. 3rd ed. Rev. C. L. Barber. London: Oxford UP, 1958.

McLuhan, Marshall. *The Gutenberg Galaxy: The Making of Typographic Man*. Toronto: U of Toronto P, 1962.

McMichael, George, gen. ed. *Realism to the Present*. Vol. 2 of *Anthology of American Literature*. 2 vols. New York: Macmillan, 1985.

Miller, J. Hillis. *Poets of Reality: Six Twentieth-Century Writers*. Cambridge: Belknap, 1965.

Moody, A. D. *Thomas Stearns Eliot: Poet*. Cambridge: Cambridge UP, 1979.

———, ed. The Waste Land *in Different Voices*. London: Edward Arnold; New York: St. Martin's, 1974.

Mowry, George E., ed. *The Twenties: Fords, Flappers, and Fanatics*. Englewood Cliffs: Prentice, 1963.

Murray, Gilbert. *The Classical Tradition in Poetry*. Cambridge: Harvard UP, 1927.

Nevo, Ruth. "*The Waste Land*: Ur-Text of Deconstruction." *T. S. Eliot*. Ed. Harold Bloom. New York: Chelsea, 1985. 95–102.

The New English Bible with the Apocrypha. New York: Oxford UP, 1976.

Nims, John Frederick, ed. *The Harper Anthology of Poetry*. New York: Harper, 1981.

O'Brien, Flann. *At Swim-Two-Birds*. New York: NAL, 1976.

Olney, James. "*Four Quartets*: 'The Pattern More Complicated.' " *Metaphors of*

Self: The Meaning of Autobiography. Princeton: Princeton UP, 1972. 260–316.

———, ed. *T. S. Eliot.* Anniversary issue of *Southern Review* 21 (1985): 873–1174.

Perkins, David. *A History of Modern Poetry: From the 1890s to the High Modernist Mode.* Cambridge: Harvard UP, 1976.

Perkins, George, et al., eds. *The American Tradition in Literature.* 6th ed. 2 vols. New York: Random, 1985.

Perl, Jeffrey N. "The Language of Theory and the Language of Poetry." *Southern Review* 21.4 (1985): 1012–23.

———. *The Tradition of Return: The Implicit History of Modern Literature.* Princeton: Princeton UP, 1984.

Perrine, Laurence. *Sound and Sense: An Introduction to Poetry.* 6th ed. New York: Harcourt, 1982.

Picasso, Pablo. *Daniel-Henry Kahnweiler* (1910). Art Institute of Chicago.

———. *Portrait of Ambroise Vollard* (1909–10). Hermitage, Leningrad.

Pope, John C. "Prufrock and Raskolnikov." *American Literature* 17 (1945): 213–30.

———. "Prufrock and Raskolnikov Again: A Letter from Eliot." *American Literature* 18 (1947): 319–21.

Pound, Ezra. *Ezra Pound: A Critical Anthology.* Ed. J. P. Sullivan. Baltimore: Penguin, 1970.

———. *Gaudier-Brzeska: A Memoir.* London: Bodley, 1916. Rpt. as *A Memoir of Gaudier-Brzeska.* New York: New Directions, 1970.

———. *Literary Essays of Ezra Pound.* Ed. T. S. Eliot. London: Faber, 1954.

Radhakrishnan, S. *The Principal Upanishads.* New York: Harper, 1953.

Rajan, Balachandra, ed. *T. S. Eliot: A Study of His Writings by Several Hands.* London: Dennis Dobson, 1947.

Ricks, Beatrice, comp. *T. S. Eliot: A Bibliography of Secondary Works.* Metuchen: Scarecrow, 1980.

Rosenthal, M. L. *The Modern Poets: A Critical Introduction.* London: Oxford UP, 1975.

Sanders, G. D., et al., eds. *Chief Modern Poets of Britain and America.* 5th ed. 2 vols. New York: Macmillan, 1970.

Schuchard, Ronald. "Eliot and Hulme in 1916: Toward a Revaluation of Eliot's Critical and Spiritual Development." *PMLA* 88 (1973): 1083–94.

———. " 'First-Rate Blasphemy': Baudelaire and the Revised Critical Idiom of T. S. Eliot's Moral Criticism." *ELH* 42 (1975): 276–95.

———. "T. S. Eliot as an Extension Lecturer 1916–1919." *Review of English Studies* 25 (1974): 163–72, 292–304.

Schwartz, Sanford. *The Matrix of Modernism: Pound, Eliot, and Early Twentieth-Century Thought.* Princeton: Princeton UP, 1985.

Scott, Nathan. "The Broken Center: A Definition of the Crisis of Values in Modern

Literature." 1959. *A Casebook on Existentialism*. Ed. William Spanos. New York: Crowell, 1966. 162–83.

Sencourt, Robert. *T. S. Eliot: A Memoir*. New York: Dodd, 1971.

Shackleton, Ernest. *South*. London: Heinemann, 1919.

Sinfield, Alan. *Dramatic Monologue*. New York: Barnes, 1977.

Smidt, Kristian. *Poetry and Belief in the Work of T. S. Eliot*. 1949. Rev. ed. London: Humanities, 1961.

Smith, Carol H. *T. S. Eliot's Dramatic Theory and Practice: From* Sweeney Agonistes *to* The Elder Statesman. Princeton: Princeton UP, 1963.

Smith, Grover. *T. S. Eliot's Poetry and Plays: A Study in Sources and Meaning*. 1956. 2nd ed. Chicago: U of Chicago P, 1974.

———. *The Waste Land*. London: Allen, 1983.

Soldo, John. *The Tempering of T. S. Eliot*. Ann Arbor: University Microfilms International, 1983.

Southam, B. C. *The Student's Guide to the Selected Poems of T. S. Eliot*. New York: Harcourt, 1968.

Spanos, William. "Hermeneutics and Memory: Destroying T. S. Eliot's *Four Quartets*." *Genre* 9 (1978): 523–73.

———. "Repetition in *The Waste Land*: A Phenomenological De-struction." *Boundary 2* 8 (1979): 225–85.

Spears, Monroe K. *Dionysus and the City: Modernism in Twentieth-Century Poetry*. New York: Oxford UP, 1970.

Spender, Stephen. *T. S. Eliot*. New York: Viking, 1975.

Spurr, David. *Conflicts in Consciousness: T. S. Eliot's Poetry and Criticism*. Urbana: U of Illinois P, 1984.

Stead, C. K. *The New Poetic: Yeats to Eliot*. London: Hutchinson, 1964.

Stevens, Wallace. *The Palm at the End of the Mind*. New York: Vintage, 1972.

Stock, Noel. *The Life of Ezra Pound*. London: Routledge, 1970.

Sullivan, Sheila, ed. *Critics on T. S. Eliot*. London: Allen, 1973.

Tate, Allen, ed. *T. S. Eliot: The Man and His Work*. New York: Delacorte, 1966.

Time-Life Books Editors. *This Fabulous Century: 1920–1930*. New York: Time-Life Books, 1969.

Torrens, James. "Charles Maurras and Eliot's 'New Life.' " *PMLA* 89 (1974): 312–22.

———. "Eliot's Poetry and the Incubus of Shakespeare." *Thought* 52 (1977): 407–21.

Trilling, Lionel. "On the Teaching of Modern Literature." *Beyond Culture: Essays on Literature and Learning*. 1966. New York: Viking, 1965. 3–30.

Unger, Leonard. *T. S. Eliot: Moments and Patterns*. Minneapolis: U of Minnesota P, 1956.

———, ed. *T. S. Eliot: A Selected Critique*. New York: Rinehart, 1948.

Virgil. *The Aeneid*. Trans. Allen Mandelbaum. 1971. New York: Bantam, 1972.

———. *Eclogues*. Trans. Guy Lee. New York: Penguin, 1984.

———. *Virgil*. Trans. H. Ruston Fairclough. Rev. ed. 2 vols. Cambridge: Harvard UP, 1953.

Wagenknecht, Edward C. *Cavalcade of the American Novel*. New York: Holt, 1952.

Wagner, Linda W., ed. *T. S. Eliot: A Collection of Criticism*. Contemporary Studies in Literature. New York: McGraw, 1974.

Warren, Austin. "Continuity and Coherence in the Criticism of T. S. Eliot." *Connections*. Ann Arbor: U of Michigan P, 1970. 152–83.

———. "T. S. Eliot's Literary Criticism." *Sewanee Review* 74 (1966): 272–92.

Wellek, René. "The Criticism of T. S. Eliot." *Sewanee Review* 64 (1956): 398–443.

Weston, Jessie L. *From Ritual to Romance*. Cambridge: Cambridge UP, 1920.

Williams, Helen. *T. S. Eliot:* The Waste Land. 2nd ed. Studies in English Literature 37. London: Edward Arnold, 1968.

Williamson, George. *A Reader's Guide to T. S. Eliot*. New York: Noonday, 1953.

Wilson, Edmund. *Axel's Castle: A Study in the Imaginative Literature of 1870–1930*. New York: Scribner's, 1931.

Wimsatt, W. K. "The Structure of Romantic Nature Imagery." *Romanticism and Consciousness: Essays in Criticism*. Ed. Harold Bloom. New York: Norton, 1970. 77–88.

Wollheim, Richard. *F. H. Bradley*. Baltimore: Penguin, 1969.

Wyman, Linda. "*Murder in the Cathedral*: The Plot of Diction." *Modern Drama* 19 (1976): 135–46.

Yeats, W. B. *Collected Poems*. New York: Macmillan, 1956.

Recordings

Eliot, T. S. *British Poets of Our Time: T. S. Eliot:* The Waste Land, Four Quartets, "The Love Song of J. Alfred Prufrock," "Journey of the Magi." Read by Alec Guinness. 2 records. Arts Council of Great Britain in association with BBC. Decca-Argo, PLP 1206/7, n.d.

———. *Four Quartets*. Read by T. S. Eliot. Caedmon, TC 1403, [1947].

———. *Old Possum's Book of Practical Cats*. Read by John Gielgud and Irene Worth. Caedmon, CP 1713, 1983.

———. *T. S. Eliot:* The Family Reunion. Dir. Howard Sackler. With Paul Scofield, Flora Robson, Sybil Thorndike, et al. Caedmon, TRS 308, n.d.

———. *T. S. Eliot:* Murder in the Cathedral. Dir. Howard Sackler. With Paul Scofield, Cyril Cusack, Julian Glover, Michael Gwynn, Alec McCowen, et al. Caedmon, TRS 330, n.d.

———. "T. S. Eliot." *The Poet's Voice: Poets Reading Aloud and Commenting upon Their Works*. Comp. Stratis Haviaras. Cambridge: Harvard UP, 1978.

———. *T. S. Eliot Reading Poems and Choruses*. Caedmon, TC 1045 (LP), CDL 51045 (cassette), 1955.

———. *T. S. Eliot Reading* The Waste Land *and Other Poems*. Caedmon, TC 1326 (LP), 51326 (cassette), 1971.

———. *T. S. Eliot Reads* Old Possum's Book of Practical Cats. Spoken Arts, 758, [1959].

Genesis. "The Cinema Show." *Selling England by the Pound*. New York: Atlantic-Charisma, FC6060, 1973.

Persichetti, Vincent. *The Hollow Men*, op. 25. For trumpet and string orchestra. Turnabout, 34705, n.d.

Rawsthorne, Alan. *Practical Cats*. For narrator and orchestra. ("Overture," "The Naming of Cats," "The Old Gumbie Cat," "Gus, the Theatre Cat," "Bustopher Jones, the Cat about Town," "Old Deuteronomy," and "The Song of the Jellicles.") Angel, 30002, [1954?]; Seraphim, M 60042, 1967.

Stravinsky, Igor. *Ave Maria. Anthem: The Dove Descending Breaks the Air. Pater Noster*. Crystal, S890, 1976.

———. *The Dove Descending*. Canby Singers. Nonesuch, H-71115, n.d.

Webber, Andrew Lloyd. *Cats*. Musical with libretto based on *Old Possum's Book of Practical Cats*. 2 records. London: Really Useful, 1981. Geffen, 2GHS 2031, 1981.

Films

Eliot, T. S. *The Cocktail Party*. BBC tv film.

———. *The Confidential Clerk*. BBC tv film.

———. *The Family Reunion*. BBC tv film.

———. *Murder in the Cathedral*. BBC tv film.

———. *Murder in the Cathedral*. Dir. George Hoellering. 1951. (Available from Films, Inc., Entertainment Div., 5547 N. Ravenswood, Chicago, IL 60640.)

The Mysterious Mr. Eliot. Writer and dir. Stephen Cross. Narr. Keir Dullea. BBC and WNET, n.d. (Available from McGraw-Hill Films, Dept. 455, 1221 Ave. of the Americas, NY, NY 10020.)

T. S. Eliot. Voices and Visions: A Television Course on Modern American Poetry. The Annenberg-CPB Project. New York: New York Center for Visual History, 1987. Shown on PBS tv, 1988. (Available from Annenberg-CPB Collection, 1111 16th St., NW, Washington, DC 20036.)

SELECTED MUSICAL
COMPOSITIONS

ApIvor, Denis. The Hollow Men: *The Poem by T. S. Eliot*. For baritone solo, male voice chorus, and orchestra. Oxford: Oxford UP, 1951.

Baaren, Kees van. *The Hollow Men*. For soprano, baritone solo, choir, and small orchestra. Amsterdam: Donemus, 1948.

Berio, Luciano. *Epifanie*. For orchestra. Stuttgart: Reclam, 1972.

Britten, Benjamin. *Canticle IV: Journey of the Magi*, op. 86. For countertenor, tenor, baritone, and piano. London: Faber Music; New York: Schirmer, 1972.

———. *Canticle V: The Death of Saint Narcissus*, op. 89. For tenor and harp. London: Faber Music; New York: Schirmer, 1976.

Christou, Jani. *Six Songs*. For mezzo-soprano and orchestra. ("New Hampshire," "Death by Water," "Mélange Adultère de Tout," "Eyes That Last I Saw in Tears," "Virginia," "The Wind Sprang Up at Four O'Clock.") Wiesbaden: Impero, [1959?].

Crawford, John Charlton. *Ash-Wednesday*. Oratorio for narrator, mixed chorus, soprano and baritone soloists, and symphony orchestra. Unpublished.

Diamond, David. *For an Old Man*. For voice and piano. (A setting of "Lines for an Old Man.") New York: Southern Music, [1951].

Freund, Don. *The Waste Land*. Four movements for winds and percussion. New York: Seesaw Music, 1977.

Gruen, John. *Two Eliot Poems for Voice*. ("Time and the Bell" from "Burnt Norton" and "Eyes That Last I Saw in Tears"). [1959?]. Unpublished.

Hanson, Howard. *New Land, New Covenant*. For narrator, chorus of mixed voices, soprano and baritone soloists, children's chorus (optional), organ, and small orchestra. Text comp. Howard C. Kee from the Scriptures, colonial American writings, 17th- and 18th-century hymns, and the poetry of T. S. Eliot. New York: Fischer, 1976.

Harvey, Jonathan Dean. *The Dove Descending*. Anthem for soprano, alto, tenor, and bass with divisions and organ. Borough Green: Novello, 1975.

———. *Inner Light*. For soprano, soprano, alto, tenor, and bass soloists; for instrumental ensemble and tape, seven players and tape, and orchestra and tape. Texts from Kipling, Blake, T. S. Eliot, St. John's Gospel, and Rudolph Steiner. London: Faber Music, 1979.

Holloway, Robin. *Five Madrigals*. For unaccompanied mixed voices. Texts by James Joyce and T. S. Eliot. London: Oxford UP, 1976.

Howell, Dorothy. *The Song of the Jellicles*. Two-part song, for two voices and piano. London: Edward Arnold, [1953].

Keats, Donald. *The Hollow Men*. For soprano, alto, tenor, and bass; clarinet, three trombones, and piano. New York: Boosey & Hawkes, 1952.

―――. *The Naming of Cats*. For soprano, alto, tenor, bass, and piano. New York: Boosey & Hawkes, [1962].

Leighton, Kenneth. *The Light Invisible*, op. 16. Piano-vocal score and score for tenor solo, chorus, and orchestra. Words from the Bible and T. S. Eliot's *The Rock*. London: Novello, 1958.

Lourié, Arthur. *The Dove Music*. For voice and piano. (A setting of "Little Gidding" 4.) New York: Arthur Lourié, 1945. In *The Third Hour*. New York, 1949.

MacInnis, Donald. *The Waste Land*. (A setting of "Death by Water.") Charlottesville: 1957. Unpublished.

Matuszczak, Bernadetta. *A Chamber Drama*. For baritone, baritone from tape, reciting alto voice, bass clarinet, cello, double bass, and percussion. Text from T. S. Eliot's *The Hollow Men*. Polish trans. by A. Piotrowski. Krakow: Polskie Wydawnictwo Muzyczne, 1970.

McCabe, John. *Five Elegies*. For soprano and chamber orchestra. 1958. Elegies by Thomas Nashe, Ben Jonson, T. S. Eliot ("Eyes That Last I Saw in Tears"), Robert Herrick, and Dylan Thomas. Unpublished. [Available from Oxford UP, London].

Paynter, John. *Landscapes*. Choral suite for mixed voices and optional oboe. London: Oxford UP, 1972.

Persichetti, Vincent. *The Hollow Men*, op. 25. For trumpet and string orchestra. Philadelphia: Elkan-Vogel, [1948].

―――. "Dust in Sunlight and Memory in Corners" (from "A Song for Simeon"). *Poems for Piano*. Vol. 2. Philadelphia: Elkan-Vogel, 1947.

Pizzetti, Ildebrando. *Assassinio nella cattedrale*. Tragedia musicale in due atti e un intermezzo. Testo originale di T. S. Eliot ridotto per la propria musica dalla versione italiana di Monsignore Alberto Castelli da Ildebrando Pizzetti. Trascrizione per canto e pianoforte di Italo Delle Cese. [Milano]: Ricordi, [1958].

Rawsthorne, Alan. *Practical Cats*. For narrator and orchestra. [1954?]. ("Overture," "The Naming of Cats," "The Old Gumbie Cat," "Gus, the Theatre Cat," "Bustopher Jones, the Cat about Town," "Old Dueteronomy," and "The Song of the Jellicles.") Unpublished. [Available from Oxford UP, London.]

Reif, Paul. *Five Finger Exercises*. A song cycle for piano and voice. ("Lines to a Persian Cat," "Lines to a Yorkshire Terrier," "Lines to a Duck in the Park," "Lines to Ralph Hodgson, Esqr.," "Lines for Cuscuscaraway and Mirza Murad Ali Beg" [called "Lines to Mr. Eliot" on the title page].) New York: Leslie Productions, 1957.

Sanders, Robert L. *The Hollow Men*. For male chorus and piano. © Robert L. Sanders, 1950.

Searle, Humphrey. *Two Practical Cats*. For speaker, flute (doubling piccolo), guitar, and cello. ("Macavity: The Mystery Cat" and "Growltiger's Last Stand.") London: Oxford UP, [1956].

Shaw, Martin. *The Builders: Song from* The Rock. London: Cramer, [1934].

————. *The Greater Light Anthem.* For tenor solo, double choir, and organ. (A setting from *The Rock.*) London: J. Curwen; New York: Schirmer, 1966.

Smith, Gregg. *Landscapes.* For mixed voices a cappella. ("New Hampshire," "Virginia," "Usk," "Cape Anne" [sic], "Rannoch, by Glencoe.") New York: Schirmer, [1962].

Stravinsky, Igor. *Anthem: The Dove Descending Breaks the Air.* For chorus a cappella. (A setting of "Little Gidding" 4.) London: Boosey & Hawkes, 1962.

————. *Introitus: T. S. Eliot In Memoriam.* For male chorus (tenor and bass) and chamber ensemble (harp, piano, four percussion players, viola, and double bass). London: Boosey & Hawkes, 1965.

Swanson, Howard. *Four Preludes.* For voice and piano. New York: Weintraub Music, [1952].

Thomas, Alan. *Five Landscapes.* For voice and piano. ("New Hampshire," "Virginia," "Usk," "Rannock, by Glencoe," and "Cape Ann.") Bryn Mawr: Theodore Presser, [1957].

Togni, Camillo. *Coro di T. S. Eliot*, op. 34. Per coro misto a cappella. (Di *Assassinio nella cattedrale*, parte 2, coro 4.) Traduzione dall'inglese di Alberto Castelli. Milano: Zerboni, [1962].

Vogt, Hans. *Vier Englische Lieder.* For soprano and instruments. Texts by Fry, Auden, Eliot, and Hopkins. Stuttgart: Recalm, 1972.

Webber, Andrew Lloyd. *Cats.* Musical with libretto based on *Old Possum's Book of Practical Cats.* Music by Andrew Lloyd Webber; photographs and drawings by John Napier. San Diego: Harcourt, 1983.

Whettam, Graham. *The Wounded Surgeon Plies the Steel*, op. 41. Anthem for unaccompanied soprano, alto, tenor, and bass. (A setting of "East Coker" 4). London: Boosey & Hawkes, 1960.

Wills, Arthur. *The Light Invisible.* For chorus (soprano, alto, tenor, bass) and instruments (percussion, harp, and organ). London: Weinberger, 1976.

INDEX

DATE DUE